Your Natural Health Makeover

Dr. Lauri M. Aesoph

PRENTICE HALL PRESS

Library of Congress Cataloging-in-Publication Data

Aesoph, Lauri M., N.D.
    Your natural health makeover / Lauri M. Aesoph, N.D.
        p.   cm.
    Includes index.
    ISBN 0-13-628652-6 (PPC)   0-13-628660-7 (C/J)
    ISBN 0-7352-0071-8 (P)
        1. Health.   2. Diet therapy.   3. Naturopathy.   I. Title.
    RA776.5.A37   1998   97-36541
    613—dc21   CIP

Acquisitions Editor: *Doug Corcoran*

Production Editor: *Eve Mossman*

Formatting/Interior Design: *Robyn Beckerman*

© *1998 by Lauri M. Aesoph, ND*

Printed in the United States of America

10   9   8   7   6   5   4   3   2   1   *(PPC)*

10   9   8   7   6   5   4   3   2   1   *(C/J)*

10   9   8   7   6   5   4   3   2   1   *(P)*

ISBN 0-13-628652-6 (PPC)

ISBN 0-13-628660-7 (C/J)

ISBN 0-7352-0071-8 (P)

PRENTICE HALL PRESS
Paramus, NJ 07652

A Simon & Schuster Company

On the World Wide Web at http://www.phdirect.com

Prentice Hall International (UK) Limited, *London*
Prentice Hall of Australia Pty. Limited, *Sydney*
Prentice Hall Canada Inc., *Toronto*
Prentice Hall Hispanoamericana, S.A., *Mexico*
Prentice Hall of India Private Limited, *New Delhi*
Prentice Hall of Japan, Inc., *Tokyo*
Simon & Schuster Asia Pte. Ltd., *Singapore*
Editora Prentice Hall do Brasil, Ltda., *Rio de Janeiro*

For Chris, Adam, and Will.

Thank you for all your love and support—and for disappearing when I needed to work.

Acknowledgements

I'd like to acknowledge all those individuals who helped me pull this book together: Deb Carlin and Barbara Papik from Lommen Health Sciences Library at the University of South Dakota School of Medicine—thank you for finding last-minute references and searching obscure topics for me. Warm gratitude to the staff at Sioux Valley Hospital Library for allowing me to monopolize your time, computers, and journals. Thank you to JoEllen Koerner, Hal Fletcher, MD, and Karen Fletcher and the other health care practitioners in and around Sioux Falls who have supported my work here.

Thanks to my many colleagues for their pearls of wisdom and encouragement. Thanks to Dr. Joe Pizzorno for his scientific vision of natural medicine, and to Dr. Steve Austin for making nutrition class so much fun and so informative. My gratitude to John Weeks for handing me opportunities and Paul Bergner for mentoring me during the early years.

Thank you, Doug Corcoran, for being a wonderful editor with a sense of humor.

Finally, thank you to my grandparents for making "natural" seem normal. (Kim and Steve, I can't forget you.) And a great big hug and thanks to my parents, Jim and Pat Baillie, for raising me right and getting me started on this path called natural medicine.

Contents

Chapter 3
Defend Your Body for Total Revitalization—21

Chapter 4
Revitalize Your Digestive System—39

Chapter 5
Better Inner Cleansing—63

Chapter 6
Maximize Your Immunity—75

Chapter 7
Lasting Stress Relief—91

Chapter 8
Improve Circulation and Live Longer—105

Chapter 9
Attain Tiptop Muscle Tone—121

Chapter 10
Regain Your Sexual Vitality—137

Chapter 11
Build Stronger Bones and Teeth—149

Chapter 12
Secrets of Beautiful Skin—167

Chapter 13
The Keys to Keener Vision—179

Chapter 14
Supercharge Your Brain—193

part two
Natural Remedies for Over
Thirty Common Ailments

Introduction

How many times have you picked up a natural health book and said: "There's no way I can do this! It's too weird. It's too strange. It's too natural!"

Well, I hope *Your Natural Health Makeover* is the book that changes your mind.

Rather than tell you what you're doing wrong, rather than insist you give up chocolate forever (Heaven forbid!), rather than demand you give up coffee today, I'm going to build on all those healthful things you're doing right now. (And you are.) I'm going to take you by the hand, and step-by-step, show you simple, natural, non-threatening ways to make over your entire body from head to toe.

Let's face it, while there is a minority of people who can maintain a perfect diet, exercise three hours each and every day, and do those other things we all should, the fact is most of us don't. I live in the real world. I know about those days when exercise is out of the question and the only answer for stress is a chocolate chip cookie. The person eating tofu next to you who runs 10 miles every day—rain or shine—is not better than you; taking healthful steps is not a moral issue. But I also want you to feel and look the very best you can. *Your Natural Health Makeover* is a very good idea, and something that you can incorporate into your daily schedule, and fall back on as health needs arise. For those sick times during and after your makeover, turn to Part Two for dozens of natural health ideas for common ailments.

Your Natural Health Makeover came about because I saw people struggling with making health changes all the time. Has your doctor ever said, "Eat better!" but didn't tell you how or why? Maybe you're not sick, but don't quite feel right—tired, tense, slightly achy—and don't know what to do. I wanted to take all those suggestions I've handed out to audiences, readers, and patients during the past decade, and compile them into a simple format: a Natural Health Makeover format.

To make this makeover a truly personal one, I give you the choice of what you want to change and offer you practical, easy ideas that you can "plug" into your current way of doing things. You'll find over one hundred Makeover Hints with specific, do-now tips. I also explain the principles behind natural health; for true health is more than popping a vitamin pill or drinking herbal tea. It's an attitude and a way of life.

Also included are hundreds of scientific studies backing up these very practical makeover steps interwoven with personal stories. I purposely put a lot of myself into this book—my stories, frustrations and triumphs—so you don't feel alone in making these difficult health revisions.

Don't feel ashamed if you can't carry out all the Natural Health Makeover recommendations in order and immediately. Just do your very best. Take a break. Then try a health touchup. Pursuing good health habits is a lifelong venture, and one worth striving for. It's fun and feels good (and yes, is sometimes frustrating). You might feel out of place occasionally, especially when you become the person eating tofu at the dinner table or insist on stretching your body every hour at work. But that's O.K. All of America (and the world) is turning to natural health for help; be a leader and include your family, friends, and colleagues in your Natural Health Makeover.

How to Use This Book

This book is laid out so you can either read it straight through (I suggest you do this the first time) or use it as a reference. Begin by reading all of Chapters 1 and 2; these will give you background on natural health and useful thoughts for a smooth makeover. Next proceed to Chapter 3, and onward through the rest of Part One, to begin your Natural Health Makeover journey. Try not to vary the order in which you use these makeover chapters, as they've been placed in sequence for a reason. The first six chapters set the stage for better digestion, elimination, circulation, immunity, and stress management, so that the rest of your Natural Health Makeover will be more effective. For example, Chapter 3 shows you how to protect your body from poisons. Detoxification, or poison control, is an important first step in building and maintaining health. Next is Chapter 4 on how to make over your gastrointestinal tract. Without well-functioning digestion and absorption, you are unable to use all those good foods you'll be eating.

How quickly or slowly you work through the Natural Health Makeover depends on you. If you're already practicing the suggestions in a particular step, then move on. If the information in a certain section is new, take a little time to practice and absorb it. It's been my observation and experience that if you give yourself some time to become accustomed to a new habit, you'll be more likely to stick with it.

A Full Body Makeover

For first-time customers, I recommend a head-to-toe body makeover beginning with Chapter 3 and working all the way through Chapter 14. Think of this as spring-cleaning your entire body—inside and out. Not only will you touch on all aspects of health, but you will learn about your body in the process. (See the sixth principle of natural health: education.) If you get stuck along the way, do your best, and move on. You can always go back and repeat a chapter.

Health Touch-ups

Taking care of your body is a lifetime commitment. If, after completing your Natural Health Makeover, you slip here or there (and we all do sometime), use this book to touch up your health habits. Think of this as a body tune-up. Good health habits aren't an ethical issue. Also, health care information and techniques are continuously evolving. Through your readings or practices, you may find a better or different way to clear your skin or treat your cold. If you do, let me know. (See Appendix E.)

How to Make Over Your Illness

Even those who live a natural and healthful existence sometimes get ill. There are factors beyond our control—stress, pollution, genetic weaknesses—that shape health. This is why I've included a section called Natural Remedies for Over Thirty Common Ailments (Part Two); you can apply the same natural health principles when you're sick as you did while well.

Often the medicines we use give only temporary relief for specific symptoms—itchy skin, a stuffy nose, constipation. They do nothing to enhance overall health or assist the body to heal. Side effects are a common problem with both over-the-counter and prescription conventional medicines. Aspirin and acetaminophen (Tylenol®) can cause liver damage when taken in large enough dosages. These same medicines when used to squelch pain or a fever during a cold, have been shown to suppress immune response, boost viral action, and make your runny nose even worse. Many drugs are known to cause nutritional havoc by changing nutrient absorption, metabolism, utilization, or excretion.

In addition to your Natural Health Makeover, start to use effective, safe natural health therapies when you're sick. Begin with suggestions in Part Two. Note what works for you, and learn from there. Read magazines and other books on natural health, talk to friends who use these methods, visit your local health food store, and for complex and hard-to-treat problems, consult with natural health practitioners in your area (see Appendix D).

Now sit back, take stock and enjoy a makeover like you've never experienced before. Grasp hold of those time-tested lifestyle steps that will grace you with a natural and healthy beauty.

Lauri M. Aesoph, ND

part one

Make Over Your Health

Chapter 1

What Is a Natural Health Makeover?

A beauty makeover may make you look more attractive, but only a Natural Health Makeover does the job in depth. Rather than brighten your outer body with curlers and cosmetics, a Natural Health Makeover reaches your core, resulting in health and beauty. And unlike a beauty makeover, this isn't a plan that will go out of date as hair styles or clothes do; good health is always in fashion.

A Natural Health Makeover also helps you fight chronic disease like arthritis, clogged arteries, and high blood pressure; it saves you money as well. Americans spend $600 billion annually—in the most expensive health care system in the world—fighting these and other illnesses.[1]

Save your money and your health. Rather than fight an uphill battle to health while racked with pain, why not take care of business now while you feel good enough to make over your health? Contrary to what you might think, you can take steps to enhance well-being. Diseases of old age are not inevitable; many illnesses are due to factors within your control.

A couple of years ago I had the good fortune to interview Dr. Ronald Klatz. Knowledgeable and effervescent about the topic of growing old, this president of the American Academy of Anti-Aging Medicine told me that the average American life span will eventually increase to 120 years and beyond. If this is true, I don't want to spend the last 40 or 50 years hurting or relying on false teeth to chew my food. Do you? How well you live in those latter years depends on how well you live now. Today's Natural Health Makeover can mean the difference between savings spent on medical treatment or exotic travel. Let's face it, it's cheaper to prevent illness than treat it.

The trick is how to avoid falling victim to heart disease and other lifestyle-linked ailments efficiently and effectively. How do you stay healthy for as long as possible? That's what I'm going to teach you. I've supervised, witnessed, and personally undergone many Natural Health Makeovers over the last 20 years. One of the first involved a young college student.

This young woman was studying for her pre-medical degree at the University of Victoria in British Columbia. Even so, she found herself reading more and more on nutrition and vitamins. It was 1976, and natural medicine was making a comeback. One day, while researching a paper, this student started talking with a fellow named Leonard who told her he ate no meat or sugar, and feasted only on natural foods. Thrilled to meet a real live vegetarian, the young woman quizzed Leonard about how he changed his diet. "No big deal," he replied, "I just decided to eat naturally. It wasn't hard at all."

The pre-med student couldn't believe her luck. Up to now, she'd read about the new natural ways of living, but had been afraid to try them. According to her new friend, there was nothing to it! The next day, the young woman began her life as a vegetarian. She quit caffeine, meat, and sugar, and gave her life over to tofu and brown rice. After a full day on this diet, the young lady felt terrible. Her head ached from coffee withdrawal. Her sweet-tooth cried out for a Kit Kat™. Plus, she had no idea how to cook tofu. What had gone wrong?

This is a perfect example of how not to begin your makeover. Perfect health cannot be achieved in a day, and health habits don't change overnight. I was that young college student, and it took me many years to learn that lesson. I'm sure there are other Leonards in the world who find switching to healthful living a breeze. But as you've read, I'm not one of them.

If you're like me, let me take you by the hand, and show you step-by-step how to gain better health using my Natural Health Makeover plan. You don't need to be a doctor to take care of yourself. In fact, the foundation upon which natural health care rests is lifestyle—what you select to eat and drink, how and if you exercise, the relationships you enter into and the work you do. Your doctor can suggest a diet, tell you to exercise, recommend you relax more, but the style of your life is ultimately your own choosing.

Unfortunately, changing your appearance with cosmetics and clothes is a lot easier than altering health habits. Real health can't be painted on or coiffured; a touch of rouge won't replace the rosy glow of health. A Natural Health Makeover is also more lasting than a beauty touch-up. If you're truly well, you'll still feel rosy even when the lipstick (or aftershave lotion) wears off.

Before we get started, let's look at the six principles that rule natural health. Reading and understanding these not only give you basic knowledge about this fascinating field, but will ensure a successful makeover.

Whole Health Means a Whole-Person Approach

This book is about how to stay whole and healthy using natural means. By doing this, you're practicing the first principle of natural medicine: prevention. Some of you probably already use techniques to stay well such as wearing a seat belt when you drive and having a yearly physical examination. While these are important, there's much more to preventive health care. True prevention involves taking steps that enhance overall health.

According to the Surgeon General's 1988 *Report on Nutrition and Health*, half of the top ten causes of death in America—heart disease, cancer, stroke, diabetes, and atherosclerosis—are linked to diet.[2] These chronic diseases are not only killing us, but stealing our money, too.

Principle number one: Practice an ounce of prevention to save dollars (and illness) down the road.

Body, Heal Thyself

The body is a wondrous entity. Under the right circumstances, it has tremendous healing abilities. Thus the second principle of natural medicine refers to the inherent healing power of nature. It's not the doctor or medicines or herbs that cure you when you're sick, it's your body. The immune system, a complex assemblage of cells, organs, and other factors, is your defense against germs, toxins and other foreign matter, and the equipment your body uses to recover from most illnesses or injuries. Natural health practitioners recognize this, so they do their utmost to support this system, and when that's done, get out of its way.

An example of which works better—drugs or the body—is illustrated with a classic study conducted 20 years ago by European researchers Marcus Diamant, M.D., and Bertil Diamant, M.D. They wanted to find out if antibiotics were really necessary for the treatment of ear infections, a condition that plagues many young children. After observing over 10,000 cases over a 14-year period, they discovered that 88 percent of their young patients didn't need antibiotics, due to what they termed "spontaneous healing." Even more surprising, the antibiotic-free kids had fewer recurrent infections than children treated with these drugs during the first week of illness.[3] The body's ability to heal, largely via the immune system, improves when given the chance to work unencumbered by drugs or other obstacles.

My youngest son, Will, came into this world with weak lungs. During his first Midwest winter—he was healthy in the summertime—he not only suffered from a continuous runny nose, but was finally struck down with pneumonia. Rather than give him antibiotics, I used various means to build his immunity. By his second winter, I noticed a slight improvement in his health. He was still susceptible to colds, but his symptoms were less severe and frequent. During his third winter, he was mostly well. I attribute this gradual health improvement to the natural building of his immune system. (Caution: Whenever treating young children with natural therapies, especially for severe ailments, seek the advice of a qualified physician.)

Principle number two: The body knows how to heal itself, given half a chance.

Natural Is Not a Four-Letter Word

Every doctor takes an oath to "do no harm." Naturopathic physicians take this promise very seriously by using the most natural, safe, and non-invasive therapies possible. This is the third principle of natural medicine: Do no harm by using safe treatments. According to Webster's dictionary, natural is defined as "pertaining to nature," "to be expected" (I like this one), "innate," and "reproducing the original state closely." So natural health simply refers to the way our bodies are meant to be—healthy. Even the word physician, based on the French word "physicien," means *natural* philosopher.

It pleases me to see more conventional medical institutions becoming interested in these therapies. Yet in truth, natural health care is no different from conventional medicine in its complexity—both deal with the human body. Still the former is often given short shrift because in many people's minds natural equals "simple" or "ineffective."

Now, don't get me wrong. I'm tremendously grateful for modern medicine and its technology. Without it, my grandfather, a robust 81-year-old who was advised by his naturopathic doctor a few years ago to have a hip replacement, would be sitting in a wheelchair. Antibiotics, used judiciously, are lifesavers for serious bacterial infections. However, I also recognize that straying too far from our original (natural) way of doing things is hard on our "natural" bodies. Life in the city exposes us to polluted air and water, excessive noise, sedentary jobs, and too little leisure time.

Principle number three: Use safe and natural therapies whenever possible.

Health Is More Than Skin Deep

The fourth principle of natural medicine says you must search out the root or cause of a health problem in order to heal completely. In a sense, naturopathic physicians are the anthropologists of the medical world. We piece together the information we unearth during an office visit in order to solve the mystery behind a patient's health. You can help your doctor, and yourself, on this healing expedition by paying attention to how your body feels under different conditions—after eating, when ill. In some cases, using natural therapies, like homeopathic medicines, requires you to pay attention to very subtle sensations that you may have ignored in the past or didn't realize were there.

For some this is difficult. In a society where fast food feeds us, correspondence travels by e-mail and instant financing is expected, it's hard to slow down. Taking time to listen to your body can be as difficult as asking an active three-year-old to sit still for half an hour. However, failure to do so can mean relying on drugs and medical procedures fraught with annoying, and sometimes harmful, side effects.

You only need to open a copy of the *Physician's Desk Reference* or other such drug guide to learn that most medications carry with them lists of adverse reactions and situations where they shouldn't be used. For example, some antibiotic acne creams can cause your skin to burn, peel, itch, feel tender, dry out, or turn red while clearing up pimples. Sleeping pills, like Nembutal® (pentobarbital), allow you to drop off—but at a cost. This addictive drug may bring on nausea, vomiting, constipation, headaches, liver damage, dizziness and, ironically, may create insomnia and nightmares.[4]

Principle number four: You can only solve a health problem by finding and curing the cause.

■ Makeover Hint #1—Body Scan

Makeover artists begin their work by stepping back and surveying the outer appearance of their client's face, posture, and clothes. In order for you to be successful during your Natural Health Makeover, you must do the same—only you're scanning your body from the inside. Use this exercise to help you understand how your body reacts to different situations.

1. Select a situation. This could be after eating, upon waking, after sitting, after exercise, after or during work.
2. Close your eyes.
3. Take note of all bodily sensations. These could include pain, perspiration, breathing, muscle tightness, stomach upset, gas, bloating, itching, feelings, fatigue.

The Whole Person Makeover

The fifth principle of natural medicine is that one must address the whole person in order for treatment to be effective. Depending on whom you talk to, the word "whole" can mean many things. To say you're "whole" might mean you're healthy or uninjured. A wholesome body is one that is well. Wholeness indicates something that's complete—another way of stating health. "Whole" also refers to a state in which every part is accounted for, a process that natural health care and a Natural Health Makeover are very good at.

When you take care of the whole body, not just the part that hurts—like the head or big toe—other complaints often disappear as well. The billions of cells in your body are like individual members of an expansive community. Each operates independently, but can also work together to form, for example, an organ like the heart or stomach. And, like most communities, your body works best when each member or cell is getting along and pulling its own weight. When one or a group of cells gets sick or injured, others are affected either directly or indirectly. While the big toe might be way down there and the head up here, they're both housed in the same skin covering. They both receive the same blood supply, are influenced by the same immune system, and are fed by the same foods. Thus chronic headaches and an aching toe (gout) could be clues there's a digestive problem going on.

Even though the Natural Health Makeover plan is laid out in twelve different stages for a dozen body systems, you will be addressing your whole health by following all these steps. This is evidenced by specific recommendations repeated throughout many sections. For example, the advice to eat whole foods is suggested in every makeover chapter. That's because consuming healthful foods has body-wide effects. The same goes for quitting smoking, avoiding drugs, and other makeover steps.

Principle number five: *Keep the whole body healthy and everything else will work better.*

The Motions of Emotions

I recently spoke at a half-day health care seminar to a group of counselors, psychologists, and psychiatrists about the relationship between the body and mind. I told this group that we talk about body-mind or psychosomatic medicine as if the body and mind are two distinct and separate factions. The doctor treats physical ailments, while the counselor cares for feelings. As health care practitioners, we need to remember that this separation is artificial, and that physical and emotional components often overlap and influence one another.

It's understood that chronic pain or other physical ailments can be emotionally upsetting. But, psychoneuroimmunology (PNI), the study of how emotions and thoughts influence physical symptoms and immunity, is a growing field. So now when you say your headache or other pain is from stress or worry, know that the scientific world is backing you up. Recent research has found that treating feelings can help a wide scope of physical ailments such as leukemia,[5] breast cancer,[6] psoriasis,[7] gum disease,[8] and colds.[9]

Let the Spirit Cure You

The spiritual side of healing is as old as shamans and faith healers, and as modern as the chapels found in many hospitals. However, including religious belief as part of conventional health care treatment has been taboo, or, at the very least, irrelevant in past decades. That is changing as spirituality slowly makes it way into medical discussions and research.[10] Mary Ann Miller, R.N., Ph.D., an associate professor at the College of Nursing, University of Delaware, writes: "If one believes that spirituality permeates all human experiences rather than being additional to them, one must accept it as integral to health or a sense of *wholeness* (my italics) or well-being." She points out that not only does this "belief in something greater than the self" give meaning, value, and direction to life—a wonderful stress reducer—but many religions advocate healthy living habits. Seventh-Day Adventists, for instance, discourage alcohol and cigarette use.[11]

Finding your own spiritual niche, be it attending church each Sunday, meditating silently each morning or going for a reflective walk in the evening, will help you complete your circle of health.

Educate Yourself to Health

The final and sixth rule of natural health is education. The more you know about your body and how to take care of it, the healthier you'll be. I'm constantly amazed by how many people are ill-informed about the state of their health. When I met Muriel, an 82-year-old California woman with excruciating back pain, I asked her what was wrong. She said: "I have osteoporosis." Then she paused a moment. "Or is it osteoarthritis? I'm not sure." I suggested she call her doctor for the correct diagnosis. "Oh no," she replied, "I couldn't do that. My doctor's far too busy. Besides, I trust that he'll take care of me."

Don't become a Muriel. Use this and other books and your doctor to learn about the state of your health. In fact, "doctor" is derived from the Latin word *docere,* which means "to teach." So a doctor is (or should be) your private instructor, ready to educate you about your illness and your health, and then guide you toward wellness. To make the most of this situation, be a good student. Ask a lot of questions, do your homework by reading up on what concerns you, and attend health classes that interest you. See Appendix C for books and magazines you can read.

Principle number six: The more you know, the healthier you'll be.

Chapter 2

Making the Most of Your Natural Health Makeover

The Importance of a Healthy Foundation

To be successful in business you must plan for the future. If you don't, your business can end up bankrupt. Health is much the same way. If you take care of business now, there's less chance your health will go bankrupt later on. This can be difficult to do when you feel fine. Practicing naturopathic medicine is my motivation to embrace healthy habits. Not only do I see how ill people can become from years of lifestyle indiscretions, but I get to witness how healthful living helps reverse disease.

If you need convincing in this regard, talk to your older relatives. With any luck, you'll have different people in your family living different lifestyles with the results to prove it.

The other plus to living the healthy life is that you have more room for moderation. In other words, if you make over your health now, your body will better tolerate the odd glass of wine or the occasional cookie. A healthy body has reserves, ready to handle stress. Very ill people who decide to pursue natural treatments are often required to make radical and immediate changes in order to get well. Limited reserves often require them to stick with these changes if they want to return to health. It's like the difference between maintaining your car with regular tune-ups or waiting until it breaks down and then having to replace expensive parts.

Turn Everyday Habits
Into Health Enhancers

Changing or even building upon your current lifestyle is a powerful way of boosting wellness and treating sickness. Most people have at least some habits that are healthful and can be used as a foundation during a Natural Health Makeover. Before you begin, make a list of all the health-enhancing factors in your life. These can include drinking water (any amount), eating fruits or vegetables, sleeping, or having fun. Save this sheet so you can list additional items or modify your current ones as they apply during your makeover plan.

Your Talkative Body Is Your
Makeover Guide

The body is constantly chattering about how it's doing and what it needs. Uncomfortable or intense needs, like pain or fever, are simplest to listen to. The quieter the need, the easier it is to ignore. How often have you put off going to the bathroom because you're busy? Or eaten past the point of satiety because the food tastes good? If you continue to discount these requests, your body will speak up. Dismissing thirst, for instance, may result in constipation or chronic urinary tract infections. Neglect these pleas and your body will eventually scream at the top of its lungs with even more serious ailments.

When I first started teaching people about natural health, I'd tell them to listen to their bodies, assuming they'd know what to do. While what I said was true, I often got blank stares from my audience because they didn't know what I was talking about. They didn't know how to listen; and even when they did hear their bodies talk, they didn't know how to respond.

Attentive body listening also clues you into, and helps you prevent, sickness that can take a foothold. In getting to know your body, you need to determine what your warning systems are, that is, what are the signs that you've pushed it too far, health-wise. Perhaps a stiff neck or upset stomach are signals that you need a Natural Health Makeover tune-up. Each of us also has an Achilles heel that falls victim most easily to stress or neglect. Identify yours, so you can concentrate on the section or sections in this book that address your frailest body system.

■ *Makeover Hint #2—How to Converse with Your Body*

Acquire body-listening skills by learning how to consciously listen to, not merely hear, what your body has to say. Merely find a quiet spot to sit, and pay close attention to how your entire body feels, starting with your head and slowly working down to your toes.

Twelve Practical Tips to Overcome Makeover Blocks

Your Natural Health Makeover needn't be difficult. Read on for practical tips to help you get started and stay motivated.

- Get ready, get set—make over. If you find it difficult getting started, pick a date when to begin. Circle that day on your calendar; tell friends and family if it helps. Then enjoy the anticipation of getting ready for the big day.

- Groom yourself for success. Setting forth on a makeover is like quitting smoking. It's only going to work if you want to do it.

- Use your imagination. Picture the results when you're done—a vibrant, energetic, healthier you. Know what you want, and then take steps to get there.

- Follow your passion. A Natural Health Makeover works best when you identify and follow those aspects that excite you the most.

- Accessorize your life. Although this book is laid out as a specific plan, feel free to insert your own ideas where you want, when you want, how you want. Think of a Natural Health Makeover as a powerful way of integrating your current lifestyle with healthy new ways of living.

- Take baby steps. Make one or two small, easy-to-swallow changes that you'll stick with at a time.

- Try it on for size before you say no. Before turning your nose up at tofu or flaxseeds, try them—you might like them.

- Let your taste buds guide you. Fortunately, Mother Nature gave us a vast variety of foods—as well as exercise, relaxation, and natural treatments—to choose from, to fit our many tastes.

- Learn to mix and match. Combining old lifestyle ways with new in a way you find comfortable is an important part of this health makeover plan.

- Make over your schedule. You must make room in your regular routine for exercise, sleep, and learning about new foods. If at first the scheduling-in of makeover steps feels forced, wait for a month or two. You'll soon adjust to—even yearn for—everyday exercise and wholesome meals.

- Rest up for the big makeover. Make sure you're sufficiently rested before you dive into your Natural Health Makeover plan. Fatigue can make lifestyle changes harder.

- Stay motivated. Last, but certainly not least, know that with each step you make, you'll feel better. This is your motivation to continue. Once people understand that a health makeover and maintenance is a lifelong endeavor, they are more inclined to make permanent changes and stay the course.

Before and After—Snapshots of Your Health

The Before-and-After Chart is not unlike the before-and-after pictures you see of a beauty makeover. Not only is it a good record of the progress you've made during your Natural Health Makeover, but because the results of a health makeover can be subtle—a few pounds lost here, slightly more energy there—it will serve as a reminder of where you started health-wise.

There are a couple of ways to rate symptoms: both by intensity and by frequency. For intensity, I use a 1 to 10 scale to assess a patient's health, where the number 1 indicates feeling poorly and 10 is perfect health. This works especially well for those vague, hard-to-define symptoms like fatigue and malaise. Under the frequency column, record whether a symptom occurs daily, weekly, monthly, or several times during the day, week, or month.

With that in mind, fill out the Before section of this chart. You'll complete the After part once you've finished your Natural Health Makeover. I've grouped symptoms according to the different body systems you'll be working on; some fit under many categories but I have listed each one only once.

Table 2.1
THE BEFORE-AND-AFTER CHART

| | Before | | After | |
	Intensity (1–10)	Frequency	Intensity (1–10)	Frequency
LIVER				
Itching				
Bad breath				
Sensitive to chemical smells (paints, solvents, perfumes)				
Sensitive to cigarette smoke				
Food intolerances or allergies				
Foul-smelling stools				
Prone to infections				
"Toxic" feeling				
DIGESTION				
Weight (lbs)				
Abdominal bloating				
Excessive gas				
Excessive belching				
Heartburn/indigestion				
Nausea				
Constipation				
Diarrhea				
KIDNEYS AND URINARY TRACT				
Urinate frequently				
Urinate at night				
Pain/burning with urination				
Weak urine stream				
Difficulty starting urine stream				
Bladder doesn't feel empty after urination				
Retain water throughout body				
Dull mid-backache				
Side ache				
Weakness				
Loss of appetite				

Table 2.1, cont'd.

	Before		After	
	Intensity (1–10)	*Frequency*	*Intensity (1–10)*	*Frequency*
IMMUNE SYSTEM				
Difficulty recovering from illness				
Poor wound healing				
Chronic infections				
Recurring warts				
Cold sores				
Canker sores				
Genital herpes				
Yeast infections (anywhere)				
Nail fungus				
Athlete's foot				
ADRENAL GLANDS				
Fatigue				
Frequent colds/flus				
Headaches				
Upset stomach				
Insomnia				
Irritable				
PMS				
Many allergies (foods, pollens, animals, drugs etc.)				
Feel "stressed out"				
HEART AND CIRCULATION				
Shortness of breath when exerting self				
Bruise easily				
Cold arms/legs				
Irregular heartbeat				
MUSCLES				
Joint pain				
Joint stiffness				
Body aches				
Tight muscles				
Chronic backache				

Table 2.1, cont'd.

	Before		*After*	
	Intensity (1–10)	*Frequency*	*Intensity (1–10)*	*Frequency*
LOVE LIFE				
Low libido				
Impotence				
Vaginal dryness				
BONES AND TEETH				
Mid-back pain				
"Bad" teeth				
Frequent fractures				
Bleeding gums when brushing teeth				
Bad breath				
SKIN				
Acne				
Rashes				
Dry skin				
Oily skin				
EYES				
Dry eyes				
Eyestrain				
Red eyes				
Decreased central vision				
Difficulty adapting to light changes				
Difficulty reading				
Shade/color contrasts are fuzzy				
FEELINGS/THINKING				
Sense of well-being (good or bad)				
Depression				
Anxiety				
Memory				
Concentration (good or bad)				
Mood swings				

How You Can Expect to Feel After a Natural Health Makeover

What can you expect after completing this makeover plan? It all depends on you, your current health, your age and sex, and how diligently you stuck with this layout. I find that patients who take my advice to heart invariably feel better. Here's some of what I hear:

- More energy
- Constipation improves or resolves
- Digestion is better
- Sleep is more sound
- Headaches decrease or leave
- Thinking clears
- Skin clears
- Get sick less often
- Sex drive increases
- Pain diminishes
- Hope returns

There are occasionally instances when health doesn't improve—usually for a reason. Look at the end of each chapter where I summarize the steps you've just taken. Also listed here are references to conditions related to the body system you just made over. If following these two steps doesn't set you right, seek the counsel of a natural health practitioner or your physician. A list of laboratory tests conclude each chapter for your benefit and that of your doctor.

Chapter 3

Defend Your Body for Total Revitalization

Your Multi-Talented Liver

The liver is one of the largest and busiest organs in your body. Tucked under the right-hand side of your ribcage, it makes bile for fat digestion, stores blood, iron, and vitamins like A, B_{12}, D, and K (that's why your mother tried to get you to eat liver), and is involved in most of the body's metabolic functions. This versatile structure is also a respected member of the digestive system. Did you know that the liver helps stabilize your blood sugar levels? Were you aware that the liver breaks protein down into its most basic building blocks—amino acids? Has anyone ever told you that fat metabolism, including cholesterol production, happens in your liver? Arthur Guyton, M.D., author of *Textbook of Medical Physiology*, states that "the liver has so many and such varied function that it is impossible to separate its actions from those of other organ systems."[1]

Natural health practitioners are enthralled by the liver's part in digestion, and its dual role as body defender and blood cleanser. A direct blood line runs from the gastrointestinal (GI) tract to the liver; another feeds this industrious organ with blood from the general circulation. This means the amazing liver must filter and clean a total of one and a half quarts of blood every minute. While blood from the digestive tract is full of nutrients needed by the liver (and rest of the body), it also carries with it bacteria and other undesirables like drugs you've taken and chemicals you've been exposed to. All of these need to be pulled from the blood to keep your body safe. Kupffer cells, the liver's resident immunity guards, are extremely efficient at grabbing bacteria, and handling bothersome substances trying to sneak into the body via the GI tract. Special chemicals in the liver detoxify drugs like penicillin, erythromycin, and ampicillin and toss them into bile which is then carried away. Similarly, several hormones like estrogen, cortisol, and thyroxine are inactivated by the liver so as not to poison the body.[1] Premenstrual syndrome and other conditions aggravated by elevated estrogen are often solved by treating an overburdened liver so it becomes more efficient at breaking down estrogen, which in turn lowers estrogen blood levels.

Bile, which is made by the liver but stored in the gallbladder, is another important piece of the liver story. Besides helping you digest fat, the four cups of bile your liver produces each day also carts toxins away into the feces. This is one reason why a well-functioning colon and regular bowel movements are vital, in addition to a picture-perfect liver. If you're constipated, stool remains in the colon longer than it should—along with toxic bile—and some of those toxins are reabsorbed into the bloodstream.

A Regular Liver Makeover Is a Must

Some of the poisons deactivated by the liver come from your body. But living in today's world has made health problems much more complicated than they were even 20 years ago, partly due to all the chemicals we're currently exposed to. Pollution, medications (over-the-counter and prescription), alcohol, tobacco, drugs, pesticides, food additives, junk food, plastics, solvents, and other factors have placed an additional burden on the modern liver. Some people work in professions where chemical exposure is an everyday occurrence, like factory employees or dry cleaners. When you consider that blood cleansing is only one of the many tasks your liver must perform, you begin to understand why a regular Liver Makeover is a good idea.

Naturopathic physicians talk about a "sluggish," "toxic," or "congested" liver. This doesn't refer to overt liver disease like hepatitis or cirrhosis, but a condition where the liver isn't functioning up to par. Besides asking about possible toxic exposure, naturopathic doctors look at a person's medical history for signs that the liver needs help. One hint is when someone has used or is using therapeutic hormones, like levothyroxine (Synthroid®), estrogen (birth control pills, hormone replacement), or anabolic steroids. Even pregnancy—

when estrogen levels soar—may be reason enough for a liver cleanse. Note: Never embark on a Liver Makeover when you're pregnant or nursing a baby.

A poor diet can add to the liver's burden. The busy liver, and every other bodily organ, needs nutrients to operate efficiently. The liver is no different.

So what are the signs that your body and liver might be toxic? They include unexplained itching, bad breath, headaches, sensitivity to many things—including chemicals and foods, constant fatigue, increased susceptibility to infection, acne, foul-smelling stools and a general "toxic" feeling as if you have a hangover.

Super Healing Foods

The place to start with a Liver Makeover is to screen all the foods you eat. I'll be harping on the need for sound nutrition again and again—that is, after all, the foundation of good health—but for now, let's begin with how foods affect the liver.

As a general rule, the more whole, unprocessed foods you eat—fresh fruits and vegetables; raw, unsalted nuts and seeds; dried beans and legumes; fresh poultry, fish and lean meats; whole grains—the better. While processing supplies us with food when fresh is unavailable, eating products with synthetic preservatives, colorings, flavorings, and other additives is hard on the liver. Study content using the labels on all packaged foods you buy; if you can't pronounce it, you may not want to eat it. Some additives are fine. For example, annatto added for color, or extra vitamins aren't going to hurt you.

When foods have been processed so much that they barely resemble true food, beware. Potato chips, for instance, look like nothing from nature and are worthless when it comes to nutrition. That goes for most of the creatively colored, sugared, and shaped food-like items you find in the grocery store.

As you begin to make the switch from food-like edibles to true foods, find out if your grocer carries organic produce. A recent study published in *Plant and Soil* (Volume 167, 1994) showed that barley fertilized with manure—in other words, organic barley—contained three times as much vitamin B_{12} as the commercial variety fed with synthetic fertilizers; spinach treated the same way had almost twice as much B_{12}.[2] Since only vitamin B_{12} was measured in this experiment, we don't know if amounts of other vitamins and minerals are also higher, but we can assume that some, if not most, probably are. Past experiments have shown us that animals fed organic grains grow much better than those feasting on foods treated with inorganic fertilizers. This has led scientists to believe that good old-fashioned manure, compost, and other natural fertilizers enhance at least the B vitamins in foods. Thus eating organic foods not only allows you to avoid liver-damaging pesticides, but also gives your liver more of the nutrients it needs.

Check for Food Intolerances

Sometimes avoiding pesticides, food additives, and processed foods isn't enough. For reasons we're not entirely sure of, allergies or just plain food sensitivities seem to be on the rise. These intolerances may be due to our modern lifestyle fraught with pesticides, irradiated foods, processed and refined foods, hybridized foods, genetically manipulated foods, stress, poor digestion due to faulty eating habits and general liver overload. Whatever the reason, food intolerance is more common than we think and a party-crasher when it comes to health.

Food allergy symptoms are varied and unpredictable. When I mention to patients that food allergies could be behind their health troubles, they often say, "But my stomach doesn't hurt! How can that be?" Food allergies don't just affect the digestive tract. According to scientific research, they've also been linked to rheumatoid arthritis,[3] migraine headaches,[4] eczema,[5] asthma,[6] irritable bowel syndrome,[7] and several other conditions. Many times when a patient comes to me with a chronic complaint and displays a personal or family history of allergies—not necessarily to food—I suggest testing for foods. Invariably, after avoiding those allergic foods for two to four weeks, they feel better. You'll notice in Part Two that I frequently suggest checking for food allergies when simple measures don't work.

If you suspect you're intolerant to one or more foods, consider food allergy testing. This can be done with a blood test; I recommend the test which measures both IgE and IgG antibodies, and picks up both immediate and delayed food reactions. Or you can test for intolerances on your own using the Elimination and

Challenge diet. If you know or suspect you have severe reactions to certain foods, do not use this method.

- Begin by making a list of foods you eat every day. These are the foods you're going to eliminate for four days.
- Add to this list (if not already included) the foods that most commonly cause reactions in people. These foods will also be eliminated for four days:

    alcohol (wine, beer, and hard liquor)

    chocolate

    citrus fruits (grapefruit, oranges, lemons, limes, tangerines)

    coconut

    coffee and black tea

    corn (often in the form of corn syrup)

    dairy products (milk, butter, cheese, ice cream, yogurt, cottage cheese)

    eggs

    fish

    nuts (including nut oils and butters)

    peanuts and peanut butter—peanuts are a legume, not a nut

    pineapple

    soy (a common additive)

    strawberries

    sugar, and products containing it

    tomatoes

    vinegar

    wheat (bread, pasta, cookies, cereals etc.)

    yeast

- For four days, eat a diet of foods that rarely cause allergies (unless they're on your list of frequently eaten foods). These include:

    apricots

    artichokes

    asparagus

barley

broccoli

carrots (organic only)

grapes (organic only)

honey

lamb and mutton

lettuce

oats

peaches

pears

raisins (organic)

rice

rye

sweet potatoes

- On the fifth day, eat one of the suspected intolerant foods on your list. This is called a Challenge. It helps you determine, after clearing your body of all suspected allergenic foods, which ones are causing you troubles. Keep a detailed journal of what you eat and any reactions you have to any food. If you react (watch for symptoms for two days), remove that food from your diet. If you have no reactions, feel free to keep it in your diet.
- Continue introducing a new food every other day until you've finished the entire list.

This is a very time-consuming process that takes patience, observation, and perseverance. The advantage of the Elimination and Challenge technique is that it gives you immediate, firsthand knowledge of which foods are troubling you. Once you've experienced the stomach upset, headache, or foggy thinking caused by an allergenic egg, you're less likely to eat it again. The downside to this method is the willpower and time involved. Also, this test is not very adept at picking up delayed reactions that last longer than two days, or reactions caused from eating a combination of foods. Most of my patients prefer the simplicity of having blood drawn for the IgE/IgG test, and like the clear black-and-white information it provides. Either way, investigating for food intolerances can make you and your liver happier.

Don's Sensitive Stomach

Don, a 67-year-old retired farmer, came to see me for high cholesterol; the usual dietary changes hadn't helped. However, after visiting with him for awhile it was apparent that a more annoying problem for Don was his sensitive stomach. He had a difficult time taking most medicines or supplements, and eating a variety of foods, because they hurt his gut. This roadblock made it difficult for me to suggest nutrients or herbs for Don, so before beginning any treatment plan, I recommended he be tested for food allergies.

When the test results came back, many foods showed up as highly allergic, including all milk products, eggs, and most grains. Don agreed to avoid these foods for one month to see if that would help his constantly sore stomach. Thirty days later Don came to see me and happily reported that his once delicate abdomen was ever so much better. All gas was gone and he no longer needed antacids. The pleasing side effects of this temporarily restrictive diet were a 75-percent drop in fatigue, clear sinuses, less joint pain, and an end to his once ongoing leg pain. He now found dinner-time enjoyable, and he could take most pills with ease. This first step now allowed me to direct Don to nutrients that would help with his cholesterol problem.

Wash Away the Poisons

The next step to reviving a sluggish liver is to remove all the poisons you can from your life. These include toxins at home, work, and play. Once you have identified these potential poisons, look for safer alternatives.

One of the most common household toxins is cleaners—the window sprays; tub scrubbers; cleaning fluids for the floors, walls, and counters; carpet spot removers; and sink decloggers. Wherever possible, replace these smelly poisons with non-toxic cleaning products either purchased from a natural foods store or homemade. If you're a gardener, consider replacing synthetic fertilizers with more natural alternatives like compost and manure. Call your local gardening shop for options to garden pesticides; there are also many mail order companies specializing in these products. For you interior decorators, be cautious when working with paint, paint thinners, paint strippers, and other harmful solvents. Again, search for safer options. If you can't locate substitutes, be sure to ventilate well while working with these products. Everyone should be cautious around gasoline and similar fuels.

Some people are faced with toxins every day in their work. Anyone who works in a dental office, farms, cleans offices or homes for a living, paints houses or does other building repair or remodeling that involves solvents or chemicals is in danger of hurting the liver. Again, where possible, use safer chemical alternatives. Otherwise, practice safety techniques when handling these chemicals such as ventilation, wearing protective clothing, gloves and masks, and taking breaks from exposure. Discuss using less toxic substances with your employer.

Last, take a close look at any medications you're currently taking. The liver must break down most of these drugs when your body's done with them. One way to protect your liver is by minimizing the number of synthetic medicines you take. You should have less need for some medicines after completing your Natural Health Makeover. In the meantime, consider using natural treatments instead when you're sick (see Part Two). For help with serious health conditions, consult with a practitioner knowledgeable in natural therapies.

■ *Makeover Hint # 3—Less Is More*

Many times we use poisons unnecessarily. You don't have to use a spray cleaner every time you wash the kitchen counter. You don't have to spray insecticide around your house every month to prevent ants from creeping in. You don't have to bleach your clothes every time you wash them. Adopt the motto: Less is more, especially when it comes to chemicals and your liver's health.

Your Liver's Favorite Foods

Your liver has many favorite foods that nourish it and help it work better. Brussels sprouts, cauliflower, cabbage, and other members of the brassica family boost its detoxifying abilities.[7] Beets, both the greens and red-staining root, are famous as liver foods due in part to their nutritious state.

If you're looking to spice up a bland meal and heal you
at the same time, lace your food with onions and garlic.
smelly bulbs are loaded with sulfur that help restore the liver's sulfate reservoir, necessary for detoxification. Turmeric, that yellowish-
orange spice that gives prepared mustard and curry their festive colors, contains curcumin. This bright pigment works by enhancing the
liver's bile flow.[8]

A favorite liver beverage is green tea. Japanese research tells us
that the more cups you drink each day, the more your liver is protected. When subjects drank very high amounts of this tea daily (10
cups and more), laboratory tests showed that serum markers like
aspartate aminotransferase were favorably influenced.[9]

■ *Makeover Hint #4 Make Ruby Beet Soup*

For those cold winter nights, prepare a steamy pot of ruby beet
soup. You'll please both your tummy and liver with these ingredients.

Add the following items to one quart of stock (chicken, beef,
or vegetable). Add more liquid as needed. Let simmer for two hours
(or six hours in a crock pot), and serve with a crusty loaf of bread.
Add a dollop of sour cream to your soup bowl if you like.

2 cups of beets, cubed

1 cup of red and/or green cabbage, shredded

3 cloves of garlic, diced

1 onion, diced

1/2 cup carrots, diced

Season to taste with sea salt, fresh ground pepper, and other
favorite spices.

Fill Up on Fiber

Your liver, your digestive system, in fact your entire body adores
fiber. Fiber, also known as roughage, is the indigestible stuff found
in whole grains, beans, legumes, and fresh vegetables and fruits.
Unfortunately, the more we tamper with these virgin foods, the more
likely they are to lose both fiber and other nutrients. The vitamins

and minerals you lose when you eat fiber-less, processed foods is reason enough to become a roughage enthusiast. However, there are other reasons as well.

More fiber means less chance of constipation. Efficient digestion decreases both your body's and liver's exposure to toxins either created by the bacteria in your colon or those consumed. A healthy serving of fiber several times daily also helps sweep away bile, which carries with it more toxins for disposal outside. The water-soluble fibers in particular, found in vegetables and fruits, increase bile secretion. Finally, too little roughage creates an upset in the bug population in your intestine. There are over 400 good bugs residing in your GI tract keeping the bad bugs at bay. When delinquent germs increase in number and take over, they make poisons like endotoxins—one more thing for your liver to deal with. Yeast overgrowth and infections from pathogenic bacteria are also more likely.

Here are 10 easy ways to increase your fiber intake:

- Munch on carrot and celery sticks before each meal (when you're hungry).
- Eat brown rice instead of white; or mix it half and half with the white.
- Have a piece of fresh fruit instead of juice for breakfast.
- Add beans or barley to your homemade soups.
- Eat hot oat bran cereal for breakfast (or as a snack).
- Eat whole-grain bread, not white.
- Top your yogurt with fresh banana slices or other fresh fruit.
- Crumble shredded wheat on top of casseroles.
- Eat the skin on your baked potato (this is safest if the potato is organic).
- Add a tomato slice, lettuce, cucumber slices and/or bean sprouts to your sandwich.

Super Nutrients for Your Liver

The next step in revitalizing your liver is to ensure that you're giving this hardworking organ all the vitamins and minerals it needs.

Antioxidants top the list—those that fight organ-damaging, make-you-look-older-than-you-really-are free radical molecules. These super nutrients are found far and wide in nature, both in foods and herbs. The most brightly colored fruits and vegetables contain the most antioxidant carotenoids (the autumn-colored pigments) and flavonoids (red, blue, and purple colorings). Be sure to feast on these brilliant foods. For added protection look to the antioxidant nutrients selenium, vitamins E and C, and glutathione. Your whole foods diet should keep you well stocked. Look to a well-balanced multiple vitamin pill as additional insurance. The more diverse the antioxidants you consume, the better they work.

There's also a class of liver nutrients called lipotropics which guard the liver from fatty buildup. Exposure to toxic substances like pesticides or birth control pills increases fat infiltration in your liver and drags down function. Lipotropic compounds include choline, folic acid, vitamin B_{12}, methionine, betaine, and carnitine; lipotropic formulas often include other liver-friendly herbs and nutrients as well. If you feel a need to use such a formula, start by taking one pill a day and gradually increase dosage by one pill daily until you reach the recommended amount. Unless you are under the guidance of a health practitioner, take lipotropics for no more than two months. If you experience any adverse effects while taking these pills, like nausea, decrease your dose. If this doesn't help, discontinue taking them.

Four Helpful Liver Herbs

Some plants serve as both food and herbs; we find several among the liver herbs. You can use some of these in everyday cooking like turmeric, known in professional circles as *Curcuma longa*. Or, if you prefer, take the active pigment found in turmeric, curcumin, as a pill. You can eat artichokes, *Cynara scolymus*, or take its leaves in medicinal form—pills, tea, or tincture. Researchers suspect that cynarin, one of artichoke's active ingredients, is what boosts bile secretion.[10]

One of the most fascinating liver herbs is milk thistle, or *Silybum marianum*. Researchers have discovered that milk thistle actually protects the liver from poisonous substances by offsetting free radical damage, and through regeneration of new liver cells.[11] You can see that milk thistle is a most valuable plant to have around for both liver damage due to diseases like hepatitis and cirrhosis, or exposure to toxins ranging from alcohol to drugs to chemicals. I have a very low tolerance to anesthetics, and typically feel spacey and ill afterward. A few years ago I needed a sebaceous cyst removed from my scalp, and was dreading the operation only because I knew I'd be injected with a local anesthetic. As an experiment I took milk thistle several days before and directly after the procedure. That day and the few following, when I usually took to my bed, I felt fine. Milk thistle had done its job.

A simple way to start using this herb is to include milk thistle seeds (available at many fine natural foods markets) as part of your daily meals. Merely grind up a week's worth in your coffee blender or food processor. Sprinkle one tablespoon of this seed meal on your food each day. Store unused portions in the refrigerator.

Dandelion (*Taraxacum officinale*) is famous as a liver herb. The root of this "weed" works in three-step fashion: by promoting bile production in the liver, its flow to the gallbladder (where it's stored) and finally release from the gallbladder into the digestive tract.[12] Remember that without proper bile flow, toxic substances can't be adequately flushed from your body. Drink dandelion root tea made from the unsprayed weeds in your backyard, one to three cups a day. If you're unfortunate enough to have a dandelion-free lawn or are worried about what the neighbors will think, look to your local herb or health food store. You can also spruce up salads with a few dandelion leaves thrown in.

■ Makeover Hint #5—Live on the Wild Side

The first place to look for liver herbs is your backyard. Those #$%@ dandelions, specifically the long tap root clogging up your lawn, are some of the best medicines for your liver. During the summer collect your dandelions, cut off the root and cut it into small pieces or chop up in a blender. For a fresh cup of liver tea, boil a pot of water, add a handful of root, and simmer for 30 minutes. Drink three cups of tea daily for one to two weeks. If you'd like to dry the root for later use, split it longitudinally first.

Practice Regular Inner Cleansing

Like regular exercise, routinely cleansing your body by eating simple foods is a healthy idea. By doing this you decrease the toxic burden on your liver and ease up on digestion. Think of this as a liver vacation. In fact, I suggest you follow a cleansing diet for a day or two each month instead of attempting an annual week-long cleanse.

There are several types of cleansing routines. Fasting with water only is the most traditional way to cleanse. It's simple and requires minimal preparation. The disadvantage is that some people find the idea of going without food both difficult (due to hunger and social pressures to eat) and frightening. Some find drinking only water boring. I don't recommend you embark on a water fast without professional supervision.

Another choice is to follow a liquid-only diet where fresh vegetable and fruit juices, vegetable broth, herbal teas, and water are on the menu. This requires slightly more preparation, but it also gives you some nutrients and a variety of tastes. Again, be cautious before starting this sort of cleanse. Only do it if you're experienced; alternately try this plan for one to two days.

A third option is to follow a simple cleansing diet. While not as effective as a fast, this menu is less apt to induce hunger because it includes food. Also these cleansing foods are highly nutritious and can actually help your liver (and other organs) function more efficiently. But most important, a cleansing diet such as this retrains your taste buds to appreciate the whole foods we should all eat most of the time. After a few months of regular cleansing "vacations" you may find that your everyday menus don't vary appreciably from your monthly cleansing weekends. Those of you unaccustomed to a high-fiber diet may find this cleansing regimen causes bloating and gas. Drink plenty of water, chew your food well and drink gas-relieving teas like peppermint and ginger.

Here is a list of foods you can consume during a cleanse. Eat mostly vegetables, with small portions of other foods. Drink one to two quarts of fluid daily. Eat organic foods where possible:

- Amaranth
- Brown rice
- Dried beans and legumes (soaked, then cooked)

- Fresh raw fruits
- Fresh vegetables (raw or lightly steamed)
- Fresh vegetable juices; can include small amount of fruit in these juices to taste
- Herbal teas
- Homemade vegetarian soup or broth
- Kamut
- Millet
- Oils such as canola, flax seed, and olive—cold pressed (use sparingly as seasoning or dressing). Don't heat flax seed oil.
- Nuts (raw and unsalted; not peanuts)
- Quinoa
- Seeds (raw and unsalted)
- Water (pure—either distilled or filtered)

■ *Makeover Hint #6—The Mini-Cleanse*

Can't stand the idea of a two-day cleanse? Then start out small, very small. Begin with a one-meal cleanse, say breakfast. The following week or month, follow your cleansing routine for two meals—breakfast and lunch. The third month, cleanse for an entire day. Continue at this snail's pace until you're cleansing for a whole two days.

How to Calm an Angry Liver

Natural and conventional medicine both recognize that emotions affect overall health. According to Chinese medical philosophy, the liver is the governor of emotions, and when feelings are excessive or insufficient, they generate illness. Or conversely, when the body is unwell, the emotional state is affected.

Traditional Chinese Medicine has developed an even more specific guide to emotions and various body organs. Seven different emotions—fear, fright, grief, joy, sadness, pensiveness, and anger—are thought to be tied to five different organs. The liver is said to be the seat of anger, and is considered, along with the heart, to be the most susceptible to emotional disruption. An angry outlook, according to Chinese Medicine, is thus responsible for liver problems. Or if the liver is "congested," you may experience frustration, anger or extreme mood swings.[13]

Use Edgar Cayce's Castor Oil Treatment

The castor oil treatment is an old-time treatment for the liver, though it can be used on other body parts and does affect other systems. I include this historical, and somewhat mystical, treatment because: (1) it works, and (2) it's tied to such an interesting story.

Edgar Cayce, born in 1877 in Hopkinsville, Kentucky, was a lay healer. The difference between him and others was that he could only offer therapeutic suggestions under a self-induced trance. With the help of his wife, Gertrude, and secretary, Gladys Davis Turner, Cayce performed almost 9,000 readings over a 40-year period for the sick that visited him. According to historical records he helped an enormous number of people, so much so that the Association for Research and Enlightenment, or ARE, Clinic in Arizona, was specifically set up to offer Cayce's health principles and remedies to patients. This clinic still thrives today.

Although used for thousands of years, the castor oil treatment was one remedy frequently suggested by Cayce. A recent study published in *The Journal of Naturopathic Medicine* proved that castor oil packs increase the number of white blood cells called lymphocytes in the body—one part of immunity.[14] This treatment is also thought to work as an antitoxin.

■ Makeover Hint #7—How to Make a Castor Oil Pack

To make your own castor oil pack, begin by collecting:

- Cloth—36" × 12" inch piece of plain wool or cotton flannel
- Bottle of castor oil
- Plastic sheet (Saran Wrap™ or plastic bag opened up)
- Towel
- Two safety pins.

Fold the cloth so you end up with a pack of three thicknesses that measure one foot by one foot. Pour the castor oil into a bowl, and dip the pack into it until it is saturated, but not dripping, with oil. Next, find a comfortable and quiet place where you can lie down for 30 minutes to an hour, and apply the castor oil pack over the right upper area of your abdomen. This would include the bottom portion of your right rib cage where your liver is housed, overlapping slightly to the area just above and to the right of your belly button. Place a piece of plastic sheet over the pack. Wrap the towel around your torso and fasten with a couple of safety pins.

For a suspected toxic liver, practice this therapy daily for a week to a month. Save your pack in a plastic bag between treatments. Oily skin can be washed with a baking soda wash, two teaspoons of soda added to a quart of warm water.

Lois Halts Hair Loss With Amazing Liver Treatment

After quitting a 10-year stint on birth control pills, 27-year-old Lois noticed she was losing her hair, so she decided to consult a naturopathic physician. Upon learning of her history, the naturopath immediately recognized that Lois's liver needed help. A decade of synthetic hormones had compromised her liver function. First the doctor prescribed a lipotropic supplement. Next she advised that Lois use a castor oil pack over her liver region. Lois followed the doctor's directions exactly. When she returned to the doctor's office two months later, she reported that her hair felt thicker and wasn't falling out at the same rate as before.

Liver Makeover Checkup

How did you do? These are the steps you've just taken to invigorate your liver:

- Began eating more whole foods, and fewer processed foods, and fewer additives.
- Checked for food intolerances.
- Checked home and work for poisons.

- Started eating liver-friendly foods like Brussels sprouts, beets, onions, and garlic.
- Ate more fiber.
- Added more antioxidant foods and nutrients to regimen.
- Took a lipotropic supplement.
- Tried some liver herbs like turmeric, dandelion, and milk thistle.
- Vowed to eat a cleansing diet for one to two days each month.
- Learned about the relationship between anger and the liver.
- Tried a castor oil pack.

For Related Problems, See

- Acne
- Constipation
- Eczema
- Headaches

Laboratory Tests Your Doctor Can Order

- Liver Detoxification Profile
- Food Allergy Panel
- Liver Enzyme Levels

Chapter 4

Revitalize Your Digestive System

Your Intestinal Lifeline

Did you know there's an 18-foot tube filled with a jungle of wildlife—at least 400 species at last count—inside of you? This is your digestive tract. The digestive system goes by many names: the gastrointestinal tract, GI tract, the alimentary tract. This remarkable body system is responsible for converting all that you eat and drink into tiny units that can be utilized for fuel, to repair broken bones and other injured tissues, make sex hormones, create the cells that defend you from germs, grow hair, and perform a staggering number of other everyday functions. When the digestive tract doesn't do its job, not only do you feel it in your gut, but in the rest of your body as well.

The Healing Power of Your Kitchen

There's a joke about a gentleman who visits his doctor. He informs the physician that he hasn't felt well for the last month and can't figure out why. After asking numerous questions, the doctor finds nothing unusual in his patient's medical history. Laboratory tests are all perfectly normal. Finally the doctor conducts a physical exam. Blood pressure is normal, temperature is fine, as are heart rate and respiration. However, when the doctor peeks into the gentleman's ears, he's surprised to see carrots lodged inside. A glance up his nose reveals bits of parsley. And when the doctor asks his patient to lift his arms, a piece of watermelon falls out.

"I know why you don't feel well," the physician announces.

"Why?" asks the desperate patient.

"You're not eating right!"

This punch line applies to many people: They feel bad because they're not eating right. The Standard American Diet—the SAD American diet—and that of most other industrialized nations is quite different from more traditional menus. In his superb work, *Traditional Foods Are Your Best Medicine* (Ballantine Books), Dr. Ronald Schmid talks about the benefits of ancestral diets—be they vegetable-based or more meat-laden. When compared to modern ways of eating, these traditional foods contained more fiber, and less fat overall. "Whether one ate more in the manner of hunter-fisher-gatherer, or more in that of the agriculturist," says Schmid, the result was people who "were healthy and largely resistant to diseases prevalent today."

The difference between eating healthy and not isn't determined by whether you're a vegetarian or one who loves meat. For each of us has our own nutritional requirements based on cultural and ethnic roots, individual physiology, and current health needs. Some people do fine eating red meat, while others thrive on strictly plant foods. It's how food is grown, handled, and processed that impacts health the most.

Before the turn of the century, most people ate foods that were whole and mostly unprocessed. This meant fresh, home-grown vegetables and fruits, wild or free-range meats, raw dairy, whole grains. Milling wheat to produce white flour wasn't available on a large scale until 1910; this process strips the wheat berry of its bran and germ, as well as of nutrients like vitamin E, B-vitamins, and minerals. Consumption of refined sugars, vegetable oils, hydroxygenated oils and margarine, additives, irradiated foods, and quick-to-fix foods in general has soared in the last 100 years.

During the last century, many indigenous peoples have moved to the city and adopted modern menus. One result has been a dramatic rise in diabetes.[1] The landmark work of Weston Price, D.D.S. revealed similar disturbing news. This Canadian dentist discovered that swapping "primitive" foods for modern, refined ones not only adversely affected people's teeth, but contributed to the swell of rheumatoid arthritis, heart disease, cancer, and other modern diseases we see today.[2] More recently Professor Sylvia Guendelman from the University of California at Berkeley reports that Mexican women who emigrate to the United States are much healthier than their American counterparts, with their low-fat, high-protein diets brimming with zinc, calcium, and folic acid. However, as these new residents become more Americanized, their diets and health deteriorate.[3]

In response to increasing ill health and the realization that food is one cause, there has been heightened interest in nutrition by both the public and researchers. Scores of articles fill the pages of both alternative and conventional medical journals; scientists probe and prod our food trying to learn which nutrients keep health humming. Magazines scramble for the newest information on nutritional advances, and how the latest vitamin, mineral, or food can cure this or that sickness. Caught in the middle of this is you—the consumer—confused and feeling guilty about not eating as well as you could.

Do you feel like giving up? Many people do. During a nutritional lecture I gave, several audience members expressed their frustration at maintaining a healthful diet amidst a culture that entices its members with commercials, restaurants, and billboards to consume more sugar, more pop, more fast food, more candy, more beer—all those things you're told to avoid. This is in addition to the bewilderment over "What foods should we eat anyway?"

Eating doesn't have to be complicated or mysterious. Or guilt-provoking. This is not an issue of morality, it's one of health. As you launch into your Digestive Makeover, keep these simple thoughts in mind:

- Choose whole foods, as close to their original state as possible, for more nutrients and fewer additives. For example, pick a baked potato over potato chips, a steak over a hot dog, an apple over a candy bar.
- Pick fresh foods. Nutrient levels fall with processing and storage.
- Include raw foods in your meals (vegetables, fruits, nuts, seeds); when you must cook, don't overdo it. Nutritional value is lost with the heat of cooking. (There are exceptions to this minimal cooking rule: poultry and eggs, for instance.)
- Select regional and seasonal foods, that is, items grown in your area and in season. Out-of-season foods and ones that must be shipped long distances are often treated with unwanted chemicals to prevent spoilage, and are less nutritious due to storage.

- Eat organic foods. This is the best way to avoid harmful pesticide and chemical exposure; there's also evidence that organic produce is more nutritious than commercially grown foods.

Remember: As you improve the quality of your food using the above suggestions, you may find the quantity of what you eat declines. Try that piece of whole grain bread; it's much more filling than white.

Signs That Your Digestion Needs a Face-lift

Most patients in my general practice complain of digestive troubles—regardless of their main complaint. Come to think of it, most don't even complain. Among the people I care for, digestive problems are so common as to be considered normal. But they're not. Does dinner give you gas and bloating? Just plop-plop-fizz-fizz your way back to comfort. Suffering from occasional irregularity? That overnight laxative will do the trick. Got a little heartburn? Pop an antacid. Some of the most important information I collect about a person's health, regardless of why they came to visit, centers around digestive function. For how and what you eat not only affects the GI tract, but the body at large. I look for clues that their digestion needs a makeover: indigestion, gas, bloating, constipation, diarrhea, nausea, cramping, or other abdominal-centered complaints.

Besides examining what people eat, I try to figure out if they're digesting, absorbing, and utilizing their food. You can eat the best diet in the world, but if your body can't use the food it does you no good. Read on for steps to improve your diet, and clues that you need help digesting and absorbing your food.

Record Everything You Eat for One Week

Before you can make dietary changes, you must know what you eat now. You can do this two different ways: Record everything you ate during the past week based on recall, or fill out a Diet Diary as you go. Both scientists and doctors recognize that retrospective data (remembering what you did) is much less reliable than prospective information (recording as you go).

Most people don't realize what or how much they eat until they actually write it down. I use Diet Diaries not only to learn what a patient is consuming, but to educate him as well. When a patient is slightly embarrassed about her Diet Diary, and tries to explain away the results with "I really don't eat like this . . . there was Aunt Martha's birthday on Friday and I had two pieces of cake. We ordered a pizza on Wednesday—we hardly ever do that. And, well, Joan brought in these fantastic chocolate chip cookies on Friday—I couldn't resist and had four," I know I'm getting the truth.

Use the Diet Diary on the following page as your guide. You must record everything that goes into your mouth including food, all beverages (water, alcohol, coffee), medicine, and vitamins. Amounts are important, too. It also helps to mark down how you felt after eating—either digestive or other symptoms, bowel movements, and emotions. After a week of using your Diet Diary, you may discover how certain foods are affecting you both physically and emotionally. You'll also see how much you eat and what foods you eat on a regular basis. You may be surprised to learn that you're drinking 10 cups of coffee daily and eating sweets every three hours. It may shock you to discover that you're low on protein. Or you might be pleased that you are actually eating five servings of vegetables and three of fruit each day.

Hang on to this record, along with your Before-and-After Chart. Use it as a blueprint during your Digestive Makeover. Begin by circling one item you'd like to change—for instance, fewer sweets. Then get to work. If it helps, use the Diet Diary throughout your Digestive Makeover as a testimony to the changes you're making.

Getting Ready with a Grocery List Makeover

You know what you eat. The next step in your Digestive Makeover is altering your shopping habits. I decided to put this step here so you'll be prepared to buy new foods as I discuss them later. Before I do that, let's stop for a moment and establish a few ground rules.

You may be feeling slightly overwhelmed, maybe even depressed at this point. Your Diet Diary isn't as sparkling as you'd hoped, and forgoing your favorite foods isn't particularly appealing.

Table 4.1
DIET DIARY

Date	Time	Item	Amount	Feeling
EXAMPLE Nov 11	8am	coffee, white toast, jam	2 cups, 1 slice, 1 tbsp	Jittery

You don't relish the idea of sprouts and tofu for the rest of your life; you don't want to be deprived of delicious dishes forever.

- Rule number one—Eating should be enjoyable. I don't know about you, but I love food. And I do my utmost to prepare and select delectable dishes. The trick, of course, is finding healthful foods that are fun.
- Rule number two—Shopping should be an adventure. I love to grocery shop. I find beauty in fresh vegetables and fruits, and love discovering new and interesting foods. Try new stores (specialty, gourmet, bakeries, health food); add one new food a week to your list.
- Rule number three—Cooking should be simple. I hate to cook, as much as I love to shop. Perhaps it's the everyday drudgery of it. Whatever the reason, I promise to show you easy, convenient ways to prepare nutritious Digestive Makeover foods.

To begin your Grocery Shopping Makeover, change nothing. That's right, just shop as usual—but make sure you make a list of what you plan to buy. (You do make lists, don't you? Like a good shopper?) The only difference with this list is that I want you to put your foods into categories: produce (mark fresh, frozen, canned, or other—sorry, ketchup and potato chips don't count), protein foods (meats, poultry, fish, beans, legumes, nuts, and seeds), dairy, grains (bread, rice, cereals, pastas), beverages (coffee, tea, water, juice, pop, alcohol) and miscellaneous. This will help you see how much of each you're buying, and where you'll want to make changes in the future. For instance, the bulk of your foods should be in the produce sections, with a good portion under grains and protein; if you're buying mainly miscellaneous items like chips, we need to talk.

Week number two, start making menus for the week and incorporate some of the Digestive Makeover ideas that follow. Rather than white bread, buy whole wheat. Add a crisp green salad to dinnertime. Stock up on fresh fruit and dish it out for between-meal snacks. Based on these dietary changes and your seven-day menu, write up your grocery list. I do this myself, and find it saves me time, money, and frustration over what to cook that night. In addition to my seven selected dinners for that week, I add a couple of easy back-up meals in case I'm too busy to make a complex meal or we feel like eating something different. Purchase ingredients for these meals, too.

Many of the items I use in everyday cooking I order in bulk or have on hand. I'm also a very lazy cook, and so in the name of convenience, supplement my nutritious cooking with some healthy convenience foods like spaghetti sauce, fixings for burritos, items to make a panful of vegetable stir-fry. Besides enjoying sandwiches and soups for lunch, I double my dinner meals for either lunch-time leftovers or freeze for future use.

Continue to make gradual changes to your shopping list as you take steps to make over your digestion and eating habits. Think of each shopping trip as a safari, with you as the hunter out to bag the wild tofu or exotic quinoa. Try foods on for size, check out their flavor and texture, and see if they fit your tastes. When you do this, keep these thoughts in mind: Number one—just because a food tastes *different* doesn't mean it tastes *bad*. Many foods are an acquired taste. (Remember the first time you tried shrimp or spinach or some other non-kid food you love now?) Number two—you don't have to enjoy every food. Some people love tofu, others don't. Bean sprouts aren't for everyone, and barley may not be your cup of tea. But there are plenty of healthful, delicious foods out there, enough for everyone's liking.

■ Makeover Hint #8—Buy Organic

An easy first step when making over your groceries is to shop organic. Organic foods are grown—by and large—without synthetic fertilizers, pesticides, livestock feed additives and/or growth regulators. The idea is to produce safer foods while preserving our environment and agricultural lands. Organic produce and meats may be slightly more expensive than commercial items, though not always. You can find these foods in health or natural foods stores, farmers' markets, and some grocery stores. Also ask your neighbors and friends who raise organic gardens if you can buy their leftovers; or grow your own.

Seven Ways to Make Cooking Easy

Do you remember Peggy Bracken's *I Hate to Cook Book*? She wrote a humorous cookbook thirty years ago, generously seasoned with complaints about cooking. One of her chief beefs was recipe books with beautiful pictures of perfect, impossible-to-prepare food; her answer was dozens of simple meals in place of those too-hard-to-cook recipes. Her easy tips hit a chord with American women, and we haven't looked back since. I've gone one step beyond Peggy's advice, and developed these seven ways to keep meals healthy, yet simple to prepare.

- Always serve raw vegetables. They're easy to make—just cut them up, no cooking involved. They're nutritious, and after they get used to them, kids and spouses love them. Try green salad, carrot and celery sticks, hunks of jicama, or tomatoes and cucumbers in an olive oil and balsamic vinegar mix. Throw together vegetables that don't belong for a new dish—for example, carrots, red peppers, and cucumbers.

- Prepare whole grains ahead of time. Brown rice, millet, and other whole grains take more than one minute to cook. I don't want to miss out on their goodness, so I make a large pot early in the day and feast on it during the week.

- Cut your meat down to size. Small pieces of chicken, ground turkey, or dabs of beef or lamb cook much faster than larger chunks.

- Crock-pot magic. I love my slow cooker—especially on cold winter days. I can throw a bunch of vegetables, stock, beans, and meat into it in the morning for soup or stew, and let its savory aroma embrace me all day long. The best part is I don't have to cook another thing.

- Undercook your vegetables. A quick steaming for broccoli (three minutes over boiling water), seven minutes for corn on the cob, keeps veggies crisp, nutritious, and saves you time in the kitchen.

- Serve fresh fruit. Dish up a platter of fresh fruit instead of vegetables during dinner or lunch. In-season melons, grapes, slices of apple, cherries, kiwi are all delicious and require little prep.

- The less the better. You don't need to serve four different platters of food at each meal. Soup and bread; stew and salad; rice and stir-fried vegetables are plenty, and easier on your digestive system (and budget).

■ *Makeover Hint #9—Prepare a Basic Snack*

There is such a thing as fast healthy foods. Instead of potato chips and candy bars, turn to these simple snacks, or make up your own:

- Fresh fruit
- Raw vegetables
- Nuts and dried fruit
- Rice cake with peanut or nut butter, sprinkled with raisins
- Celery sticks filled with soy cheese or brie
- Whole wheat toast with sugar-free jam
- Plain yogurt mixed with pineapple and sunflower seeds

A Makeover for Every Favorite Recipe

Simple cooking is important to stay motivated during your Digestive Makeover. However, there are probably several old recipes you'd like to hang on to. Making dietary changes doesn't mean giving up on old favorites; merely make over your recipes to fit with your new way of eating.

As with meal alterations, slow and steady is the key to changing any recipe. If you make too many changes at once, results can be disastrous. Instead, modify one ingredient or measurement each time you cook a dish. In pencil, record on the recipe sheet what you've altered—amount and ingredients. Jot down comments about how successful (or not) you were. For example, your great banana bread may taste wonderful with 3/4 of the flour as whole wheat and 1/4 white; any more and it's too heavy. For new, untried recipes, cook exactly as directed the first time. Then make modifications. Here are some ideas on how to convert old standbys into digestively-pleasing dishes. Natural health cookbooks offer many suggestions also.

- Substitute whole grain flours for white. Start by replacing half the white flour only, then work your way up.

- Substitute canola oil for shortening or lard.
- Use butter instead of lard.
- Substitute apple sauce or a smashed banana for one egg or fats (oil, lard, butter).
- Replace cream with low-fat milk or soy milk.
- In place of one egg, add two egg whites.

■ *Makeover Hint #10—Sneaky Vegetables*

There are hundreds of ways to sneak vegetables into your meals. (See importance of vegetables discussed later.) You can feed them to hungry kids pestering you for dinner. You can slip garlic, onions, celery, peppers, and mushrooms into spaghetti sauce. When no one's looking, throw extra potatoes, yams, carrots, peas, onions, into the stew. Serve vegetable soup. Make healthy zucchini bread or carrot cake. Chop up red cabbage, fresh tomatoes, yellow peppers, leaf lettuce, alfalfa sprouts for tacos or burritos. Carry fresh fruit and bunny carrots with you while traveling; offer them to starving passengers before you hit the ice cream shop.

Seven is a Lucky Number for Fruits and Vegetables

Adam, my older son, and his young friend, Josh, were watching me make dinner one day. Josh watched with particular interest as I put together my famous vegetarian lasagna. The next day, Josh's mother reported her son's reaction. "He came home with a puzzled look on his face," she said. "Then he looked up to me and replied, 'Mom, Lauri puts *green* stuff in her lasagna!'" When I heard that, I knew I was on the right nutritional track trying to feed my family seven servings of produce a day.

The Food Guide Pyramid says we should each eat two to four servings of fruits and three to five servings of vegetables for a total of five to nine servings of produce daily. Only 10 percent of us manage to consume five servings each day, much less seven or nine.[4] Since World War II, Americans on average eat 40 percent fewer vegetables and 45 percent less fruit. Whole grain consumption has also declined dramatically. The average American has filled this void with pastries, soft drinks, potato chips, as well as more fat, salt, and sugar.[5]

As nutritional research expands and matures, it is becoming increasingly evident that those vegetables and fruits your mother coaxed you into eating held more than a parent's guilt. Vegetables and fruits possess a host of vitamins, minerals and, of course, fiber. They retain enzymes that aid digestion. The *Journal of the American Medical Association* published a study in 1996 that found persons whose blood was highest in beta-carotene—the pigment found in vegetables like carrots and yams—were less likely to die young when compared with individuals with the very lowest beta-carotene blood levels.[6] People who eat produce rich in vitamin C, like alfalfa sprouts, citrus fruits, and broccoli, are significantly protected against cancers of the esophagus, larynx, mouth, pancreas, stomach, rectum, breast and cervix, according to the National Cancer Institute.[7] And just when you feel grown-up enough to say "no" to a helping of spinach, a dozen scientists prove that the more you munch on this dark leafy green (and its relations), the less chance you have of developing macular degeneration—a very serious and blinding condition.[8]

These and other studies that hammer home the phrase "Eat all your vegetables" are wonderful and welcoming. But I like what Kristen McNutt, Ph.D., J.D. has to say on the subject. She explains that it isn't enough that we tease apart foods—like fruits and vegetables—looking for which nutrients do what in the body. It may be that various food components are interactive, meaning that they don't act alone. Also, there are likely many nutrients and other substances in foods, herbs, and spices "for which functions have not yet been recognized".[9] It's not enough to pop vitamin pills. You need to keep eating your fruits and vegetables, and one day we'll figure out all the reasons why they're good for you—though we already have some pretty good ones.

Look to Makeover Hint #11 to learn what a serving is. And use Table 4.2 to play Vegetable One-Upmanship—a fun and easy way to increase the amount of vegetables you eat each week.

■ *Makeover Hint # 11—What's a Serving?*

Part of your Digestive Makeover is finding ways to eat seven servings of vegetables and fruits every day. If you're a light eater, five is fine. For those with a big appetite, aim for nine.

So what's a serving? Depends on what you eat. A serving can be:

- One medium piece of fresh fruit
- One cup of lettuce, spinach, kale or other fresh, raw leafy vegetable
- 1/2 cup of cooked beans, split peas, lentils, or other legumes
- 1/2 cup of cut-up fruit
- 1/2 cup of cooked corn, carrots, or other dense vegetables
- 3/4 cup of pure, fresh vegetable or fruit juice

How to Play Vegetable One-Upmanship

Rule #1—Pull out your Diet Diary and count how many vegetables and fruits you eat on average each day. Write it down on your Weekly Produce Chart on the following page under Week One.

Rule #2—Pick a time during the day to eat one more serving of vegetables. Remember: Carrot sticks and salads count.

Rule #3—Eat that extra vegetable serving all week long. Write it down on Your Weekly Produce Chart.

Rule #4—Pat yourself on the back, or reward yourself in some non-food way. (A movie, new shirt, calling your best friend long-distance count; a chocolate sundae does not.)

Rule #5—Continue to add one more fresh produce to your menu each week, and record and reward appropriately. Stop when you reach seven. If you wish to continue, that's OK too.

Table 4.2
YOUR WEEKLY PRODUCE CHART

Week #	Veg 1	Veg 2	Veg 3	Veg 4	Veg 5	Fruit 1	Fruit 2
1							
2							
3							
4							
5							
6							
7							
8							
9							
10							
11							
12							
13							
14							
15							
16							
17							

Switch to Well-Dressed Grains

Grains fulfill us in so many ways: a bowl of steaming rice, home-made bread, savory pasta, sweet banana bread. These are all fine complex carbohydrate foods—if eaten as their unrefined selves. Grain-containing foods that have been processed to achieve a whiter product, say white bread or white rice, lack the fiber, vitamins, and minerals of whole, untouched grains. To make up for this loss, many manufacturers "enrich" their breads or noodles with a smattering of thiamin, riboflavin, and other nutrients. This nutritional improvement, however, is a poor substitute for the real thing. Enriching processed grains is like mugging people, taking their clothes and money, then giving them back their raincoats and saying "You're enriched."

The next step to better digestion is to switch to well-dressed, whole grains.

Of the more than one dozen grains available to us, most people only take advantage of a very few, mainly wheat, rice, oats, and corn. Get out of your grain rut and explore some of those exotic grains and grain-like foods found in your grocery store or natural foods markets. These grains can be enjoyed in their whole state—solo or mixed together—or in related products like breads and pastas; you can also use the flour to make your own creations.

- Amaranth—actually a cereal-like herb, this teeny beige seed tastes woodsy. Cook one cup of dry amaranth in three cups of water for 1/2 hour to partake of its high protein, calcium, iron, and fiber.

- Barley—a great addition to soup; aim for whole barley rather than pearl for its higher nutrient content. In a one-to-three ratio of whole barley to water cooked for an hour, you can fix yourself a wholesome bowl of barley mush.

- Buckwheat—famous as a pancake ingredient, this seed is related to rhubarb. For buckwheat porridge, cook as you would for amaranth.

- Cornmeal—lots of colors available in the corn family: yellow, white, and blue for starters. Eat corn as is, as popcorn, or make into a porridge.

- Kamut—this ancient high-protein cousin to wheat looks like a large version of rice. It tastes chewy and rich.

- Kasha—this is a hulled, toasted version of buckwheat. Its reddish-brown color provides lots of high-quality protein, iron, calcium, as well as vitamins B and E.

- Millet—another high-protein grain, it is a yellow, small, bead-like, nutty grain loaded with potassium, B-vitamins, magnesium and phosphorus. Cook for one hour, with one cup of dry millet added to five cups of water.

- Oats—oatmeal and oat bran are already breakfast favorites among Americans. Look for whole, versus rolled, oats for your morning mush.

- Quinoa (pronounced "keen-wa")—like amaranth, this is really an herb. Varieties range from the black type to one that's more creamy in color. This delicate tasting food sports more protein than other grains, as well as greater quantities of iron, B-vitamins, calcium and phosphorus.

- Rice—besides brown and white rice, there are many colorful and fragrant varieties to choose from. Try jasmine, basmati, jasponica, and wehani. Wild rice, by the way, is really an aquatic grass seed but valuable as a nutritious food. Cooking times and amounts vary; start with one cup of rice to two of water and simmer for 30 to 60 minutes.

- Spelt—another cousin to wheat, but higher in nutrients. This whole grain is like rice but nuttier.

- Teff—this Ethiopian grain comes in white, red, or brown. All taste somewhat nutty; loaded with iron and calcium and high in protein. Cook for 30 minutes to make porridge.

- Wheat—a very familiar grain to Americans. But did you know it also comes as couscous, cracked wheat, and bulgur? Try one and see what you think.

If you're used to eating white bread, white pasta, and white rice, this step may be difficult for you. Whole-grain foods are much heavier, more robust, and taste fuller than their paler cousins. Go slowly as you make the crossover to more complete grains. Mix your white rice half and half with brown. Buy a whole wheat bread that's only 60 percent whole wheat. (Beware of the label "brown" for bread; it may only be white bread with coloring added.) Add a handful of barley to your soups and stews. And use some of the Flour Power hints listed below.

■ *Makeover Hint #12—Flour Power*

The whole grain is more nutritious than the ground flour. But if you like to bake, play around with flours made from the above grains as well as those made from arrowroot, chestnut, chickpea, fava bean, and soy bean. Each flour has its own particular taste and texture. Keep an open mind, have fun, and stay healthy with these tips:

- Buy fresh, or grind your own. Flour can turn rancid with time.
- Keep flour refrigerated or store in a cool, dark place.
- Toss unused flour after three months.
- Avoid flour-based products if ill with a cold or hay fever as they tend to promote mucus production.

Try Some Magical Beans and Other Plant Proteins

Next in your Digestive Makeover is adding the mysterious bean to your diet. Vegetarians, and natural health writers and practitioners love beans. Pound for pound they're higher in protein than eggs and most meats—17 to 25 percent—without the saturated fat. They have plenty of calcium, iron, and B-vitamins. They're a valuable fiber source. And they help keep unsteady blood sugar levels even— something meat can't do quickly.

Patients are often incredulous when I suggest beans as one solution to their gastric distress. "Beans?" they sputter. "The gas! The pain! . . . I'll have no friends left."

Not necessarily so. It's all in how you cook them. Let's take a look at these 10 helpful hints:

1. Choose fresh beans. If more than 12 months passes between harvest time and dinner-time, gas will also pass.

2. Store beans in a cool area in a sealed container. Pretty jars are fine; I use my mother-in-law's old Mason jars and display them on my counter top.

3. Wash beans before cooking. Remove any floating beans. Wash again if water is particularly grubby.

4. Soak beans several hours or overnight before cooking (four cups of water to one cup of beans).

5. Drain soaking liquid. Rinse beans again.

6. Add fresh water or other liquid (same proportions as for soaking).

7. Bring beans to a boil and skim off all foam. Turn down heat and simmer. Add water as needed to keep beans covered.

8. Add kombu, a sea vegetable, for flavor, minerals, and less gas.

9. Add 1/4 to 1/2 tsp of sea salt to last five minutes of cooking beans; works like kombu. If you add salt too soon, it'll make the beans hard. This isn't a seasoning, it's to improve your social life.

10. Serve beans first as a side dish or ingredient in an entree. Start with a small amount, and work your way up so your body acclimatizes to the beans.

Look to the many wonderful cookbooks available for specific bean recipes. Or use your imagination, and season at will.

■ *Makeover Hint #13—An Easy Dinner*

This idea comes from Dr. Amrit Devgun of Minneapolis. As a busy doctor, she doesn't have time to cook dinner at night for her husband and herself. So many mornings she prepares this easy meal in her slow cooker. From her many jars of beans and grains, she tosses in a handful of a mixture of dried beans (rinsed); the same for longer-cooking whole grains, such as wild rice, millet, and barley. Depending on her mood and cupboards, diced vegetables, crumbled seaweeds like kelp or wakame, and herbs are also part of the mix. You may chop the veggies by throwing them in a food processor and giving it a few spins. She fills her crock pot half way with water to cover the ingredients. During the week when she's gone all day seeing patients, she turns her slow cooker on low for seven to eight hours. For those lazy weekends, medium heat is fine for three to four hours. This potluck supper contains all the makings of a well-rounded vegetarian meal—and it's never the same twice. Or in Dr. Devgun's words: "Voila, you have a lovely hot soup, ready to serve when you get home!"

Remember to Chew

A major reason for indigestion is eating too fast. In order for food to digest, you must chew it properly. Incorporating more chewy, fibrous foods into your meals will help you do this. Chewing is so important because the mouth is where you begin to break down food. In fact, your mouth prepares for whatever succulent morsel you feed it before the food even touches your lips.

Has your mouth ever watered from the smell of dinner? This is saliva spurting forth from the parotid gland in your cheek and sublingual and submandibular glands hidden under your tongue, and jaw. Bite into a juicy apple, and your teeth tear it into tiny pieces for easier digestion, and along with your cheeks, lips, tongue and jaws mix it up with saliva into a soft, wet ball for easy swallowing. Before that happens, however, amylase, an enzyme in saliva, starts to chemically break the apple down—as well as any other sugars or starches that come its way. Salivary lipase, the fat enzyme, is also released, ready to disintegrate fats. (Apples, unless dipped in caramel, are fat-free.) Chewing also signals other digestive enzymes and organs to prepare. Thus the more thoroughly you chew, the better digestion will be further down the GI tract.

■ *Makeover Hint #14—Avoid the No-Time-to-Taste Syndrome*

In this day and age of fast food and faster eating, we often lose the pleasure of tasting our food. Here's a flavorful tip to slip into your Digestive Makeover: Sit down and enjoy the taste of your food. Savor each delicious mouthful, and pay attention to the subtle tastes and textures of every bite. There are four types of taste buds on your tongue: sweet, sour, salty, and bitter. Take advantage of these. Slow and lazy eating also gives your gastrointestinal tract a chance to ready itself for digestion.

Sprinkle Your Food with Laughter

Once you find the time to chew your food, you might extend your meal breaks and invite a friend or guest to join you. Congenial companionship is another way to improve digestion. The American Association of Therapeutic Laughter says humor and laughter improve digestion. Eating in the company of people you enjoy, laughter, and even prayer beforehand relaxes your stomach. Investigators at Queen's Hospital in Belfast would agree. They found that patients who complained of heartburn of unknown cause had poor social support compared to individuals whose heartburn was brought on by acid reflux.[10] More of a heartache, than a heartburn, you might say. Avoid stress and you also decrease your chance of developing constipation, irritable bowel syndrome, inflammatory bowel disease, ulcers, and indigestion.

Use Natural Digestive Aids

Laughter is wonderful. But sometimes you may need additional help digesting. Throw out your antacids. Once again, Mother Nature has blessed us with an array of foods that promote digestion and enhance enzyme release, all very naturally. To begin your meal, sip on a glass of water spiked with a squeezed wedge of lemon. Serve a heaping plate of salad before the main course (see Makeover Hint #15). Munch on pineapple and papaya as an appetizer 10 to 15 minutes before a meal for their natural fruit enzymes bromelain and papain. Include plenty of raw vegetables as part of your meal—salads before, carrot sticks, jicama, cucumber, radishes—for their enzyme content. Sip on some digestive teas like ginger, chamomile, and peppermint either before a meal, or at its conclusion. Herbal bitters include gentian, barberry, and golden seal. A small glass of wine prior to eating is also a digestive aid.

If these steps don't help with that full or bloated feeling, consider combining your foods differently. Eat simpler combinations, refrain from refined carbohydrates and fatty foods, and try this food-combining approach.

Eat vegetables and starchy foods together

Eat vegetables and protein foods together

Eat vegetables with grains and legumes

Eat fruits alone

Avoid combining starches with protein foods

Also try drinking liquids before meals, but not during. Wait one to two hours before drinking fluids again.

As a last resort, try supplemental digestive enzymes and/or hydrochloric acid. Some products contain both. Take between two and five capsules, depending on the size of your meal. Swallow the pills, one by one, throughout the meal. If you're still experiencing gastric distress, increase this amount slowly to a maximum of seven. If this still doesn't work, try a different brand. Note: If you have an ulcer or experience increased gastric distress after doing this, avoid hydrochloric acid supplements.

■ *Makeover Hint #15—The Advantage of the Raw Deal*

Make it a habit to eat a salad before every meal. It's elegant, fashionable, and so very, very healthy. A raw vegetable salad gives you fiber to stay regular and enzymes to aid digestion. Most green leafy vegetables, including lettuces, encourage enzyme release from your digestive tract due to their slightly bitter quality and taste. The more biting the leaf, the better it works. Try endive, radicchio, escarole, watercress, and dandelion greens.

Custom-Tailor Your Food

While certain basic rules on eating can apply to everyone, not everyone should necessarily eat the same foods, or the same amounts. As a finishing touch to your Digestive Makeover, take into consideration these idiosyncrasies and how they apply to you. Make adjustments as needed.

1. Ethnic and cultural background. What did your ancestors eat? If you come from a tradition of feasting on fish, perhaps you should eat more.

2. Blood type. Dr. Peter D'Adamo writes about how blood type can affect food choices in his book *Eat Right for Your Type* (G.P. Putnam's Sons, 1996). This is based on ancestral heritage, and one more way you can determine what's best for you. Briefly, Dr. D'Adamo says that people with type O blood are like the hunter-gatherers of long ago and do well eating meat. This is the majority of the population. Blood type A does better on a vegetarian diet; type B thrives on dairy products. And the most modern and least prevalent blood type—AB—can consume a variety of foods comfortably.

3. Individual physiology. If you find you don't feel well eating bread, but do fine with beef, that may be your body talking. People with unstable blood sugar often need more protein spread throughout the day than the average person. Take into account all digestive symptoms; be sure to listen to the rest of your body, too.

4. Personal health. The healthier your digestive (and overall) health, the more foods you will tolerate. Some people are intolerant or allergic to certain foods, and do better when those are avoided or eaten only occasionally.

■ *Makeover Hint #16—Start Your Own Nutritional Support Group*

Making food changes is lonely. Gather together your like-minded compatriots and form a nutritional support/educational group. Meet weekly and exchange recipes, spots to shop, how to prepare tofu—any helpful tip to make your Digestive Makeover easier. Choose a theme for each meeting—grains, vegetables, food allergies—and ask members to take turns leading the group in discussion. If you like, use this book as a guide. Or begin a weekly Natural Health Makeover party.

Digestion Makeover Checkup

You're on a roll. So far, you've wiped away the poisons and found new ways to soothe digestion. These are the steps you've taken in your Digestive Makeover:

- Filled out a diet diary.
- Made over your grocery list.
- Cooked simple, nutritious meals and snacks.
- Converted some favorite recipes.
- Began increasing the vegetables and fruits you eat each day.
- Discovered a world of grains—and enjoyed them!
- Found more protein foods. Made beans without the gas.
- Chewed each bite 10, 20, 30 times.
- Shared a meal with a friend.
- Tried some natural digestive aids.
- Customized your eating style and needs.
- Gathered together friends for nutritional support.

For Related Problems, See

- Constipation
- Diarrhea
- Food Poisoning
- Heartburn
- Hemorrhoids
- Indigestion
- Ulcers

Laboratory Tests Your Doctor Can Order

- Complete Digestive Stool Analysis
- Intestinal Permeability Test

- Lactose Intolerance Breath Test
- Bacterial Overgrowth of the Small Intestine
- Breath Hydrogen/Methane Test
- Helicobacter Pylori (for ulcers)
- Comprehensive Parasitology

Chapter 5

Better Inner Cleansing

Scouring the Body with the Kidneys

The underrated kidneys are remarkable organs. Not only do they help the body toss out garbage, in the form of metabolic waste products and other foreign substances, via urine, but they also have a hand in maintaining proper body fluid balance—including volume, pressure, and composition. The kidneys also help change vitamin D to its active form, assist with red blood cell production, aid with insulin breakdown, and influence blood pressure.

Normally, the kidneys are very good at what they do, no matter how much or what you eat or drink. For instance, when you drink more water than usual, you expel excess fluid with additional trips to the bathroom. Thirst is your cue to drink more water when fluid levels drop. The anti-diuretic hormone (ADH) is a very descriptive term for the pituitary chemical that puts the brakes on when enough water (that's urine) has been released. The adrenal hormone, aldosterone, helps kidneys out by monitoring sodium and potassium excretion.

To do all this, the kidneys must filter and monitor approximately two gallons of fluid each day. Most is reabsorbed into the body, while a quart or so is discarded as urine. Besides hanging on to most of your body's water, the kidneys also reabsorb most of the nutritionally important substances like protein and sugar. Toxins and artificial substances, many of which are made water-soluble by the liver, are released into the urine for disposal.

Cleansing the body and blood so thoroughly is a daunting task—and one the kidneys do well. Most of the blood that enters the kidneys is reabsorbed. Excess water, waste products, and toxins are

sent through a tube called the ureter into the bladder, a hollow muscular balloon, for storage. This happens all day and all night, drip
by drip. When the bladder is full (just over a cup), the sensation of
"having to go" begins and urine is released through the urinary tract,
or urethra, and out.

You Need an Elimination Makeover When This Happens

There are several serious kidney diseases that require you visit your
doctor immediately, such as:

1. Acute kidney failure, when the kidneys stop working
2. Chronic kidney failure, when the kidneys stop working gradually
3. Hypertensive kidney disease, when kidney disease causes high
   blood pressure but not kidney failure
4. Nephrotic syndrome, when the glomeruli are so porous that
   large amounts of protein are lost in the urine
5. Specific tubular abnormalities, when reabsorption of certain
   substances by the kidney is abnormal

   You certainly can't diagnose these problems on your own. Some
people with kidney problems have no symptoms. But you can still
be aware of what to watch for, particularly if members of your family have kidney disease. Patrol your body for these symptoms: dull
mid-backache or side ache, fever, malaise, changes in urination
amount. Changes in urine color should also be checked out with
your physician, though be aware that color is also influenced by food
and drugs. Other signs to be alert for include general body swelling,
sudden or unexplained weight loss, weakness, fatigue, shortness of
breath, loss of appetite, nausea, vomiting, itching, or convulsions.
   Other more subtle signs to watch for that may indicate you need
a Kidney Makeover are: frequent urination (normal is four to six times
daily), getting up during the night to void, urgency, urinary dribbling,
difficulty starting urination, weak urinary stream, pain or itching upon
urination, a "full" feeling in the bladder, a sensation that not all urine
has been expelled. Some of these symptoms can indicate a urinary

tract, bladder, or kidney infection. When men reach middle age (50 and above), a weak urinary stream, difficulty starting and stopping urine, and inability to completely empty the bladder, can point to an enlarged prostate which subsequently presses down on the urinary tract. Again, visit your doctor for a proper diagnosis in these cases.

Also, if you have a history of exposure to toxic materials, chemicals, drugs, or medications—substances that your kidneys must expel—a Kidney Makeover is warranted.

Don't Hold It

The first step toward healthier kidneys is common sense. When you have to urinate, do so, don't hold it! This may sound like ridiculous advice, but I've met plenty of people who've admitted to resisting the urge to void because of time, work, inconvenience or other annoyances. Part of maintaining good health means listening to bodily urges (be it urination, defecation, thirst, or hunger) and carrying through. This is particularly important with urination as the urine holds waste products, substances you don't want to voluntarily hold onto.

Water—Nature's Own Cleanser

The next phase in maintaining healthy, body-cleaning kidneys is learning how to drink water. Don't laugh. In this country, soft drink consumption exceeds water intake1 and from what I've seen in clinical practice, many people forgo water in favor of other beverages. Water should always be your first, thirst-quenching choice—not pop, not juice, not milk, not coffee, not beer. Besides their stimulating and sedating effects, respectively, coffee and alcohol are diuretics causing fluid loss, not gain. Soda, with its sugar and artificial additives, is another diuretic and impairs health in other ways. While milk provides protein and calcium, it's best served as a food, not as a primary beverage. Fruit juice is fine occasionally, but eating fresh fruit is preferable to gain fiber.

Here are eight more reasons why water is a superior fluid for your kidneys and body:

1. Water (not soda or juice) makes up 70 percent of the adult body.

2. Water helps clear the body of waste material.

3. Water helps fight constipation and aids digestion.

4. Water helps lubricate joints.

5. Water aids cell function and is an important solvent in the body.

6. Water vapor in the lungs helps control oxygen concentration there.

7. Water helps control body temperature.

8. Inadequate water intake may result in fatigue and general body aches.

Working toward the recommended six to eight 8-ounce glasses of water each day seems impossible to many people. This may be partly habit, i.e. they are used to drinking other beverages; perhaps they've been downing tap water and the taste is disagreeable; maybe they mistake thirst for hunger. It could be that their sense of thirst has diminished and they truly don't yearn to drink. Whatever the reason, you can begin to teach your body to enjoy and even desire water again.

Start by choosing only clean, pure water. If you know of a reputable bottled or mineral water to buy, that'll do. Otherwise, rely on filtered or distilled water cleaned in your home. (See Chapter 12, Makeover Hint #65—How to Ensure You Have Clean Water.) Next, make sure you have water available to you at all times. Third, reintroduce water to your life slowly. If you're currently drinking one or two glasses a day, begin by drinking three cups for awhile. Then up it to four. Continue this trend until you're drinking six to eight glasses each day. Also, make note of thirst. And, like urination, don't ignore it.

■ Makeover Hint # 17—The Sip Tip

To ensure you drink enough water during the day, carry a special bottle filled with delicious, clean water, and sip liberally. If the idea of carting water around is embarrassing, maybe this story will help. During a getaway to Minneapolis, my husband and I decided to treat ourselves and checked into the downtown Hilton. Being thirsty folks, each of us, in addition to our luggage, toted a hefty jug of water. We did our best to blend in as we casually walked through the lobby of this posh hotel, where well-dressed ladies and gentlemen strolled and limousines were the preferred mode of transportation. No one gave us a second glance. Who says class and good health don't mix?

Cindy's Restaurant Trick

Cindy doesn't make a habit of bringing her own water to hotels, but she has discovered a way of getting her family to drink more water and save money at the same time. As a working mother, Cindy and her husband take their three children out to dinner about once a week. Instead of allowing her sons and daughter to order pop, it has been a long-time tradition that each family member asks for water. Her children, says Cindy, don't even think twice about asking for soft drinks and are very content with water as their quencher. (If you're concerned about the quality of a restaurant's water, ask if it serves tap, filtered, or bottled water. For spots where only tap is available, pull out your own or wait until you leave to drink.)

Prestigious Protein

Protein is certainly a vital nutrient; its name—literally "of first importance"—tells us so. It is the raw material used to build and repair muscle, bones, teeth, blood, and bodily fluids. It form enzymes and hormones. When sick or injured or stressed-out, our body cries out for more protein so it may regain health. Kidneys, particularly when under-the-weather, do better when fed the right protein. Consider this.

British scientist Dr. W.G. Robertson surveyed over 2500 vegetarians about their eating habits and whether or not they'd had kidney stones. Judging from the answers received, Dr. Robertson discovered that vegetarians (this group included pure vegetarians—vegans—as well as those who ate eggs and/or dairy) were about half as likely to get kidney stones as their meat-eating counterparts.[2] As part of your Kidney Makeover, incorporate more plant proteins into your daily fare: beans, legumes, nuts, seeds, soy products like tofu, tempeh, soy cheeses and soy milk, nut milks, and whole grains.

■ *Makeover Hint # 18—Eat a Handful of Nuts*

Raw, unsalted (preferably organic) nuts like walnuts, almonds, Brazil nuts, and hazel nuts are an admirable choice for a snack high in protein and healthy essential fatty acids, vitamins and minerals. You can even mix them with a sprinkling of dried fruit like raisins or figs. Use your cupped hand as a measuring device to approximate how much to eat each day.

The Cranberry-Kidney Connection

If you're prone to any type of urinary system infection, you'll want to read this. Cranberry juice is a well-known anecdotal cure for urinary tract, bladder, and possibly kidney infections. The question remains, however, does it really work? According to doctors at Harvard Medical School and Brigham and Women's Hospital in Boston, 10 ounces of *Vaccinum macrocarpon* (cranberry) juice every day did the trick for 60 women with chronic urinary tract infections (UTIs). After six months, these cranberry-drinking individuals had significantly fewer bacteria in their urine than a matched group that sipped on fake juice, and their antibiotic use for urinary tract infection was half.[3]

Ocean Spray™ products, which contain one-third pure cranberry juice, are typically used in these studies. Unlike what's available in grocery stores, these juices were sweetened with saccharin, not sugar. Sugar is known to depress immunity[4,5] and saccharin has the potential to promote cancer. Your best bet is to purchase cranberry juice that has been sweetened with other juices, rather than sugar or artificial sweeteners. You can eat fresh cranberries too.

If 10 ounces of cranberry juice every day is too much for you to stomach, take heart. Another study found that four to six ounces of cranberry juice was enough to prevent future UTIs and bladder infections.[6] If blueberry juice or blueberries are more to your liking, try them instead. They have also been found to deter these infections.[7]

How Cathy Fought Back

Cathy was always getting urinary tract infections. They would begin with a tingling sensation when she urinated, followed by burning, and the urge to run to the bathroom constantly. Every month or two, it seemed, she was also running to the doctor's office for a new antibiotic prescription. After a year of this, Cathy decided to pursue other options. Not only were these treatments getting expensive, but she was concerned about the long-term use of antibiotics. In her reading, Cathy learned about the cranberry-kidney (and urinary tract) connection. She made a habit of drinking one or two glasses of cranberry juice each day, as well as switching from soft drinks to a couple of quarts of water. To her pleasant surprise, Cathy's troubles diminished to the point where such infections bothered her only once or twice a year—a vast improvement from earlier.

Foods That Help the Kidneys Cleanse

One way the kidneys cleanse the body is through diuresis, the act of urination. You can urge urination on by drinking lots of pure water. Alcohol and caffeine are also diuretic substances, but their less-than-desirable health effects and the fact that they don't hydrate the body like water does make them beverages to avoid.

Physicians often use diuretic medications to enhance urination and help patients eliminate surplus fluid for conditions such as hypertension and congestive heart failure.[8] Many herbs and foods also have this ability—albeit much gentler. As we scrutinize fruits, vegetables, grains, and beans, it's becoming increasingly apparent that edibles also possess physiological effects. Consuming foods with a mild diuretic action helps the kidneys flush your body of poisons; drinking water has a similar effect.

Maybe you're eating some of these foods already? Celery sticks are naturally diuretic, as are parsley and asparagus. Note that parsley can promote kidney stones in some people; yet asparagus is a natural kidney stone therapy. Artichokes encourage urine flow, and folklore says corn does the same thing. Not too many people toss fresh dandelion leaves into their salads, but if you do, you'll enjoy their diuretic properties too.

■ *Makeover Hint # 19—Make a Parsley Paisley Salad*

Parsley is often set on dinner plates as a garnish—and left untouched. It is, however, a flavorful ingredient you can add to many dishes including salads. Here's one of my favorites.

1 cup red leaf lettuce, torn

1 cup fresh spinach, torn

1/2 cup radicchio, torn

1/2 cup fresh parsley, chopped

1 medium tomato, cubed

1/2 cucumber, diced

Mix the above ingredients and toss in a large salad bowl. Serve as a side dish with an olive oil and balsamic vinegar dressing, or enjoy as a snack or main entree.

Gorge on Garlic for Greater Kidney Gusto

Eating a couple of cloves of germ-stopping garlic each day adds cleansing power to your kidneys. Bugs that succumb to garlic include bacteria,[9] yeast,[10] and other fungi,[11] protozoa like *Entamoeba histolytica*[12] as well as flu viruses and the herpes bug.[13] In addition, garlic promotes cleansing through its diuretic effects.[14] Raw garlic is always best; cooking steals away some of its medicinal attributes. The fresh-extract garlic pills are another option, though certainly not nearly as tasty. (And a true makeover, I believe, should incorporate as many dietary and lifestyle alterations as possible, and rely less on pill popping.)

■ *Makeover Hint # 20—A New Pizza Topping*

Garlic is a tasty and outlandish topping you can add to your homemade pizza. Simply dice the garlic finely and sprinkle it on your pizza creation while you add other healthful and tasty ingredients, such as pineapple, green peppers, fresh tomatoes, shiitake or portabello mushrooms, onions, red cabbage, crumbled tofu, artichokes, and parsley. With a pizza like that, who needs pepperoni? For more kick and therapeutic effect, add garlic after the pizza has been cooked or five minutes before it's done. Serve with Parsley Paisley Salad (see Makeover Hint #19).

Watch for Kidney Poisons

Because the kidneys are elimination organs, they're particularly susceptible to poisoning. For example, uranium (used in industry), aluminum (in cookware, aluminum cans, foil, baking powder, and deodorant), mercury (in alloy plants and some batteries) and other heavy metals poison the kidneys.[15] Cadmium, found in glass factories, metal alloys, electrical equipment, and cigarette smoke, can concentrate in the kidneys and cause problems like kidney stones.[16] Other kidney toxins to watch for include lead, arsenic, thallium, copper, nickel, antimony, and silver. Be careful of lubricants and solvents, paints and petroleum-based mineral oils.[15] A colleague of mine was a landscaper years before she entered naturopathic medical school. The pesticides she was exposed to during her gardening days caused her kidneys to fail years later.

The kidneys are also the route of excretion for many medications. Unfortunately, during the cleansing process, the kidneys not only excrete but must consolidate medicinal leftovers. This is a dangerous job because the kidneys are then swimming in toxic concentrations of these substances. When medication doses are high or use is prolonged, the kidneys are harmed, a condition called toxic nephropathy. *Brenner & Rector's: The Kidney* (5th edition), a respected textbook on the subject, offers an entire chapter on the subject. Here is some of what this authoritative tome has to say.

Immunosuppressive drugs used during kidney (ironically) and heart transplants, like FK-506, can damage kidneys. Cisplatin, cyclophosphamide, streptozocin, and other chemotherapeutic agents are also guilty. Those using gold, penicillamine, methotrexate, and high doses of pain-killers like aspirin and acetaminophen for rheumatoid arthritis need to be cautious. Even antibiotics, like neomycin, cephalosporin, and amphotericin, need to be prescribed with care. When antibiotics from the gentamicin and tobramycin family were first introduced in 1969, kidney injury among patients was 2 to 3 percent. Almost 25 years later, this number rose to 20 percent. Even acyclovir, used to treat herpes, is risky. While we all must be wary and work with our doctors to avoid such problems, those at greatest risk are the elderly, people with existing kidney troubles, diabetics, patients with cancer or congestive heart failure, and anyone who's dehydrated.[15]

Nature's Own Pantry

What's more delicious than a big, juicy T-bone steak served with mashed potatoes swimming in gravy, white dinner rolls dripping with melted butter, followed by a big hunk of apple pie a la mode, all washed down with a brew? In my younger days, I too enjoyed such a feast and my South Dakotan husband regularly points out the steakhouses he and his father used to frequent 20 years ago. Unfortunately, if this is your normal supper, your kidneys are probably in need of a face-lift. (By the way, I'm not adverse to T-bones, just a daily diet or them.)

Adhering to a simple, whole-foods eating plan full of fresh fruits and vegetables keeps the most common type of kidney stones—90 percent are composed of calcium—to a minimum.[17] It has been demonstrated by noted scientists that some of our favorite foods—white buns,low in fiber;[18] gravy, butter and T-bone steak— high in fat;[19] apple pie,refined carbohydrates;[20] sugar[21]— increase calcium in the urine and thus calcium stones. Alcohol is another culprit.[22] Calcium supplementation and vitamin-D enriched foods seem to aggravate this problem in susceptible individuals.

Read Chapter 11, and you'll see that some of the same foods that cause calcium stones rob the bones of calcium. In other words, the calcium is being pulled from the skeleton into the urine for excretion, where it runs the risk of concentrating in the kidneys and forming a stone.

■ *Makeover Hint # 21—Follow This Menu for a Day*

You've already been introduced to the idea of cleansing diets in Chapter 3 (see Makeover Hint #6—The Mini-Cleanse). At the risk of repeating myself, I offer you a slightly different version here and a few more reasons why both are a good idea. When implemented in a non-threatening, sensible manner, they also help you readjust your eating patterns (get you used to all those fruits, vegetables, and whole grains) and give your kidneys a rest. Follow this menu for 24 hours, with plans to do the same every month or two.

Begin the morning with a glass of water flavored with a slice of fresh lemon. Enjoy a piece of fresh fruit.

> Breakfast is a large bowl of oatmeal or other whole grain cereal, topped with fresh fruit and soy milk.
>
> Morning snack consists of one piece of fruit or raw vegetable sticks.
>
> Lunch is a raw vegetable salad. Use your imagination.
>
> Afternoon snack is one cup of steamed or raw vegetables.
>
> Dinner can be vegetable soup or steamed vegetables and a large bowl of brown rice or millet.

During this cleansing time, drink fluids liberally: pure water, vegetable broth, and vegetable juice. Fruit juice is all right, if diluted half and half with water. Avoid taking nutritional supplements and unnecessary medications. When I have patients dependent on strong medication—prednisone, for example—I modify this plan for them. If that describes you, work with a skilled natural health physician.

Kidney Stones and Calcium

High-calcium foods and supplements have the reputation of adding to kidney stone problems—particularly since 90 percent of stones contain calcium. So what should you do if you're, on the one hand, concerned about maintaining strong bones (see Chapter 11 for other skeletal strengthening tips), yet don't want to harm your kidneys? One way is to carefully choose your calcium source. On the food side, select dark leafy greens like kale and collard greens, and serve them with your favorite tofu dish. (The body absorbs calcium from kale better than from milk.) As far as calcium pills go, calcium citrate stands head and shoulders above other calcium forms. For one, citrate limits calcium stone formation,[23] even though calcium citrate is better absorbed than calcium carbonate, found in most calcium-containing antacids.[24] Another way to keep your kidneys safe is to take supplemental calcium with meals.[25]

With the increasing threat of osteoporosis—especially for aging baby boomers—doctors are recommending that their patients drink more milk and take antacids for extra calcium. Yet taking these supposedly bone-building steps may increase your chance of developing kidney stones through a condition called milk-alkali syndrome.

Kidney Makeover Checkup

Do you feel cleaner after your Kidney Makeover? These are the steps you took to get there:

- Urinating as soon as the need hits.
- Drinking at least one quart of pure water daily.
- Eating more of those darn'd beans and tofu.
- Sipping on cranberry or blueberry juice as needed.
- Turning to celery, asparagus, and other cleansing foods.
- Gorging on garlic.
- Watching for kidney poisons.
- Taking one more step toward whole foods.
- Taking calcium supplements with meals.

For Related Problems, See

- Backaches
- Fever
- Gout
- Urinary Tract Infections

Chapter 6

Maximize Your Immunity

Fight Off Sickness Naturally

Have you ever noticed that not everyone gets sick during cold season? Why is that? Is it the luck of the draw, or is this something you have control over? Your body, when in tip-top shape, has the ability to fight off most bugs and noxious substances. Individuals who are most susceptible to sickness need an Immune System Makeover.

When natural doctors talk about "the body healing itself," in effect they're praising immunity. To be "immune" means you're protected. In the case of the body, the immune system guards you from germs like bacteria, viruses, fungi, and parasites, and diseases like cancer. It does this through a complex collection of organs, cells, lymphatic vessels, and other factors that work together with help from non-immune body parts, such as searing stomach acid and skin.

Don't Let Your Immunity Down

One of the first signs that you need an Immunity Makeover is when you seem to catch everything that's going around: a cold, the flu. People with poor immunity also have a difficult time shaking illness—the cold that never goes away. Or you might just be tired all the time. If it takes a long time for a cut to heal up, it could be your immunity is dragging. Chronic infections, too, can be a signal that either your defenses are low or the infection itself could be causing depressed immunity. Watch for recurring warts, cold sores, genital herpes, athlete's foot, fungal infection of the nails, or yeast infections

75

(anywhere—vaginal, intestinal, skin or mouth). If you've had mononucleosis in the past, and have never felt well since, think Immune Makeover. Those with AIDS or infected with HIV should also groom their immunity.

If you have multiple sensitivities either to food, chemicals, inhalant substances, or all of the above, consider the following. Some white blood cells—members of your immune system—can create an allergic reaction. This is an overreaction by your immune system to harmless matter. Also remember, for reasons we don't quite understand, the immune system sometimes turns against its host—you. These are called autoimmune diseases and can include rheumatoid arthritis, multiple sclerosis, diabetes, lupus, Hashimoto's thyroiditis, pernicious anemia, Goodpasture's syndrome, and others. Caring for your immune system, and removing other suspected allergens from your life—be they foods, chemicals, or inhalants—often help these conditions.

Kick the Sugar Habit

The simplest way to bolster sagging immunity is by avoiding or minimizing the sugar you eat. This includes white, yellow, and brown sugar, corn syrup, fructose, honey, maple syrup, dried fruit, and fruit juice. Also look for sugar aliases, especially in packaged foods, such as dextrose, sucrose, maltose, turbinado sugar, raw sugar, glucose and cane juice. In some cases, side-stepping sugar, particularly at the first inkling of illness, is enough to turn a slumped immune system around. Try it and see.

More than 20 years ago a group of dentists showed us that sugar doesn't just cause cavities. Using dental students as their subjects, they discovered that drinking a 24-ounce container of soda depressed the germ-eating activity of some white blood cells called neutrophils by 50 percent. This occurred 45 minutes after downing the pop[1]. That's a substantial kick-in-the-pants to your immune system. It's especially rattling when you consider that not only does the average American consume 120 pounds of sugar yearly, but that pop outdistances water as the beverage of choice.[2]

Further research by Loma Linda University in California revealed that sugar's effect on immunity lasts for at least five hours, possibly longer. This pattern occurs not only with white table sugar, but fructose, glucose, and honey as well.[3] Again, the implications of a sweet tooth are great when you consider that a dose of sweetness every three to four hours dampens your defenses all day long. Last but not least, sugar is the preferred food of bacteria[4] and yeast.[5] Eating sugar is like stoking the infectious fire.

■ *Makeover Hint # 22—KO the OJ*

At the first sign of a cold you should start drinking lots of orange juice. That's the conventional wisdom. But according to the Loma Linda study, orange juice is just as damaging to immunity as other sugars. And the vitamin C you gain from this beverage is minimal. So skip the OJ, and drink plenty of water with a frequent dose of vitamin C—in pill form—when you start feeling sick.

Watch the Fats

Too much fat in your diet or on your body appears to hamper the immune system. Not only does your susceptibility to infection increase, but various immune cells and tissues are depressed. Obviously the fats we usually associate with illness—dietary cholesterol and saturated fats—can interfere with immunity. Even polyunsaturated fats, the healthful lipids found in vegetable oils, may impair immunity when eaten in excess. However, don't cut these fats out of your diet entirely. Eating foods and oils that supply you with a balance of omega-6 and omega-3 essential fatty acids, like fish, flax seeds, flax seed oil, walnuts, and other nuts and seeds, should be a regular but moderate part of everyday eating. These essential fats, when deficient, interfere with some aspects of immune operations.[6]

How about when you're ill? Researchers from the University of Texas Medical School in Houston demonstrated that a low-fat diet was best for immediate healing.[7] Why is this? First, stress caused by disease or surgery lowers your body's fat metabolism. Also, scientists have shown the liver's energy reserves, in the form of glycogen, are lower when a lot of fat is consumed. This means an ailing body has less energy to draw from. Carbohydrates, not fats, spare protein. The body has more raw materials for rebuilding wounded or diseased parts when glycogen levels are up. Finally, some experts theorize that high-fat diets may increase free radical levels, those internally produced molecules blamed for accelerated aging, cancer, and impaired healing.

■ *Makeover Hint #23—How to Keep Your Oils Healthy*

Have you ever sniffed a bottle of vegetable oil that smells funny? This is a sign that your otherwise healthy oil is rancid and full of free radicals, those harmful molecules that contribute to degenerative disease and aging. To get the most out of healthful oils, be sure to follow these steps:

- Buy only cold-pressed, when possible, organic oils.
- Store your oil in a cool, dark place such as the refrigerator.
- Use only fresh oil. Toss unused portions two to three months after purchase or if the oil smells "off."
- Take two vitamin E capsules, cut them open and empty the contents into your bottle of oil. This antioxidant quenches free radical molecules and is good for your heart.

Rest and Resist Disease

Rest. Sleep. Laze around. This is the next stage in making over your immunity. Sound hard? It shouldn't be, yet most adults find it difficult to fit rest, relaxing breaks during the day, and eight hours of nighttime sleep into their busy lives. Whenever I'm tempted to skimp on my shut-eye, I need only turn to my three-year-old son for guidance. Willie is a remarkable toddler with an uncanny knack for sleeping. (Actually, this trait runs in the family.) If Will starts coughing or his nose begins to run, he promptly takes a nap. And I don't mean a cat-nap; William is a super napper, dozing for three to five hours at a stretch. When he awakes, he's perky and he's usually symptom-free.

Studies show that Willie is on the right track. Animal research has provided considerable evidence that sleep and immunity are inseparable. It's been just recently that scientists have explored the same connection in humans. Nevertheless, exciting studies are confirming that not only does sleep support immunity and help you fend off illness, but that parts of your immune system may regulate sleep.[8] Just as the field of psychoneuroimmunology (see Battle Stress for Better Defense following) has demonstrated the scientific link between emotions and the immune system, investigators are now drawing similar conclusions about sleep and immunity.[9]

■ *Makeover Hint #24—Nip Sickness With a Nap*

The signs are there. A tickle in your throat. A wave of fatigue. Loose stools. You're getting that cold that's going around the office. There's no stopping it, right?

Wrong! Taking heed of those very warning signals and stopping it in its tracks are a vital part of being a health makeover artist. The best thing to do is listen to your tired body and take a nap. A snooze today could prevent a sick day or more tomorrow.

Don't Starve Your Immune Soldiers

The many cells, glands, and vessels that comprise your immune system are a hungry bunch. That's why it's important to eat nutritious foods, and when necessary, take a general vitamin/mineral supplement. The immune system requires a wide range of vitamins, minerals, and other nutrients to keep it operating in ideal fashion.

One of the most dramatic illustrations of this was a 1992 study done at Johns Hopkins University by Professor Ranjit Kujmar Chandra. He gathered together 96 healthy and independent people 65 and older. To half he gave a multiple vitamin and mineral pill every day for a year; the other 48 received a sugar pill. This minor lifestyle adjustment produced major results. The women and men who took a moderate helping of extra nutrients each day for 12 months were sick half as many days as their placebo counterparts. Also, they used antibiotics less frequently and blood tests showed a significant reduction in nutrient deficiencies, especially vitamins A, B_6 and C, iron, zinc and beta-carotene.[10]

Lest you think nutrients only help the immunity of the elderly, know that your immune soldiers can starve at any age. Young medical students, between 18 and 21, who took 1000 mg of vitamin C everyday for one and a half months enjoyed a substantial immunity boost.[11] Young children who are deficient in vitamin A (a problem that can be solved with minimal supplementation) are more susceptible to illness.[12] The best way to ensure that your immunity is well fed is first, to eat a varied and wholesome diet; second, to add a comprehensive multiple vitamin and mineral supplement as an insurance policy.

■ *Makeover Hint #25—If a Little Is Good, Is More Even Better?*

There are still gaps in our knowledge of immunity and nutrition. However, we do know that single nutrient deficiencies, excessive amounts of certain vitamins and minerals, and a general imbalance among the range of nutrients can upset your defense system.[13] Don't take too many extra vitamins or minerals unless you know what you're doing. Too much of a single nutrient can be as detrimental to your immunity as too little.

Nancy's Swiss Chard Account

Nancy discovered an easy and secret way to keep her family— husband, two daughters and son—healthy all winter long using Swiss chard. During the summer months, Nancy planted a mound of this zesty beet-like vegetable. Throughout July and August she watched the deep green leaves grow, and picked the young shoots often to add to salads and the older ones for other dishes. One year, after a successful vegetable garden, she was saddened to think that all the leftover chard was going to go to waste. Suddenly she had a thought. She'd recently purchased a food dehydrator, so she decided to dry the extra chard she had in the garden. She carefully stored her dried treasure in airtight containers.

That winter, Nancy pulled out her Swiss chard jar whenever she made any dishes that required seasoning, be it stew or soup, and sprinkled the highly nutritious spice-looking substance on it. To Nancy's delight, her family never once complained about the unusual addition to their meals. In fact they seemed to like it because the chard made her dishes taste slightly salty. So without their knowing it, Nancy was able to boost her family's defenses against winter-time germs.

Protein is a Positive Step

A forgotten nutrient when making over immunity is protein, found in beans, legumes, nuts and seeds, eggs, milk and dairy foods, meats, poultry, fish, and whole grains. So many of the cells, tissues, and other parts of your defense system rely on protein for their structure and function. Illness, hemorrhaging, surgery, broken bones, infection, and severe burns accelerate protein breakdown[14] and increase your body's need for good-quality protein. Indeed, being sick tends to depress appetite and thus protein consumption, when protein is most needed. Diarrhea contributes to this problem as well.

During immune-demanding times, look for these signs that you need a protein boost. Enhance your protein intake through either meals, or a protein drink if appetite is down.

- Weight loss
- Skin changes (moist, or dry and scaly)
- Increased susceptibility to infection

I'm sure you're somewhat confused reading this information, only because our culture has been shooed away from protein (and fat). I've had patients, who feast mainly on vegetables, breads, and fruits, look at me as if I'm crazy when I suggest they increase their protein intake. The trick, of course, is finding suitable protein sources and amount that are healthy not only for your immunity but for the rest of your body.

Begin by following my basic rule of eating: stick to whole foods. When you apply this to meats, it means avoiding processed meat products like hot dogs, bologna, and luncheon meats. Many of these contain undesirable additives. Eating rule number two: choose fresh, organic sources. This applies to meats, dairy, and eggs as well as fruits and vegetables.

You can even combine your protein foods. There's no rule saying that tofu can't join chicken or hamburger in an entree. As part of your Recipe Makeover, replace half the meat in all hamburger recipes with crumbled up tofu or tempeh. If you don't say anything, I'll bet your family won't be able to tell the difference.

Also, load your plate up with salads and other vegetables as well as a good portion of lean steak, broiled salmon, skinned chicken, or braised tofu. Continue to snack on fruit as well. Scatter your protein throughout all meals so you're consuming some at each meal and snack; this means breakfast too. This will avoid that draggy feeling between meals. In order to fit all this good-quality protein and vegetation into your menus, you'll have to toss more and more refined foods out.

■ *Makeover Hint # 26—How Much Protein is Enough?*

There's no easy answer to the "how much protein is enough?" question. Each of you has individual requirements; it'll take a little experimentation to determine your optimum amount. If a high carbohydrate diet with 12 percent or so protein is what you've been eating—this is what most Americans do—and you don't feel so great, try boosting that to meals with one-third protein calories, 40 to 50 percent carbohydrates, and 20 to 30 percent fats. If you're overweight, have heart problems, are diabetic, have blood sugar problems or feel sickly, you may need more protein. Also take into account individual differences, activity levels, health or other needs. See Table 6.1 for how much protein is found in common protein foods.

Table 6.1
PROTEIN SOURCES

- 1 cup of soy milk is almost 8 grams
- 1 cup of whole cow's milk is 8 grams
- 1 cup of cottage cheese is 25 grams
- 1 cup of cooked lentils is 15 grams
- 1 cup of cooked beans (e.g., kidney, navy) is 14 grams
- 8 ounces of chicken (light meat) is 12 grams
- 8 ounces of turkey (light meat) is 20 grams

Table 6.1, cont'd.

- 8 ounces of sirloin steak is 41 grams
- 8 ounces of venison is 47 grams
- 1/2 cup of almonds is 13 grams
- 1/2 cup of walnuts is 7 grams
- 1/2 cup of pumpkin seeds is 20 grams
- 1 egg is 6 grams

Vegans can also look to vegetable protein powders, tofu, tempeh, and other soybean-based products for additional protein.

Battle Stress for Better Defense

It's a well-documented fact that stress is an enemy of your immune system. In fact, there's a field of study solely dedicated to the relationship between psychological stress, the nervous system, and the immune system called psychoneuroimmunology (PNI). During the past twenty years, PNI scientists have connected the dots between tension and cancer,[15] upper respiratory infections,[16] periodontal disease,[17] psoriasis[18] and slow wound healing[19]—to mention a few.

Hans Selye, M.D., Ph.D. changed our lives forever when he published his 1956 work *The Stress of Life* (McGraw-Hill), and planted the word "stress" in our minds. Stress is many things, said Selye. It can be emotional turmoil, mental anguish, pain, surgery, a car accident, arthritis, a bad cold, starvation, overeating, or just overdoing it. It's also a poor diet, a couch potato existence, not enough sleep, or any of those other lifestyle no-nos. Stress is anything that fits a very broad category of factors that upset your body's natural balance.

Forty years later, we're confirming Selye's original contention that not only can stress be caused by many things, but it also has widespread effects in the body. Besides rattling the adrenals (see Chapter 7) and other hormone-producing glands, stress stomps on the thymus gland, lymph nodes, white blood cells, and other members of the immune system. So many ways to get sick, so little time.

You'll never remove stress from your life, and you wouldn't want to. A little bit of tension is good; it's what keeps you primed for life. It adds spice to everyday living. You wouldn't want to avoid that thrilling Caribbean cruise just because thinking about it makes your heart race a little bit faster, would you? The trick is to keep your stress load to a level where it doesn't impede immunity and health.

The "Cold" War Experiment

In 1991 a group of American and British scientists proved what most of us already know—stress can make you sick.

They began by choosing almost 400 people and asking them how stressed-out they felt, either from past major events or current demands. Then these perfectly healthy individuals were purposely inoculated with cold viruses. Isolated from the everyday world, this group of human guinea pigs was observed to see if any sneezed, coughed, or showed any other signs of a cold. The scientists even counted how many tissues their subjects used to blow their noses. After one week, it was discovered that those who felt the most stressed-out were most likely to get a cold.[20] In other words, stay calm and you remain well.

■ *Makeover Hint #27—The Stress-O-Meter*

To keep stress—be it physical, mental, or emotional—at arm's length, keep an eye on your stress-o-meter. These are some signs that the stress in your life is passing into the danger zone:

• Exhaustion
• Tension headaches
• Insomnia
• Lack of concentration, forgetfulness
• Mood swings, and erratic emotional behavior
• Nightmares
• Recurrent infections, like colds
• Tearfulness
• Tight muscles
• Muscle spasms
• Vague pain

Minimize the Negative;
Accentuate the Positive

The next phase in your Immunity Makeover is to minimize those substances that put a strain on your defense system (and other body parts, like the liver). These range from tobacco to recreational drugs to unnecessary medications. I realize that abandoning an addictive habit, like smoking, is easier said than done. And offering a comprehensive plan for battling addictions is beyond the scope of this book. However, a short treatise on why taking such a step is best for you and your immune system is outlined below.

Tobacco

Cigarette smoking is the main avoidable cause of death in the United States[21], and possibly an immunity depressor.[22] Nicotine is most often blamed for tobacco's deleterious effects. However, carbon monoxide, tar and an array of other toxic materials support nicotine's role in inviting a variety of cancers, heart disease, atherosclerosis, cataracts (see Chapter 13), chronic lung disease, and increased susceptibility to illness in general.[23] In addition, cigarette smoking steals from you immune-hungry nutrients, such as folic acid and vitamin B_{12}.[24]

This advice isn't just for smokers, but also for those who live with second-hand smoke—so called passive smokers. No longer is it cool to sit among your smoking friends; for doing so also tramples on your immunity. Passive tobacco smoke may increase your risk of lung cancer.[25] Children who live in smoking homes are more prone to ear infections, inflamed tonsils (which are often removed as a result), respiratory infections, Sudden Infant Death Syndrome, as well as asthma in susceptible youngsters.[26] Stop smoking tip: Sip on dandelion tea to help remove tobacco toxins.

Recreational Drugs

Marijuana, heroin, cocaine, and other fun-drugs can make your immune system miserable. It's the opinion of some experts that these recreational substances may be what makes an individual vulnerable to AIDS and other viruses.[27] Intravenous cocaine, for instance, decreases the white blood cells called lymphocytes in rats; the more they're given, the greater the fall.[28] Other immune-devastating drugs include the opiates (morphine, opium), marijuana, and nitrite inhalants ("poppers").[29] Besides their direct bombardment on body defenses, these drugs rob immune vitality by pilfering away vitamins and minerals[30]—the very same nutrients used to uplift your germ guard.

Alcohol

Alcohol often goes hand in hand with smoking and drug use; well over 80 percent of alcoholics also smoke.[23] So, what's that got to do with an Immunity Makeover? Plenty. Besides depleting nutrients used to fuel your defenses, alcohol has been shown to slow down white blood cells in nutritionally intact people.[31] So much for that hot brandy cold cure.

Medications

An Immunity Makeover accomplishes many things, one of which is better health so you have less need for strong medication. Unfortunately, there's a Catch-22 when you're ill. Often the very medicines you rely on for relief come with a laundry list of side effects, including immune suppression. Our most common painkillers— aspirin, acetaminophen (Tylenol®) and ibuprofen (Advil®, Motrin®)— also stomp on body defenses. Australian researchers discovered that taking aspirin and acetaminophen for achiness during a cold not only crushed subjects' defenses, but *increased* nasal stuffiness.[32] While antibiotics are a welcome treatment for serious bacterial infections, their overuse has created "super-bugs" resistant to this medicine. In addition, chronic[33] and frequent[34] antibiotic use diminishes the body's ability to resist such bugs—super or otherwise.

Then there are medications prescribed purposely to impair immunity. I see many patients using these drugs, like gold and methotrexate for rheumatoid arthritis; prednisone used to curtail inflammation, or steroid nasal sprays for chronic sinus infections also harm immunity.

While I make it a policy never to suggest that a patient or reader discontinue medication prescribed by their other physician, I do encourage everyone to learn about the adverse effects of these substances and help each find safer, immune-friendly options. These may include lifestyle changes (as discussed in this chapter), herbs, and nutrients. Part Two offers many ideas for a variety of conditions. However, anyone who is afflicted with a serious condition or who has been taking a prescription medication for months or more should work with the prescribing doctor and a practitioner experienced in natural therapies before making changes. We want to make over your immunity, but not at the expense of your safety.

■ *Makeover Hint #28—Fewer Chemicals, More Immunity*

Get rid of the superfluous chemicals in your life, and you'll enliven your immunity. California researcher Aristo Vojdani, Ph.D., found that individuals chronically exposed to industrial chemicals— trimellitic anhydride, formaldehyde, aromatic hydrocarbons—from working in computer manufacturing plants for a decade or more suffered from significant immune system malfunction.[35] For hints on how to rid your life of poisons, see Chapter 3.

Boost Your Immunity with Plants

One final step to defending your immune system is through the use of herbs. Mother Nature has covered our world with immune-strengthening plants to keep us healthy and cure us when sick. Barrie learned the value of one such herb when she and her one-and-a-half-year-old son were both sick with pneumonia. Barrie knew a little bit about medicinal herbs but hadn't used them much. Her young son wasn't getting better from the penicillin the doctor prescribed, so she began giving him capsules of garlic and Echinacea, a wildflower native to the state where she lived, South Dakota. Within three days, Barrie saw an improvement in her son; a couple of weeks later he was completely well. And he's been pneumonia-free ever since. Now Barrie always relies on this formula to treat her family when they come down with winter illness. "It takes a little longer before their symptoms turn around," she admits, "four days, compared to the 48-hour improvement you see with antibiotics. But their sickness doesn't recur, something I never saw with penicillin."

The purple coneflower (Echinacea) works by not only killing bacteria and viruses (antibiotics only attack the former), but also by kickstarting your immune system into action—something most medications can't do. You can also turn to goldenseal (*Hydrastis canadensis*), licorice (*Glycyrrhiza glabra*), *Astragalus membranaceous* and *Ligustrum lucidum* to stimulate your defenses. Unless you are skilled in herbal medicine, reserve these herbs for acute infections, taking them for a maximum of 10 straight days. If you want to repeat this cycle, take a four-day rest first.

Many foods are natural immune beautifiers and can be a regular part of meals. Garlic takes first place as an immune-enhancing bug fighter, in addition to its role in warding off cancer and protecting your heart from disease. Take heed: don't cook the medicine out of your garlic. That pungent, garlicky smell comes from volatile oils like allicin and is responsible for most of garlic's good deeds. The more you cook it, the less healing it is. Also, crush it prior to eating for the most benefit.

Campbell's (of soup fame) is now distributing fresh shiitake mushrooms (*Lentinus edodes*), found in many grocery stores. While rather expensive, these succulent, meaty fungi contain a polysaccharide called lentinan that supports immune function.[36] If you can't find shiitakes in your local market, try a natural foods store or Asian shop where the dried versions are often sold. Revitalize these dried mushrooms by submerging them in water for three hours or overnight; add both the fleshy mushroom and soaking water to your cooking.

Inflammation, be it from a nasty cut or arthritis, is part of immunity and can be tempered with ingredients in your spice cupboard. Ginger, as a powder, root, or tea, has been shown to decrease joint and muscular swelling when eaten daily for several months.[37] Turmeric also works this way.[37]

■ *Makeover Hint #29—Brew a "Cuppa" Purple Coneflower Tea*

To keep your immune system humming, drink purple coneflower tea on a regular basis. This majestic daisy-like wild flower is an attractive addition to any garden, for those who enjoy growing their own herbs. Or you can purchase the dried plant loose or in tea bags from most health food stores and some grocery stores. For prevention drink a cup every other day; as a treatment drink three cups a day while sick or during stressful and susceptible times like winter. Here's how you make it:

- Add one tea bag or one tablespoon of dried herb to a mug.
- Fill your cup with boiling water.
- Cover, and let steep for 10 minutes.
- Relax and enjoy.

This tea recipe works for most teas containing the leaf, flower, or other soft parts of a plant. If your dried herb is made of the hard woody portions, boil and then simmer it in a covered pot for 30 minutes. Strain before drinking.

Sunbathe Sensibly

Contrary to what you've read about avoiding sun exposure, sunlight is essential to our well-being. For example, 15 to 20 minutes of the sun's warm rays help our bodies convert vitamin D to its active form. However, too much of this good thing may harm immunity. Studies suggest that long-term exposure to the sun's ultraviolet-B (UV-B) rays not only increases risk for sunburn, skin cancer, and eye damage, but dampens immunity as well.

People with a history of basal or squamous cell skin cancer are most susceptible. Skin pigmentation is not protective. Ironically, UV radiation (both therapeutically and with sunlight) is used medically to treat skin conditions like acne and psoriasis. However, research now suggests that over-indulgence lowers resistance especially to infections like herpes, and may in fact increase how often, how long, or how severe each outbreak is.[38] So what should you do? Practice moderation with daily, short periods in the sun.

Immunity Makeover Checkup

You should be feeling sick-free and alive. These are the steps you've just taken to get there:

- Kicked the sugar habit.
- Watched your fats.

- Took naps, breaks, and slept eight hours each night.
- Kept working on your diet. (I told you I'd harp on nutrition.) You added a general vitamin/mineral multiple to your day.
- Made sure protein levels were adequate.
- Took a look at the nicotine, alcohol, and drugs in your life; assessed medications and consulted with your doctor if needed.
- Tried some immune-boosting herbs.

For Related Problems, See

- Bronchitis
- Canker Sores
- Colds & Flu
- Coughing
- Ear Infection
- Fever
- Hay Fever
- Sore Throat
- Urinary Tract Infection
- Yeast Infections

Laboratory Tests Your Doctor Can Order

- Complete Blood Count
- Food Allergy Panel (combined IgG4 and IgE)—ELISA
- Adrenal Test: Comprehensive Hormone Profile

Chapter 7

Lasting Stress Relief

Your Body's Stress Alarms

Perched on top of each kidney is an adrenal gland. While they perform many functions, their role as "stress alarms" is particularly pertinent to modern-day life. The middle portion of the adrenals, called the medulla, produces the hormones epinephrine (adrenaline) and norepinephrine during fear or stress. Your body reacts to these hormones with a "flight or fight" response—pounding heart, faster breathing—all indications that your body is preparing to either go into battle or run from it. A pounding heart means your muscles are getting more nutrient and oxygen-rich blood; increased breathing pulls more oxygen into your lungs.

As stress alarms, adrenal glands are lifesavers during real crises—like a bear attack. But in our world, danger is less tangible. Things like a demanding boss, traffic jams, and money troubles can't be beaten off with a stick (I suppose you could, but this creates a whole new set of crises) or fled from easily. And because of that, the adrenal alarm system seems primitive. For one, all that heart-pounding adrenaline just sits there while your blood pressure soars during rush hour. During a bear attack, running or fighting wears it off. Secondly, today we are faced with many more intangible hazards than the average bear fighter of long ago.

But the adrenals are more than stress alarms. They're responsible for producing steroid hormones such as aldosterone, which maintains normal blood pressure by balancing sodium, potassium, and fluid levels. Glucocorticoids, namely the hormones cortisol

osterone, regulate blood pressure, support normal muscle function, promote protein breakdown, distribute body fat, and
increase blood sugar as needed. This hormone class is most noted
for its anti-inflammatory properties, hence the popularity of artificial cortisone as a medication. Adrenal glands also make sex hormones, namely testosterone and estrogen, and dehydroepiandrosterone (DHEA), which is currently gaining fame as an anti-aging
supplement.

Signs Your Adrenal Glands Need a Makeover

Speeding through life, while at times exhilarating, is also tiring. Yet
rather than learn how to relax and take time to sleep, we cover the
dark circles of fatigue with make-up and rely on caffeinated energy.
Minor aches and pains are ignored—after all, we're not getting any
younger—or temporarily treated with a pain pill. Then we wonder
why this swift and surface-like way we care for our bodies results in
bigger problems down the road.

Relentless stress without outlet also tires out your adrenal glands
and causes them to atrophy or shrink. A little stress is OK, and in fact
saves us from danger. But when these alarms are rung continuously
without a bear in sight—kind of like the little boy who cried wolf—
then the adrenals get tuckered out. What you feel is exhaustion,
stomach upset, insomnia or sleepiness, irritability, headaches, and
that all too familiar stressed-out feeling. Some women may develop
premenstrual syndrome as elevated cortisol levels leave the body
progesterone-poor. Others develop allergies easily or are open to
every cold, flu, and other infection floating by (see Chapter 6). Look
at making over your adrenals, as well, if you've taken prednisone or
other cortisone medications for a long time.

Secrets of Stress Reduction

What is stress? That's easy, you might say. It's the boss yelling at me,
the kids yelling at me, my spouse yelling at me—any situation that
makes me uptight. True, but stress is not strictly mental or emotion-

al. It's anything, physical, mental, emotional, environmental, social, that attempts to push your body out of balance. This means illness is a stress. Injury, be it a cut or broken leg, is a stress. Surgery, traveling, Christmas (whether you like it or not), getting married, having a baby, winning the lottery, drinking alcohol, smoking cigarettes, eating a bag of chips and a 24-ounce cola are all stresses. Why? Because they challenge your body. Fatty foods, in fact, have been shown to hurt your ability to deal with stress.

Beth Tannenbaum, a neuroscientist from McGill University's Douglas Hospital Research Center in Montreal fed 60 rats a high-fat diet; another 60 were served low-fat fare. She placed some of her subjects in tense situations and found that the fat eaters recovered more slowly from stress than those rats that watched what they ate.[1]

So does this mean all this stuff is bad for you? Not necessarily. Certainly you want to keep junk food down, and stick as much as you can to a wholesome diet. But when it comes to mental/emotional stress, it can be a good thing. It's what keeps us animated and alive. It's the reason for living. I, for one, wouldn't mind winning the lottery at all, and would welcome the stress it brings. For I know that our adrenal glands and body are equipped to handle a certain amount of pressure, and when healthy, bounce back rather nicely. The trick is for you to recognize the stresses in your life, and to keep them in line so they don't overtax your adrenal glands. This is the first step in your Adrenal Makeover. (For more hints on dealing with stress, see Battle Stress for Better Defense and Makeover Hint #27 in Chapter 6.)

■ *Makeover Hint #30—List Your Stress Excesses*

Take 15 minutes, and write down everything that you feel creates tension in your life and on your adrenals (besides making lists). Include pressures at work and home, dietary indulgences, too much or too little exercise or sleep, illness, surgeries, drugs (prescription, over-the-counter, or otherwise). You get the idea.

When you're done, star everything you have some control over. Then start making changes that will turn your stress excesses into vitalizing tension.

Six Adrenal Super Nutrients

In order to carry out all their duties, the adrenal glands rely on you to feed them well. Specific to their diet are vitamins B_6 and C, magnesium, and zinc. If you feast on alfalfa sprouts, citrus fruits, and broccoli, there'll be lots of vitamin C in your meals. Whole grains and green leafy vegetables give you B_6 and magnesium. Zinc is found in abundance in soybeans, pumpkin, sunflower seeds, and eggs. Lean meats gives you additional B_6 and zinc.

Potassium, plentiful in most produce, particularly bananas, as well as in whole grains, dried fruits, legumes and sunflower seeds, is another plus for hard working adrenals. In tandem with this, it's important to limit salt and salt-laden foods like pickles, processed cheeses and most canned foods. So eating canned (high salt) vegetables (high potassium) is rather pointless.

But the vitamin that appears most vital for proper adrenal operation is pantothenic acid, or vitamin B_5. When this nutrient is low—for those of you who avoid whole grains, legumes, salmon, eggs, tomatoes, and sweet potatoes—the adrenals shrink and tell-tales signs of adrenal exhaustion appear. Of course, as you slowly improve your eating habits and include whole foods, not only will your adrenals make a recovery, but your entire health will transform during the makeover process. For times when stress is particularly cruel to your adrenals, load up on these nutrients by using a high-potency vitamin and mineral multiple supplement.

■ *Makeover Hint #31—Whip Up This Adrenal Appetizer*

For some zing when you're zapped, create this flavorful snack full of adrenal-pleasing nutrients. Mix together:

1 banana, sliced up (rich in potassium)

1 cup strawberries, diced (lots of vitamin C here)

Top with a mixture of:

1 Tbsp Brewer's yeast (vitamin B_6 and zinc)

1 Tbsp of wheat germ (vitamin B_5 and more zinc)

1/4 cup of ground-up nuts, especially almonds (for magnesium)

Don't Burst your Balloon

I want you to think of yourself as a balloon, and stress as air. The more stress you add to your life, the fuller you get until one day the pressures of life are so numerous you feel like you're going to burst—not unlike an overblown balloon. The trick to managing stress, then, is to constantly gauge how full your balloon is and not let it get so full that it'll pop. How do you do that?

There are a couple of ways. One is to keep an eye on the number of stressors in your life, and to keep these to a manageable amount. (See Makeover Hint #30). The other is to make sure you have enough reserves to handle these demands. Remember, one sign of a healthy person is someone who is resilient enough to handle unexpected physical and emotional demands, like the flu, a sick child that's awake all night, bad news, a long car ride, a piece of birthday cake. You can take care of this by following all the Adrenal Makeover suggestions in this chapter; the other way is to implement some of these ideas:

- Get eight hours of sleep each night as often as possible.
- Make a wholesome diet the rule, not the exception.
- Schedule in restful breaks throughout the day.
- Pretend exercise is as important as brushing your teeth—then do it as often.
- Don't sweat the small stuff.

■ *Makeover Hint #32—Play Bullseye Bingo*

Part of stress control comes from deciding which demands in life need attention, and which do not. One way to help you prioritize, and thus lower tension levels, is to play Bullseye Bingo. My husband, Chris, a business trainer, taught me this method and uses it all the time during his Stress for Success seminars. You can use this game to gain perspective with the people in your life, work, household chores, and other time-eating, stress-inducing factors.

Grab a blank piece of paper and pen. Draw a bullseye like the one on the following page.

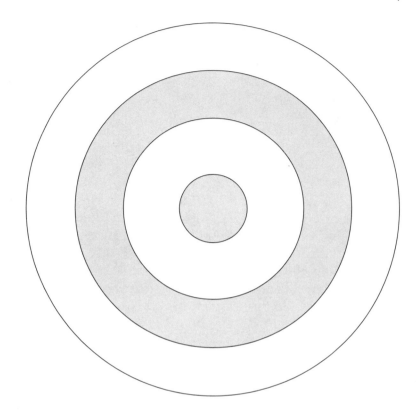

Then select a category of stress, say, the people in your life. Write your name at the center of your bullseye. Next, jot down the people most important to you in the next circle. Continue to do this with all the individuals you deal with regularly or are emotionally tied to. The farther away they are in the bullseye from you, the less important they are to you. For example, your children and spouse may be in the circle directly next to you. When there's discord between them and you, it's worth the energy and time it takes to iron out differences. On the other hand, the mailman has no VIP status in your life and sits on the most outer ring of your bullseye. It's not worth your emotional energy to ensure that you and your mailman have a smooth relationship.

This kind of diagram allows you to gain perspective on what's really significant in your daily life, and what's worth your time and energy. You have only so much time; using it indiscriminately creates stress and a drain on your adrenals.

Give Coffee a Break

"A cup of coffee is a miracle," say Heinrich Edward Jacob in *Coffee, the Epic of a Commodity*. Unfortunately this miraculous beverage and its caffeinated cousins do a number on adrenal glands. Save your adrenals, and cut coffee, black tea, colas, chocolate, and cocoa down or out of your routine. Here's why.

Sanford Bolton, Ph.D., and his colleagues from St. John's University in New York were curious about how exactly caffeine affects our stress alarms, so they enlisted the help of 11 volunteers. After serving them the equivalent of one cup of coffee a day for a week, the researchers found that adrenal function declined in subjects who were not regular caffeine users. Subjects who labeled themselves as moderate to high users (two to six cups daily for two or more years) were unaffected, probably because their adrenal function was already diminished—by chronic caffeine consumption—before the experiment began.

One of the researchers, Dr. Martin Feldman, reported that 65 percent of his new patients who complained of fatigue drank three or more cups of coffee or black tea each day. As these patients' fatigue worsened, they increased caffeine to boost their energy. Caffeine bolsters adrenal function by increasing epinephrine and norepinephrine release.[2] Not the thing for stressed-out, adrenally-sapped individuals.

■ *Makeover Hint #33—Drink a Soothing Cup of Tea*

Instead of sipping on coffee during breaks, look to herbal teas as a non-stimulating, adrenal-friendly way of relaxing. Teas with a calming influence include peppermint, chamomile, valerian, passion flower, or skullcap. Drinking these teas also helps you avoid the over-stimulating effects of caffeine.

Curing the Blood Sugar Blues

If missing a meal makes you grouchy; if you shake, rattle, and roll between meals; if your eyes glaze over, your mind shuts down, and you collapse within an hour of your coffee and Danish breakfast;

you may well be part of the "dysglycemic club." Dysglycemia (liter-ally "bad blood sugar") is one of the new labels being used in place of hypoglycemia, a state where blood sugar must be boosted every couple of hours with food. You may have heard the terms Syndrome X, carbohydrate intolerance, hyperinsulinemia, or insulin resistance describing this condition too. (These latter two descriptors techni-cally apply to a state where the hormone insulin—which lowers blood sugar—is ineffectual.) I bring this subject up here, because there is a link to your adrenal glands.

Those same stimulating hormones—epinephrine and norepi-nephrine—that get you hot and bothered during stress, also raise your blood sugar. The idea is that you need plenty of available food to keep you going as you run from (or fight) that bear. So if you're under a load of stress, for whatever reason, your poor adrenals are going to be pumping out higher-than-usual amounts of adrenaline. Eventually your adrenals are going to get tired; less adrenaline means less blood-sugar-raising back-up.

Adding to this is a diet heavy in sugars and refined carbohy-drates (that's white bread, pastas made with white flour, white rice). Eating these foods causes blood sugar to shoot up; the pancreas counters with a burst of insulin and blood sugar drops. Next the adrenals step in with their stimulating hormones to bring plummet-ing blood sugar to a halt and try to hoist it back up. And so begins the vicious bad blood sugar cycle. The liver, thyroid, and pituitary glands are also affected. All of this sounds like a play-by-play description of a sporting event. Candy Bar 1. Adrenals 0.

Besides keeping that stress in check, see Low Blood Sugar in Part Two for practical suggestions on how to solve this problem.

Soothing Herbal Help

Besides drinking relaxing herbal teas, like chamomile and valerian, you can turn to other plants for adrenal help. Borage boasts a pret-ty little purple flower, but it's the leaves that hold promise for your adrenal cortex. This herb is used to renew worn-out adrenal glands, whether due to unyielding stress or extensive cortisone use; it's also a good convalescent remedy. Licorice is the other adrenal-helper that comes to mind. Some of the compounds in the licorice plant, called glycosides, are very similar in structure to steroid hormones in the body. Like borage, licorice helps make over adrenal health after steroid medication or merely a trying time. Note: Don't use licorice for more than six weeks without a one- to two-week break as it can cause water retention, sodium retention and elevated blood pressure in some people. Eating plenty of high-potassium foods—most vegetables and fruits—helps offset this potential effect. Anyone who currently or previously had kidney problems or hypertension, or is now taking digitalis, should likely avoid licorice.

Wild yam provides the raw materials for drug manufacturers to make birth control pills, steroids, progesterone, and other medicinal hormones in the laboratory. Some herbal companies sell wild yam claiming the untouched version possesses these hormonal properties. There's no firm evidence that this is so. However, many herbalists add wild yam to their adrenal restorative formulas.

Ginseng is the other well-known herb used for Adrenal Makeovers. Actually ginseng refers to a group of plants, the most common of which are *Panax ginseng* (Asian ginseng) and *Eleutherococcus senticosus* (Siberian ginseng). These tonic herbs—also referred to as adaptogens because they help you *adapt* to stressful situations—are useful for those physically and emotionally draining times. And unlike stimulants like caffeine, ginseng energizes you only during time of stress, not when you take it.

■ Makeover Hint #34—How to Use Ginseng

There are many ginseng products on the market with varying prices to match. Since ginseng only works well if you purchase a good-quality product, follow these tips to get the most out of what you buy:

- Make sure you're getting the right species. See Appendix A for how to assess herbal quality.
- Use only as directed to avoid over-stimulation. Albeit rarely, some users may experience insomnia, irritability, morning diarrhea, skin rashes, or anxiety. If you do, stop using the ginseng for two weeks, then try it again at a lower dose.
- If you plan to use it over a long time, take it for two to three weeks, with a one- to two-week rest in between.
- Women should use eleutherococcus rather than Asian ginseng, as the latter may cause abnormal periods and cyclical breast pain.[3]

Revitalize With Hormonal Extracts

In addition to or in place of herbal help for your adrenals, you can try using adrenal glandular supplements. These products are derived from cattle, so may not be preferred by anyone eating a vegetarian diet. Nevertheless, using endocrine glands (adrenals, thymus, thyroid, pancreas, ovaries, testes) or their hormones is common practice in both natural and conventional medicine, though orthodox medicine favors the latter.

Adrenal (and other) glandulars provide your body with hormones, enzymes, building blocks for hormones, and nutrients required by that particular endocrine organ. For maximum effectiveness, you need to choose a product that has been prepared in such a way that these vital components have not been destroyed. According to Dr. Michael Murray in his excellent work, *Encyclopedia of Nutritional Supplements* (Prima Publishing, 1996), the "predigested soluble concentrates" are the most effective. For a more in-depth discussion on this topic, refer to his book.

I can personally attest to the benefits of using adrenal glandulars. Immediately following graduation from naturopathic medical school, I was a wreck. Although I attempted to stick to a healthful existence during my training (after all, that is what I was taught everyday), the stress of study, a new marriage, the death of my husband's mother, and a long list of other pressures finally wore me down. I was exhausted and my adrenals were shot. On the advice of a colleague, I began taking an adrenal glandular supplement. Within one month I felt considerably better. After three months, I was well on the road to recovery. Of course, putting my natural health ideas into practice—like managing stress, breathing, eating right, exercising, sleeping—was mandatory; yet, I believe the glandular supplement was a helpful boost.

■ *Makeover Hint #35—What about DHEA?*

You may have heard about dehydroepiandrosterone (DHEA), an adrenal hormone that is the precursor for other hormones, and in some cases mimics other hormones (see Chapter 10 for more info). Because of its central role in hormonal biochemistry, supplemental DHEA has many effects on people, most reported of which is a sense of well-being. It's also tempting to use DHEA as an adrenal rejuvenator. DHEA is sold in most health food stores and drugstores. But before you run out and stock up, read this:

- DHEA is a hormone, not an herb or vitamin.
- We don't know the long-term effects of indiscriminate supplementation.
- It is most effective in people who are deficient. You can be tested for this by your doctor.
- DHEA is helpful as a treatment. Sometimes dosages are very high; you should not take more than 10 mg of DHEA a day without professional supervision.
- Women have more side effects from DHEA than men. (DHEA is an androgen or male hormone.)
- It's better to first try boosting your DHEA levels naturally by reducing stress and following the other suggestions in the Adrenal Makeover.

The Laughter Remedy

Laughter truly is the best medicine. Norman Cousins, author of *Anatomy of an Illness*, helped popularize the notion that laughing and humor were crucial to healing. Diagnosed with the crippling disease of ankylosing spondylitis, Cousins was informed by his physician that he had one chance in 500 of recovering completely. Interestingly, Cousins was familiar with Hans Selye's work and knew of the connection between stress and adrenal function, and Selye's contention that negative emotions adversely affected the body. So Cousins' solution to his incurable condition was to chuckle his way to wellness, together with other immune-enhancing, adrenal-replenishing steps.[4] As an epilogue to his recuperation, Cousins spent the last dozen years of his life exploring the science behind laughter at the UCLA Medical School in the Department of Behavioral Medicine with his Humor Research Task Force.[5]

The American Association for Therapeutic Humor (AATH) has taken Cousins' work a step further with its membership of 600 physicians and health care practitioners who'd like to see laughter become part of every treatment plan. A good belly laugh not only relaxes you, but helps immunity (and adrenal function) by lowering cortisol levels.[6, 7] Many nurses and others in the medical field are taking therapeutic humor very seriously. Besides incorporating buffoonery into their protocols, practitioners can attend Clown Camp at the University of Wisconsin in La Crosse, subscribe to several newsletters and books on the subject, listen to tapes of funny songs by and about their peers (there's Nursing Notes and the Chordiac Arrest), and attend conferences. See Appendix C for more information on the AATH and humor-related newsletters, and visit the AATH website at http://www.callamer.com/itc/aath for a great collection of jokes.

■ *Makeover Hint #36—Jump Start Snickers*

Mirth doesn't always appear at the drop of a hat. If you're having difficulty getting into the mood, try this to jump-start your laughter.

- Stand up.
- Put your hands on your belly.
- Say "Ha" several times slowly until you can feel your belly move under your fingers.
- Now increase the speed and volume of your "Ha's" until they jump-start into continuous laughter.

Warning, this technique works best in a crowd.

Still Not Laughing?

Need a few more tips on how to handle stress? Try these on for size:

- Make a list of things you've already done.
- Bill your doctor for the time you spent in his waiting room.
- Use your Visa to pay your Mastercard.
- When someone says "Have a Nice Day!" respond that you have other plans.

Adrenal Makeover Checkup

Once you've stopped laughing, scan this list to make sure you've done all you can for your adrenals.

- Taken control of stress.
- Added adrenal nutrients and foods to your life.
- Put people and situations in perspective with Bullseye Bingo.
- Given caffeine a break.
- Tried a few adrenal-pleasing herbs.
- Considered adrenal glandulars.
- Learned how to laugh.

For Related Problems, See

- Anxiety
- Fatigue
- Headaches
- Insomnia
- Low Blood Sugar

Laboratory Tests Your Doctor Can Order

- Adrenal Test: Comprehensive Hormone Profile
- DHEA Levels or DHEA-Sulfate Levels

Chapter 8

Improve Circulation
and Live Longer

Understanding Your Heart
and Circulation

Heart disease is the number one killer in the United States. For that reason alone, you should pay close attention to this chapter. The heart is a muscular pump that drives blood through an intricate highway of vessels in your body, what we call circulation. If blood vessels are the body's highways, then blood is the truck that carries food particles, gases, garbage, hormones, and other chemicals from place to place as needed to keep your body going.

Arteries form the first section of circulatory highway, running from the heart to the rest of the body carrying oxygen-rich blood. Capillaries are the bridges between arteries and veins, and are the place where the body pulls oxygen and nutrients out of the blood in exchange for waste and carbon dioxide. Veins then cart the body's debris back up to the heart (and liver) for disposal.

There are four chambers in the heart: two atria and two ventricles. The right atrium, a kind of primer pump, is the first to receive "used" blood from the body. Its job is to push blood into the heart's power pump, or right ventricle. From here blood is sent up to the lungs where carbon dioxide is exchanged for oxygen. The body uses oxygen as fuel for various metabolic functions; carbon dioxide is what's left over. Once blood is recharged with oxygen, it travels down to the second primer pump, the left atrium, where it's given a boost to the left ventricle. Then this most powerful heart pump forces the blood through the rest of the body.

The Plus Side of a Good-Hearted Makeover

Once you understand what your heart and circulation do, you can see how important it is to maintain optimum cardiac function. When the highways of your body are clogged or your pump is too weak or diseased to work well, then the body can't get enough oxygen or nutrients, or dispose of its refuse.

One of the most common circulatory conditions is atherosclerosis, where blood vessels become thick and hard. Unfortunately, symptoms are often silent until heart or blood vessel disease is advanced. Most Americans can assume they have some degree of atherosclerosis; studies have shown that this insidious disease is even apparent in some children.[1] Your chance of developing this and other heart-related conditions increases when you have high blood pressure, high total cholesterol, LDL (bad) cholesterol (the kind that sticks to artery walls) and triglycerides, and low HDL (good) cholesterol (which travels to the liver for disposal). However, according to research that began appearing over a decade ago, our current method of testing blood fats is incomplete. We also need to measure something called "apolipoproteins." These molecules may actually be better markers for detecting coronary artery disease than cholesterol and triglycerides, according to the research team at the Mayo Medical School in Rochester, Minnesota.[2]

If you smoke, have diabetes, or are overweight, then your risk of heart troubles goes up. We mustn't forget that genetics play a part in heart disease; not everything's your fault. On the other hand, a sedentary lifestyle and eating a high-saturated fat, low-fiber, nutrient-void diet do make matters worse.

Now let's talk about some not so well-known risk factors for heart disease. Did you know that higher-than-average levels of insulin in the blood, called hyperinsulinemia, disturb your heart and vessels? In addition, insulin resistance—that is, insulin that doesn't do its job very well—is a problem.[3] Insulin is the hormone produced by the pancreas that helps cells grasp glucose (from broken-down food) and ultimately lowers blood sugar. When insulin is high, hypoglycemic symptoms are common. (See Chapter 7.)

Protecting you against oxidative damage (that's where antioxidants come in) helps keep your blood vessels clear and healthy.

Artery disease and high blood pressure are often attributed to blood vessel damage caused by everyday wear-and-tear and an inadequate repair system. Smoking, alcohol, rancid fats, and poor nutrition contribute to this.

If you have a personal or family history of chest pain due to angina, heart disease, or heart attack, then a Cardiovascular Makeover is for you. Fortunately, your heart and circulation are greatly influenced by lifestyle. The authors of the scientific paper, "Can lifestyle changes reverse coronary heart disease?" answer this question with a resounding probably—if you adhere to a healthful diet, regular exercise, and stress control, instead of letting stress control you.[4] So whether you have high cholesterol, high triglycerides, high blood pressure, or actually feel fine, take the Heart Makeover plunge for a longer and stronger life.

Good Fats, Bad Fats—Which Ones to Eat

Eat a low-fat diet! That's the standard recommendation of most heart specialists. And while I agree somewhat with this statement, you must also realize that there's more to the fat scenario than eradicating it from your meals. Fats are vital nutrients in every diet. The trick, especially if you're prone to heart problems or have a family history, is how to eat enough of the good fats and stay healthy. Let's start with a lesson in fats.

Fats are divided into two main categories: saturated and unsaturated. The saturated fats are solid at room temperature, and primarily of animal origin; tropical oils like palm, palm kernel, and coconut are exceptions. Plant and animal fats contain *both* saturated and unsaturated portions; some also possess naturally occurring trans fatty acids. The difference is that more animal foods like egg yolks, shellfish, whole dairy products, lard, red meats, and poultry skin are top-heavy in saturated fats, while plants favor unsaturated oils. Unsaturated fats are typically liquid at room temperature and mainly of vegetable origin. There are polyunsaturated fats like the oils from safflower, soybean, sunflower, sesame, and corn. Macadamia oil, canola oil, and olive oil are considered monounsaturated fats—liquid at room temperature, but solid in the fridge.

Piling on the vegetables and whole grains will naturally shove aside many fatty foods. But don't eliminate fats entirely. Dine cautiously on the saturated fatty foods mentioned above. And when you do, remove excess fat. Skin your chickens and turkeys. Trim that marble of fat off your steak and lamb chops. Drink non-fat milk. Fill in the fat gaps with the essential fats that your body can't make but needs. Select raw, unsalted nuts and seeds. Use olive and canola oils in your cooking and salad dressings; they don't harm arteries or raise blood fat levels. Instead they help create the HDL cholesterol that protects your blood vessels. And eat all the fish you like (see Makeover Hint #41.)

There has been some research indicating that eating too much polyunsaturated oil (safflower, sunflower, soybean) may lower helpful HDL-cholesterol. This may be because these oils tend to turn rancid faster than monounsaturated oils, and rancid fats produce free radical molecules—not good for your heart or circulation.[5] Consuming rancid oils, fried foods, and high amounts of saturated fats adds to damaging oxidation, specifically of no-good LDL cholesterol, and ultimately atherosclerosis.[6] Also, be cautious when cooking with oils, since heating them increases oxidative damage.

I should mention a third category of fats, the trans fatty acids or hydrogenated vegetable oils (they also come in the partially-hydrogenated style). These fats are vegetable oils that have been altered so that they are hard at room temperature, just like saturated fats. Hence you have margarine, and the hydrogenated fats added to many processed foods like breads, salad oils, mayonnaise, and snack foods. It's been a century since the invention of hydrogenation—the method that performs this trans fatty magic—but only 20 years of a rocket-like increase in consumption. As we search for heart-friendly foods, we've been told by margarine manufacturers to use their healthful alternative to butter. In truth, trans fatty acids boost LDL and total blood cholesterol, and drag down the good HDL cholesterol.[7]

Talking about cholesterol, do you remember all the hoopla in 1989 when we were told that avoiding cholesterol-rich foods was really unnecessary? First realize that *your body* makes most of the cholesterol you own. That's right, your liver makes up to 1500 mg of this fat-like substance from saturated fats and simple sugars;

most people don't absorb more than a third of that from foods in a day. Without cholesterol your cells would collapse without their rigid covering; you'd have no sex life because you couldn't make the sex hormones estrogen, progesterone, and testosterone (see Chapter 10); you couldn't handle stress because you'd be void of cortisone (see Chapter 7); your kidneys would be at a loss in handling fluid levels without needed aldosterone (see Chapter 5); your skin would look terrible (see Chapter 12); your bones would crumble and fall (see Chapter 11); your liver couldn't make bile for fat digestion (see Chapters 3 and 4). Without cholesterol, you'd be a mess.

It's not so much eating cholesterol that raises blood cholesterol, it's saturated fats and, possibly, refined sugars (see below, Do You Have Low Blood Sugar or High Blood Pressure?). Many cultures thrive on diets with more meat, whole dairy, and fat than we as Americans (and Canadians) think is healthy, yet don't have our high cholesterol problem. This, I think, goes back to our tendency to eat processed, refined foods rather than vegetables, fruits, meats and grains in their original and organic forms. When you get your cholesterol checked, be sure to have your doctor do a complete lipid panel (see below, Laboratory Tests Your Doctor Can Order); make sure it not only includes a total cholesterol, but HDL, LDL, and apolipoproteins. All of this information together means more than cholesterol level alone.

■ Makeover Hint #37—Eat Better Butter

Can't give up butter? You don't have to if you use this recipe to convert your butter into this healthier version—and use it sparingly.

BETTER BUTTER

1/2 lb butter, softened

1/2 cup canola oil (fresh)

Place both ingredients in a blender or food processor. Mix until blended. Store in refrigerator. Use like pure butter. Toss unused portion after two months.

Give Your Heart the Oxygen It Loves

Get a move on! That's the next step to a healthier heart. A sedentary existence of reading, watching TV, writing (oops), eating, sitting at the computer (me again), sewing, playing cards, or working at a desk is more than your heart and health can handle. Your muscular heart requires a regular workout and aerobic activity, that is, oxygen-filled exercise, to feed it. The Institute for Aerobics Research in Dallas knows this and proved it when it followed more than 10,000 men and 3100 women. After eight years of watching this large group, there was no doubt that the more fit one is, the lower the risk for cardiovascular disease (and cancer). According to this investigation, you can reach top physical conditioning with a mere 30–60 minute brisk walk each day.[8]

■ *Makeover Hint #38—Do the Potato*

The trick to having a healthy heart is to *do* the potato, not *be* a potato. In other words, find ways that keep you physically moving, not sedentary, during the day. For you, the potato might be a funky dance you enjoy practicing to an old Beatles tune while no one is looking. Someone else might find a brisk walk around the block four times a refreshing pick-me-up. Whatever it is, try not to sit still for more than 30 minutes at a time. Other aerobic activities include:

- Running or jogging
- Biking
- Rowing
- Cross-country skiing
- Jumping rope
- Rollerblading (or skating)
- Racing after children (I hope this counts)

Remember, if you haven't exercised on a regular basis for a long time, consult with your doctor first.

Feast on Fiber

I'm going to say it again: eat more fiber. There is no doubt that loading up on roughage each day helps not only your digestive tract and liver, but your heart as well. So if you haven't managed to insert fresh vegetables and fruits, whole wheat bread, brown rice, barley, oat bran, beans, legumes, and other high-fiber foods into your diet, for your heart's sake, now is the time.

Do you remember the oat bran craze of the early 1990s? It began, in part, because of a study done at Rush-Presbyterian-St. Luke's Medical Center in Chicago. Dr. Michael Davidson and his colleagues proved that people who ate just two ounces of oat bran (equivalent to three ounces of oatmeal) each day could lower their LDL-cholesterol by almost 16 percent in only six weeks.[9] Topped with a few walnuts and a sprinkling of raisins, that sounds like a mighty tasty way of staying fit. Beans, psyllium and vegetables have been shown to have similar effects.[10]

Young Andrew Barely Notices Barley in Healthy Cookies

Say the word "fiber," and many people cringe. What they don't know is that this essential heart nutrient can be delicious. One of my favorite ways to slip fiber into my children's diet is by substituting barley flour for white flour in cookies, muffins, waffles, and loaves. A couple of summers ago, I was doling out fresh homemade barley cookies. Adam's friend, Andrew, was visiting and, knowing that we served "healthy food" in our house, was slightly hesitant about sampling my baking. Nevertheless, he took a cookie and began nibbling. A few minutes later I felt a tap on my shoulder. "Mrs. Aesoph," he said, "can I have another cookie?" Of course I agreed. With a large grin on his face, Andrew ran over to the cookie dish, grabbed two, then three, and escaped outside with my son. Barley wins out again.

Eat Heart-Felt Nutrients Everyday

For years, medical experts believed malnutrition posed no threat to the heart. Modern research has proved beyond a doubt, however, that hearty eating is vital if you want your circulation and its pump—

the heart—to serve you well. The first step is to follow those nutritious steps outlined in previous chapters. Next, take a close look at specific vitamins and minerals that affect blood flow and the heart.

Antioxidants, like vitamins A, C, and E, beta carotene, and various flavonoids, are recommended not only to prevent cancer and premature aging, but also heart disease. The reason? Once again, it's because of their free radical scavenging abilities. Those darn free radicals, remember, are highly reactive molecules that damage cells all over the body, including the heart and vessels.

So where do we find free-radical fighters? The best place to start is always food. Colorful vegetables and fruits are among the most flavonoid-rich, antioxidant-full edibles available to us. Dutch researchers gave us hard evidence why eating your greens (and oranges and reds and purples) is heart-friendly. These scientists followed more than 500 men and wrote down what they ate. Five years later, they found that men who ate the most flavonoid-rich foods were half as likely to have a heart attack or die from coronary heart disease as were those eating the least amount. Flavonoids are thought to prevent atherosclerosis and reduce blood clot formation.[11]

Vitamin E, also an antioxidant found in asparagus, avocados, tomatoes, and green leafies, is famous in cardiovascular circles as a heart protector. A Scottish study revealed that men with the lowest amounts of vitamin E in their blood were two and a half times more likely to suffer from angina, or chest pain, than those with high levels.[12] Vitamin C's place in heart health is as an antioxidant, blood pressure reducer, cholesterol shrinker, and a nutrient that helps the body hold on to vitamin E.[13] Oranges, grapefruit, and other citrus fruits are vitamin C warehouses.

Magnesium deficiency has been linked to hypertension, arrhythmias, and congestive heart failure.[14] This mineral is thought to enhance blood flow, relax blood vessel walls, prevent abnormal heart rhythm and even stop blood clots from forming. Some doctors use intravenous magnesium in cases of suspected heart attack to help reduce death rates by one half.[15] Luckily, high fiber foods, like dark green vegetables and whole grains, are also high in magnesium. In addition to these nutrients, chromium, taurine, vitamin B_6, niacin, L-carnitine, pantethine, calcium, copper, and lecithin all play roles in cardiac health. Of course, these nutrients are best taken in food, or a well-balanced nutrient supplement. For specific, individualized recommendations, see a nutrition-wise cardiologist.

■ *Makeover Hint #39—When All Else Fails, Test for Homocysteine*

When nothing seems to help bring your cholesterol or blood pressure down, ask your doctor to run a homocysteine test. Too much of this, a metabolite of the amino acid methionine, hurts your arteries, and can ultimately lead to atherosclerosis and heart attack. The solution is supplementation, with the right nutrients, based on your laboratory test. Vitamin B_6 urges homocysteine to convert to cystathione (that's good), while folic acid pushes homocysteine back to methionine.[16] Vitamin B_{12} may also help.

Treating High Blood Pressure or Low Blood Sugar?

Fats are often the bad guys when it comes to rescuing your poor heart. But several studies point the finger at sugar as well. Next step to your Heart Makeover is to throw out the Valentine chocolates and look to the Low Blood Sugar section in Part Two for advice. Italian scientists examined the sugar-heart connection more closely. Their preliminary evidence showed that in some cases high blood pressure is caused by insulin resistance.[17] This means hypertension is more of a blood sugar problem than one of blood fats. When I spoke with Dr. Jonathan Wright, a well-known nutrition-expert a couple of years ago, he told me that as a matter of course he runs a glucose-insulin tolerance test on all his patients with essential hypertension. This is the most common type of high blood pressure—90 percent of cases—and has no "known" cause. More than half, he says, come back with high insulin levels and/or low blood sugar. When Dr. Wright then treats these patients for these problems, their blood pressures invariably fall.

Another interesting tidbit. Several animal and human studies have implicated sugar as the accessory in salt-related hypertension. There's a strong suggestion that white table sugar especially, in combination with salt, raises blood pressure substantially.[18] So is it the salt or the sugar? Salt-sensitive animals are more susceptible; that may be the case for people too.

The standard way to test for low blood sugar is by checking blood glucose levels with the glucose tolerance test (GTT). Most doctors look not only for a glucose level that's fallen to 50 milligrams or less per 100 milliliters of blood, but also for symptoms to occur while the glucose level is at this low point. Some natural health physicians feel this method only looks at half the picture. They also want to see insulin levels, which can rise abnormally (while glucose levels are normal) and cause hypoglycemic-like symptoms. This is the glucose-*insulin* tolerance test.

The QT on Q10

A safe and effective treatment for some types of heart disease, like angina, congestive heart failure, and high blood pressure, is coenzyme Q10. It's also known as ubiquinone because of its ubiquitous nature—it's naturally found in all plant- and animal-based foods. Specifically, it's an essential ingredient of the mitochondria or energy packs that run the cells and body; it's especially high in the heart. Heart disease increases your need for this enzyme.[19] If you decide to try this supplement, give it at least one to two months before you expect results; 50 to 100 mg daily is the usual dose.

Add More Onion, Garlic, and Spice

The heart and blood vessels love well-seasoned cooking; if you do too, you're in luck. My grandfather has been growing garlic for decades; once a week he sups on a goodly amount. It's not just his Ukrainian heritage that drives him to this bulb; he knows garlic's reputation for lowering the fats in blood—cholesterol and triglycerides—more effectively than diet alone. A group of German researchers proved this with 10 of the 20 patients they treated with garlic; all were also treated with diet. Cholesterol levels fell for all 20 patients, though more so in the garlic group. However, only the garlic-eaters saw their triglycerides fall as well. This thrilled the University of Munich scientists, who commented: "Drugs used to do this are almost invariably burdened with side effects—some of them just a nuisance but jeopardizing compliance, some of them serious, possibly out-weighing the therapeutic benefit by increasing the incidence of non-cardiovascular death. In this dilemma a harmless but efficient antilipid medication (*like garlic*) would be appreciated."[20] Onion, a cousin of garlic, offers much the same protection.[21]

For those who enjoy hot and spicy foods, you'll be happy to note that cayenne pepper is a wonderful Heart Makeover condiment. Capsaicin, one of cayenne's many constituents, promotes heart health by decreasing the clumping together of platelets,[22] tiny disk-shaped particles found in blood that assist with blood vessel repair and blood clotting. However, when arteries are damaged and not adequately repaired, for example when nutrient levels are low, platelets congregate in these areas and contribute to clogged arteries. Cayenne decreases this tendency without interfering with platelets' normal duties.

Ginger is another spice to add to your cooking as part of your Heart Makeover. Officially known as *Zingiber officinale*, ginger protects your heart through its antioxidant and tonifying effects[23] as well as its ability to diminish inflammation.[24] Rather than using aspirin as your blood-thinning medicine, rely on ginger. This way you not only avoid gastric bleeding and upset, but actually promote better digestion, help open blocked arteries,[25] and lower cholesterol.

■ *Makeover Hint #41—Spice Up Your Fish*

Eating as little as one or two fish dishes per week may prevent coronary heart disease.[26] For a tasty difference, spice up your broiled fish by flavoring it with a splash of cayenne, a sprinkling of diced garlic (fresh, not powdered) or a few thick slices of heart-loving onion.

How About Hawthorn?

I include a side note about hawthorn here because it once sat in the food category as well, in jam and wine. This plant with the rosehip-like berries is also a traditional cure for many heart ailments. *Crataegus laevigata* (or *oxyacntha*) and *Crataegus monogyna*—all are used—give us their berries, leaves, and blossoms to reduce blood pressure and serum cholesterol, prevent angina, and act as a general heart tonic. You can certainly take it in pill form, but wouldn't a cup of hawthorn berry tea be nice?

Cut Down on Caffeine

Again with the coffee, or should I say caffeine. There's evidence afloat that ingesting the stuff raises blood pressure and the risk of heart disease in people not used to this stimulant. At least that's what Drs. Dan Sharp and Neal Benowitz found in a group of bus drivers. Those who drank caffeinated beverages regularly appeared to have adjusted to this effect.[27] Perhaps it has something to do with adrenal exhaustion (see Chapter 7). I find it interesting that out of the 281 San Francisco bus drivers these doctors selected, only 10 percent used caffeine infrequently, that is, two to four times a week.

Across the Atlantic in the Netherlands, scientists found another reason to be wary of coffee when it comes to matters of the heart. Substances called cafestol and kahweol, that float around in unfiltered coffee as small oily droplets and coffee grounds, raise both cholesterol and triglycerides in the blood. The worst of these coffees are the Middle Eastern coffee brews (Turkish, Greek, and—Israeli mud?) and the boiled Scandinavian type. French press and mocha were next, followed by espresso and percolated. The most sediment-free coffees came from the drip filter; paper filter came out on top with the cleanest coffee and the least grounds.[28]

So there you have it. For a clean bill of health, avoid caffeine and coffee. As a compromise, imbibe occasionally (no more than four times weekly), and use a paper filter. Or try the next Makeover Hint.

■ *Makeover Hint #42—Drink Green Caffeine*

Drinking green tea is another coffee option. Japanese scientists found that the more of this healthful tea their subjects drank, the lower their total cholesterol and triglyceride levels were. More importantly, the good HDL cholesterol went up and bad LDL cholesterol declined.[29] I should note here that green tea does in fact contain caffeine. However, it obviously heralds benefits not found with coffee. If you're concerned about caffeine, try the decaffeinated version of green tea.

Say No to Smoking (and Sitting in a Smoky Room)

Here are two more reasons to give up cigarettes: higher triglyceride levels and less HDL cholesterol—both risk factors for coronary heart disease. Want some more? Years of puffing constricts the blood vessels traveling to your heart, raises your heart rate, and boosts your blood pressure.[30]

For you non-smokers: choose the non-smoking section of the restaurant. Avoid smoky bars and ban smoking in your home and car. If you're worried about being rude, use these facts to fortify your courage. Inhaling second-hand smoke for 20 minutes to eight hours decreases your heart's ability to receive and process oxygen. Do it on a regular basis, and your arteries get plugged, your cholesterol shoots up, blood pressure may climb, and ischemic heart disease is a possible threat.[31]

I know quitting is extremely difficult. But here's what you have to look forward to once you stop:

> In 20 minutes—blood pressure drops to normal.
>
> In 8 hours—oxygen levels in blood increase to normal; carbon monoxide drops.
>
> In 24 hours—chance of heart attack decreases.
>
> In 48 hours—nerve endings begin regrowing.
>
> In 2 to 12 weeks—improved circulation.
>
> In 1 to 9 months—energy increases.
>
> In 5 to 10 years—chance of cancer declines.[32]

Advice on Alcohol

This is a confusing topic when it comes to a Heart Makeover. Harvard's Eric Rimm, Sc.D., told us in 1991 that drinking liquor decreases your chance of coronary disease.[33] In France, where wine is consumed like soda is in this country, coronary heart disease is lower than any other developed country. Some have called this the "French Paradox." Why is this? And does this mean that we should be drinking wine or other alcohol every day as part of a Heart Makeover? There is no simple answer.

Certainly wine—even alcohol—has a positive effect on the heart and the good HDL cholesterol in our blood. Red wine, in particular, with its antioxidant flavonoids (from the purple grapes) seems helpful. It could be that in nations where wine is a regular dinner-time beverage, nutrition is better. Maybe drinking wine *with* meals is the trick to lowering blood fats and decreasing alcohol's negative health influences. However, while the French certainly have less heart disease, alcohol abuse is a major problem, as are disease and death from other causes besides heart troubles. Dr. Timothy Regan from the New Jersey Medical School in Newark reminds us that too much booze ups blood pressure and contributes to stroke.[34]

So what should you do?

This is my advice. The occasional glass of wine, especially with dinner, is not harmful for most. Sipping on this or saki (rice wine) before dinner helps digestion, and may improve the health of your heart. The key is moderation. Also take into account your personal health history and risks. Refrain from drinking if you have liver disease or a history of it, a history of alcoholism, or are unable to have "just one." If your immunity is struggling, alcohol could make it worse. Women have special circumstances to consider. Don't drink if you're pregnant or nursing. And the risk for breast cancer does increase substantially for women who drink alcohol.[35]

How to Make Over a Broken Heart

You've heard the story of the elderly woman who dies, and only a couple of months later her husband of many years also passes away, supposedly from a broken heart. Practitioners of Traditional Chinese Medicine believe that the heart not only pumps *blood* throughout the body, but also *emotions* and *thoughts*.

We also read how driving, type A personalities are more prone to heart attacks. Is there any truth to the idea that emotions affect the heart and general health? If you read medical journals, there is.

Harvard researchers discovered that mental stress causes blocked heart arteries to constrict, which in turn reduces blood flow even more. Your heart can't remain well if its life-feeding blood vessels are clogged. Healthy vessels, on the other hand, either open slightly to allow the blood to flow more freely or remain unchanged when things get crazy.[36] High blood pressure jumps even higher in tense situations.[37] And a short fuse more easily triggers the cascade of potentially damaging hormones released when you feel threatened or ready to fight.[38]

Even doctors can get caught in the feelings and heart trap. A Duke University study found that physicians who frequently felt angry, carried cynical mistrust in their hearts, and expressed hostility toward others, had seven times the death rate during a 25-year period than did their calmer colleagues. "Trusting hearts may live longer because for them the biologic cost of situations that anger or irritate is lower," says Redford B. Williams, Jr., M.D., a lead researcher of this study.[39]

What about broken hearts? A research team that fed two bunches of bunnies high-fat, high-cholesterol foods to see how much diet affected atherosclerosis development were shocked to find that one group had 60 percent less damage. It turns out that a graduate student assigned to the less sickly rabbits also fed them large doses of love by regularly taking them out of their cages and tenderly petting them.[41] The moral here is: Keep fat intake low, but if you decide to splurge on ice cream, hug someone first.

Here are some ways to keep your heart from breaking (or to mend it):

- First of all, realize that sadness, anger, and fear are part of the richness of living. Don't avoid them, but rather welcome these emotions, experience them and move on. So-called negative feelings help us grow both personally and within our relationships.

- Second, figure out the best way for you to cope with mental and emotional pressures (see Chapter 7). For some this might mean talking with a friend or writing in a journal. Others might find exercise helpful, or a nap, or deep breathing.

- Third, keep physical stressors low—caffeine, alcohol, junk food, insufficient sleep—when emotional or mental tension increases.

- During times of grief, take a dose of the homeopathic remedy *Ignatia.*

- Last, a healthy heart is more flexible to emotional demands. Follow all the other Cardiac Makeover suggestions above so your heart won't break for other reasons.

Heart Makeover Checkup

Is your heart just bursting with happiness and good health? I knew it would. These are the steps you took to get there:

- Sorted out the good fats and the bad.
- Started exercising.
- Added more fiber to more meals. (I feel like a rabbit!)
- Ate in a healthier manner; still taking a multiple; added a few antioxidant vitamins too.
- Realized that low blood sugar came up again; better read that section.
- Spiced up meals—garlic, onions, ginger, cayenne.
- Got another reminder to give up coffee.
- Decided to avoid cigarette smoke—smokers and nonsmokers alike.
- Cut alcohol down or out.
- Made up my mind to control my anger. . . . grrrrrrr.

For Related Problems, See

- Fatigue
- Heartburn
- Indigestion
- Low Blood Sugar
- Varicose Veins

Laboratory Tests Your Doctor Can Order

- Lipid Profile (total cholesterol, HDL, LDL)
- Apolipoprotein Test
- Homocysteine; Folic Acid/B_{12} Levels
- Glucose-Insulin Tolerance Test
- Other standard cardiac tests as appropriate

Chapter 9

Attain Tiptop Muscle Tone

Staying Active for a Lifetime

You wouldn't go a day without eating, drinking, or sleeping. Yet many ignore the fourth important daily requirement for health— movement. Humans beings are meant to move every day. That can mean walking, laboring, or planned exercise. Movement gives muscles a chance to work. And when we use our muscles, other body systems are indirectly affected. Other makeover musts, like nutrition-rich foods, also help keep our muscles in tiptop shape.

Muscle is a relative term. Your heart has muscle. Then there's the smooth muscle that lines many of your organs—like the digestive tract. But the muscle we'll be speaking of in this chapter is skeletal muscle, the tissue attached to bones that allows you to reach into the cupboard, shake hands, play the piano, use a computer, and move from place to place. Most, though not all, skeletal muscles can be moved at will and are sometimes referred to as voluntary muscles.

Almost half of your body is made up of muscle. Generally speaking, muscles are attached to bone or cartilage via tendons. However, there are exceptions to this rule. The face has muscles that make you smile, chew, and cry; these blend into the skin. The tongue is a muscle too. Within each individual muscle are muscle fibers. The larger the muscle, the more fibers. Smaller muscles, like those in your eye or hand that require precise movement, have fewer fibers.

Your Muscle Makeover

The modern life is typically a sedentary one. This is in large part due to all the conveniences we've adopted: cars, washers and dryers, dishwashers, telephones, vacuums, computers, and take-out food—to name a few. That's not to say we don't all appreciate these time-saving, energy-sparing luxuries. However, because everyday chores don't keep us physically fit anymore, we must schedule "movement time" into each day.

Movement is the foundation of attaining and maintaining muscle tone; food and other things are helpful supporters. But why are toned muscles and exercise so important? Healthy, firm muscles are better able to do their job of getting us from place to place, and protecting joints. You'll also notice, as you work your way through the Natural Health Makeover plan, that movement isn't just tied to musculature. Physical, muscular fitness also revitalizes digestion, maximizes immunity, helps you manage stress and regain sexual vitality, improves circulation, and is one way to live longer. For all you exercise-shy folks who are thinking, "No way. I've never exercised, and I never will. I don't have time. I can't do it!" stop and read on. You don't have to be an athlete to enjoy the benefits of regular movement. When I write of "tiptop muscle tone," I'm not referring to body building. I just want you to squeeze as much physical movement into your daily life as possible; after all, a little bit is better than none at all. Besides wearing off excess calories, the increased oxygen flow will make you look and feel better. Believe me, once you make over your muscles as outlined below, you'll never look back.

There are three main ways to introduce movement into your life: everyday movement—using the stairs instead of the elevator; recreational or play-time movement—golf, gardening, bowling, or biking; and workout time—aerobics class, morning treadmill walk—movement that ensures that you're getting a good, sweaty workout each day.

Foolproof Fitness Test

How do you know you need to move more? Number one, how much do you move now? If you sit most of the day and don't take time for 30 to 60 minutes of planned physical activity (anything from walking to aerobics class) every day or so, then you most certainly have a movement deficiency.

The other way to tell is by listening to your body. Look for these movement deficiency signs:

- Chronic muscle tension or pain (neck, shoulders, back)
- Shortness of breath with minimal movement, for example, climbing a flight of stairs. (This may be a heart problem. Ask your doctor.)
- Insomnia.
- Frequent tension headaches.
- Constipation.
- Weight gain or problems losing weight.
- Fatigue.
- Inability to handle stress.
- Vague body aches and pains.
- Depression.
- Irritability.

Longevity Success Story

Before you take the first step to firmer muscles, I want you to read this story. Mary is a very active, healthy 83-year-old living in Aldergrove, British Columbia. One of the secrets to her longevity and well-being is exercise—not the structured kind, but that old-fashioned hard work that comes from growing up on a prairie farm, living through the Depression, and raising a family. One of Mary's loves, and the source of her daily activity, is her massive vegetable and flower garden.

Mary and her husband Mike live on a four-acre lot, one quarter of which is cultivated. Needless to say, such an ambitious garden needs constant care. Most days throughout the year, Mary dons her wide-brimmed straw hat and heads out to hoe, pull weeds, prune—whatever needs tending. And the way Mary attacks those weeds, gardening becomes a triage of aerobics, stretching, and muscle toning. Because Mary and Mike don't believe in using herbicides, all the food they raise and subsequently eat is organic and deliciously fresh, just the thing for hardworking muscles.

Everyday Energy Boosters

Not everyone can be a Mary. But each of us moves every day—
even if it's just to the car and back. The best place to begin your
Muscle Makeover is by capitalizing on your current everyday activities. Begin by recording for a couple of days all activity in your
life. This could be running down the street to catch a bus, walking
up two flights of stairs at work, taking the baby for a walk, or
cleaning house. Not only will this tell you how much you move,
but it will give you a starting point to make changes. Let's look at
the following example.

Joe's Activity Record for April 14, 1997

Walked to the bus from home (two blocks).

Walked from the bus to work (one block).

Got up from desk two times to use copy machine, and one
time to use restroom (morning).

Walked to elevator down three flights, and walked from there
to cafeteria for lunch. Read the newspaper for half an hour.

Sat in meeting most of the afternoon; got up to use restroom
once and to storeroom once.

Walked to bus stop (one block).

Walked home from bus stop (two blocks).

Had dinner, watched TV until bed.

Although Joe is very sedentary, there are several opportunities
during his day to sneak in a little extra physical activity. To begin
with, his walks to the bus each day. Rather than walking to the clos-
est bus stop near his home, he could walk to the next bus stop a
block or two down the road. Similarly, when he exits the bus near
work, he could get off a stop earlier. This strategy alone could add
a quarter mile of walking to his day. Instead of taking the elevator
at work, Joe could take the stairs. Rather than merely eating lunch
and reading the newspaper, Joe could begin his lunch hour with a
brisk walk followed by lunch. His post-dinner TV watching could be
partially replaced by an evening stroll with his wife or a bike ride
with the kids.

Other ways you can slip exercise into your day might be shoveling the walk instead of using the snowblower; sweeping the walk with a broom, not the leaf blower—then jumping in the leaves, playing hopscotch with your kids, using your legs, not the channel changer?

■ *Makeover Hint #43—The Underexercising Trick*

Too many people give up on regular exercise before they have a chance to really begin. One reason is they overdo it. The trick to "exercise" longevity is to exercise too little. Let's say you want to jog for your everyday movement. Rather than running one, two, or three miles on your first outing, take an easy quarter-mile jog. If this distance winds you, run or walk even less. Continue running this distance every day until you feel totally comfortable and underexercised. Then very gradually increase your distance a fraction, and run *this* extended distance for a week or more.

I learned to jog this way from my track-and-field-star husband. In high school, he used to push himself so hard that his stomach hurt after a run. Knowing my competitive nature (and complete lack of experience running), he wisely had me follow this baby-step method to running. We began with a quarter of a mile, after which I whined, "Is that all?" (You should too.) But I was so proud that I could run any distance without huffing that I didn't mind too much. We continued with this program for a few months until the day came when I ran a total of three miles without stopping, feeling uncomfortable, or out of breath. What an accomplishment for a person with absolutely no athletic ability at all!

Make Exercise a Daily Occurrence

The next step to tiptop muscles is to add purposeful exercise to your daily routine. This is one of the basic health makeover tips I tell all my patients. For people who complain or give me that "you're-crazy" look, these are the tips I pass on.

- Begin with five minutes of exercise a day.

- If it helps, use a timer to tell you when you're done. When that buzzer goes off, stop regardless of what you're doing.

- Build exercise into your day. Rather than trying to find time to exercise around other commitments, schedule other activities around exercise.

- Don't be rigid. Once you've built your exercise time up, if you only have time for 20 minutes instead of 30, that's fine. A little exercise is better than none.

- Remember, it's more difficult to start something new than continue what you've already established.

While purposeful activity should be a daily habit, it's also reasonable to expect that unavoidable circumstances may prevent you from this goal occasionally. You may find that by planning to exercise every day, you'll actually do it five or six days a week. Better this than planning on exercising three days each week, and only accomplishing it one or two. If you're very disciplined, or after practicing the exercise habit for a month or two, you may decide to schedule one or two days off each week, perhaps the weekend or select weekdays—whatever works for you.

■ *Makeover Hint #44—Timing*

Find the best time of day for you, both schedule-wise ("Mornings are too hectic") and energy-wise ("I can't move after lunch") to exercise. You'll not only enjoy it more, but gain more as well. Also avoid exercising one hour before or two hours after a full meal. A small snack just before exercising is all right if you need an energy boost.

The Exercise Charter

Recording your daily movement for a month or two is a great way to build consistency and develop a good habit. You can either mark your calendar with each event, or use the following Exercise Chart to help introduce daily exercise in a no-sweat way.

Table 9.1
EXERCISE CHART

Activity	Minutes						
	Mon	Tues	Wed	Thur	Fri	Sat	Sun

Vary How You Move

It's no wonder people get bored with exercise. They pick a specific routine and figure they must stick with it for life. This isn't good for your body, and it's certainly not fun. We are naturally drawn to enjoyable activities—at least for the long haul—so a dull physical fitness regimen soon loses its luster and is eventually dropped.

Break the mold and learn to be one of those people who loves to move. Instead of just attending aerobics classes three times a week, mix it up with biking, walking, swimming, and dancing. If you enjoy routine for a short time, then get bored, attend your aerobics class for one or two months and be prepared to jump into a new activity before the excitement wanes. Another way to do this, is change your activities with the seasons. Here in season-rich South Dakota, I love to ride my bike in the summer, go for walks outside in the fall, and when that long, long winter begins, I dust off my treadmill.

Also choose different types of movement to give your Muscle Makeover more power. Besides aerobic activity, incorporate weight training and stretching into your regular routine. This way, not only do you flood your muscles and body with life-giving oxygen and build endurance, but your muscles attain tone and flexibility.

■ *Makeover Hint #45—Rate Your Exercise on the Fun Scale*

Do you exercise because you think you should, or because it's fun? One way to devise an enjoyable activity routine is to make it something you look forward to. Begin by listing all the physical activities you currently do, or could do. These could include walking, running, exercise class, gardening, tennis, dancing, hiking, martial arts, biking, yoga, bowling, making love. Then rate them on the fun scale. Activities you find thrilling rate a 10; activities that bore you to tears get a 1. Assign other pastimes accordingly. Any activity that rates a 5 or less, toss. Concentrate on the most fun activities for you.

Your Super Fitness Plan

Once you've practiced moving more in your everyday routine, and established a time for structured exercise, you need to think about different types of exercises, like aerobics, weight training and stretching, and when it's best to do each. Both stretching and aerobic activity are best done every day, even if it's just a short five- or ten-minute warm-up followed by a 30 minute walk. Weight training, on the other hand, should be done every other day or three days per week (see below for specific suggestions). Lift weights directly after your aerobic exercise. Not only are your muscles already warmed up, but the weight lifting will help prolong your aerobic movement a little bit. If you prefer, alternate stretching and weight lifting days. Your physical fitness schedule might look something like this:

> Monday—Stretch 5 minutes; 30-minute walk; 10 minutes weights.
>
> Tuesday—Stretch 5 minutes; 30-minute walk; 10 minutes stretching.
>
> Wednesday—Stretch 5 minutes; 30-minute walk; 10 minutes weights.
>
> Thursday—Stretch 5 minutes; 30-minute walk; 10 minutes stretching.
>
> Friday—Stretch 5 minutes; 30-minute walk; 10 minutes weights.
>
> Saturday—Game of tennis (45 minutes); warm-up included.
>
> Sunday—day off.

Of course, your chosen activities will vary from the above, and can change from day to day, as will the time you allot for each.

Aerobics—Cash in on Oxygen

Other factors to keep in mind when embarking on a structured exercise plan are clothing and breathing. Clothing should be comfortable and loose-fitting, such as jogging pants and T-shirt or leotards. Don't forget shoes that give your feet support. These don't have to be fancy, just functional. Remember to breathe as you work out so your muscles and heart receive the oxygen-rich blood you're working so hard to send their way. Consider too whether you'll get more use from or stay motivated by using a health club, joining forces with a friend or exercising alone with or without exercise equipment. As a busy mother, writer, and physician, I've found a fold-up treadmill the most worthwhile investment for 45 minutes of at-home aerobic activity. I also get bored easily, so I have my machine set up in front of the television where I can catch up on favorite programs I've taped or watch a rented movie. In this same room I perform various yoga positions for stretching, and complete my routine with small dumb-bells and ankle weights. You decide what circumstances will allow you to stick with a daily program.

Last, if you're over 35 or have not exercised on a regular basis, visit your doctor for a checkup and green flag to begin the road to physical fitness.

Stretch It!

Learn how to stretch your body every day, and you'll not only make over your muscles, but release pent-up tension, breathe more easily and gain inner peace. Stretching, whether through simple bends or with yoga, creates more flexible joints and muscles and helps alleviate stiffness that comes with age. Well-positioned stretches are also useful therapeutic tools for bodily aches and pains.

Ideally you want to incorporate a full-body stretch into your everyday routine. It needn't take long—15 to 20 minutes is fine. Here's a routine to get you started.

■ Makeover Hint #46—The Five Minute Stretch

For times when you're tense or short on time, use this quickie stretching routine. Find a door and open it. Face the door so that each hand can grasp one side of the door knob. Place your feet on either side of the door. Then very gently lean back so that you're hanging from the door knob. (Don't do this if the knob is insecure— or you are.) Slowly stretch out your back, pelvis, and neck. Hang there for one to two minutes. Pull up slowly.

Now turn around so your back is to the door. Reach behind you and grasp each side of the door knob with each hand. Place your feet on either side of the door, and very gently lean forward with your pelvis. You are now stretching your back and pelvis in the pose opposite to the previous. Hang for as long as you're comfortable. Pull up slowly.

Add a Little Weight to Your Life

It's beyond the scope of this book to instruct you about the ins-and-outs of proper weight training. However, the results are undeniably positive. Whether you're male or female, young or old, weight training can help you build strength, aid in combating chronic back pain and other health problems, give you more stamina, agility, and tiptop muscle tone. This is also an area that you can use as an adjunct to an overall exercise plan, or expand it for a more intense body-building regimen.

For most people, light weights will suffice for general muscle toning. Depending on your strength, choose dumbbells and ankle weights that are one to five pounds each. These are available in most department stores. I'm not an expert in this area, though I do lift weights myself. My advice to you is to incorporate at least 10 minutes of small weight training three times into your week. By lifting weights every other day, you allow stressed muscles to recover and build. Your other option is to lift weights daily, but alternate which body parts you work out. For example, you may want to work on your upper body Monday, Wednesday and Friday, and your lower body on Tuesday, Thursday and Saturday, taking Sunday off.

For specific instructions on weight-lifting procedures seek the guidance of a trained weight lifter or exercise teacher.

■ *Makeover Hint #47—The Soup-Can Lift*

Want to start out slowly? Don't want to invest in a set of dumbbells? Turn to your kitchen cupboard and pull out two cans of soup and use these as light, beginner weights. Just make sure that they're the same size so you're balanced on each side.

Feed Your Muscles

Adhering to a whole-foods, varied diet as described in Chapter 4 is sufficient to feed your muscles. If you suffer from muscle cramps or poor circulation, concentrate on foods high in these nutrients:

1. Magnesium—seafood, whole grains, nuts, dark green vegetables.
2. Calcium—green leafy vegetables, seaweed, nuts, dairy foods.
3. Potassium—vegetables, fruits, whole grains.
4. Vitamin E—fresh vegetable oils, walnuts, hazelnuts, peanuts, eggs.
5. Vitamin C—broccoli, green peppers, tomatoes, strawberries, citrus fruits, alfalfa sprouts.
6. B-Complex Vitamins—whole grains, Brewer's yeast, eggs, organ meats.

Also check your protein intake. Have you been experimenting with this as outlined in Chapter 6: Protein is a Positive Step? If not, now's the time.

How to Prevent Sore Muscles

If you overdo it a bit or are sore after starting your new exercise program, remember this. Be sure you've thoroughly warmed up before and cooled down after each aerobic or weight-lifting session. Also, follow your stretching routine before starting to avoid injuries and soreness.

In addition to these procedural items, there are nutrients and herbs available to prevent these problems from occurring. Katherine Tsoulas, a marathon runner and naturopathic doctor, has found a way to prevent aching muscles. (You don't need to be a star athlete to use these ideas.) She relies on extra vitamin C to strengthen connective tissue and prevent inflammation. Depending on your activity and needs, 1000 to 3000 mg each day in divided amounts should be adequate. Dr. Tsoulas also looks to calcium (1000 mg) and magnesium (500 mg) per day—this is the total amount to take, including what's in your multiple supplement.

Another marathon enthusiast, Dr. Helen Healy from St. Paul, says, "My main advice is to build up slowly and steadily so that a person does not have to deal with a lot of pain in the first place—they just get the enjoyment of the exercise program." She also advises avoiding alcohol and overly salty foods, both of which can cause dehydration. Her favorite drink at marathon time, and one you can use when you're working up a sweat, is the juice of fresh-squeezed oranges and grapefruits. It seems to give her just the right amount of fluid and natural sugars that her body needs, she reports.

If, even after taking the above precautions, you're sore the next day, turn to the homeopathic remedy, Arnica (see Appendix B). You can take this by mouth or apply the cream version directly onto aching muscles. Also helpful are the natural anti-inflammatory and pain-relieving substances curcumin, a derivative of turmeric, and bromelain, found in pineapple; use these instead of muscle relaxants and pain relievers like aspirin. Take both of these between meals. In addition, eat ginger and turmeric, found in curry, as much as you like. My only caution here is that if you're taking strong medications, you may want to avoid bromelain as it can increase absorption of some medicines.

■ *Makeover Hint #48—Soak Gingerly*

You've had a great workout, but Oh!, do you ache. Relax sore muscles with this simple at-home treatment. Pour yourself a nice hot bath. Make a strong cup of ginger tea, available in tea bags, or use one teaspoon of powdered or diced ginger root in one cup of hot water. Steep for 15 minutes. Pour the tea into your bath and then soak your body.

Follow the Cheap Fuel Rule

Here's an idea for those who not only want to make over their muscles, but delight in saving money and the environment. Instead of driving your car for every errand, follow the six-block rule. If your errand is six blocks or less away, walk (or bike). This is a wonderful way to insert physical activity into your everyday routine. Plus you'll save money on gas and spare the environment some car exhaust. For distances greater than six blocks, you may drive.

Find Ways to Move at Work

One excuse people use to not exercise is work. How about exercising at work? Here are some simple desk-bound movements you can practice each and every day as part of your Muscle Makeover. Remember to breathe during each exercise. Do these at least three times a day, or as needed.

- When no one's looking, stick your hands way up in the air as if signaling a touchdown. Then roll your shoulders back and try to bring your shoulder blades together. Do this slowly five to 10 times. Great for cramped backs caused by too much hunching over important paperwork.

- Neck stretches help unlock tense muscles and remind you to breathe. Pull back from your desk, plant your feet firmly on the ground and sit up straight. Loop your right arm over the top of your head so your right hand covers your left ear. Gently, gently pull your head down so your right ear is moving toward your right shoulder. Stop pulling if painful; this stretch should feel good. Hold for 15 seconds; slowly breathe in and out. Return head to upright position slowly. Do the same on the opposite side.

- For a full neck and back stretch, place laced hands at the back of your head. While sitting tall, slowly and gently pull your head down toward your chest. Feel the stretch, not the pain. Hold for 15 seconds. Return to sitting position slowly.

- For stressed out shoulders that creep higher as the day wears on, try this. Shrug your shoulder and hold for 15 seconds. Release with a big sigh of relief. Do this two more times. If you have a willing co-worker nearby, have her or him push down on your shoulders gently to break up shoulder tension.

Be an Aerobic Tourist

Another excuse for not exercising is travel. Whether you regularly journey for business or are taking a vacation, it's important to bring your exercise attitude along. I've never seen anyone abandon food during a trip; why forgo activity?

Putting aside all the reasons why exercise, or movement, during travel is impossible—time change, no facilities, too busy, too tired, don't want to—let's look at several tricks you can use to keep moving while you're vacationing.

- Pack running shoes and other exercise-type clothing.
- Book your room at a hotel with a gym and/or pool.
- While traveling, try different activities you don't normally do.
- Go swimming, then sit in the hot tub afterward.
- Golf 18 holes—without a golf cart.
- Play tennis or racket ball; if you don't know how, take lessons from a pro.
- Go for long walking tours of the town you're visiting.
- Go for hikes, if in the country.
- Rent a bike.
- If attending a conference or business meetings, go for walks in-between. Take prospective clients for a walk and network.
- Find the exercise channel on your hotel room TV and do floor exercises.
- Go skiing, sledding, or ice skating.

What if You're too Sick to Move?

While it's important to maintain a regular exercise regimen, sometimes you'll want to put your exercise leotards aside for a day or two. If you're experiencing the beginning stages of a cold or other illness, you may find a sweaty workout just the thing to stall it. Couple this with plenty of sleep, and an anti-infection diet (no sugar, caffeine, alcohol, or junk food; take extra vitamin C and drink echinacea tea). For times when illness slams you to the ground (or bed), take care of yourself and give yourself up to bed rest. Sensible exercise habits not only include consistent activity when you're well, but also recognizing when it's OK to sleep and rest so your body can heal. When you're very ill, your body needs all its energy to recover. Part of this mature attitude toward exercise is the ability to re-enter an exercise program once you're well without making excuses. You may need to ease back into your program, depending on how long you've been benched.

These rules also go for when you're severely or acutely injured. Obviously a broken leg is going to stop you from biking or jogging, and immediately following the fracture you won't feel like doing anything. However, there are ways of sneaking some activity into your down-time. Find ways to move the uninjured parts of your body while sitting—including your free leg. Lift small arm weights. Practice stretching your neck, shoulders, and arms. For acute injuries, rest for up to three days depending on how critical the damage; then begin gradually to move again. Ask your doctor or physical therapist for guidance in both of these situations.

Muscle Makeover Checkup

Isn't exercise great? Don't worry, you'll get used to it eventually. In the meantime, continue to practice these Muscle Makeover tips:

- Build on your everyday movement.
- Exercise each day—if only for five minutes.
- Don't overdo it.
- Variety is the spice of exercise.
- Do some aerobics.
- Try stretching.
- Take a shot at weight lifting.
- Are you having fun yet?
- Feed your muscles.
- Take steps to prevent sore muscles.
- Walk, don't drive, when close.
- Move at work.
- Move when you travel.
- Be cautious when sick.

For Related Problems, See

- Backaches
- Gout
- Sprains and strains

Chapter 10

Regain Your Sexual Vitality

Hormone Power

Sex hormones are what make us sexual beings. They help shape our reproductive organs, feed sexual drive, and grace us with those characteristics that make us female—soft skin, breasts, and a menstrual cycle—or male—deep voice and facial hair. Everyone has exactly the same hormones floating around. That's right, men have the female hormones estrogen and progesterone, and women have testosterone and other androgens. The difference between men and women is how much of each they possess.

There are dozens of hormones in the body, chemicals that act as messengers and tell different tissues how to act. Because sexuality is influenced by overall health, an imbalance in any number of hormones can affect your sexual desire. Also consider ways to keep your liver humming (see Chapter 3)—for this is where sex hormones are converted into less powerful forms—and care for your adrenals, another sex hormone factory (see Chapter 7).

What Causes a Lagging Libido

Lack of desire is caused by many things. It may be a sign of discord within a relationship. If so, consider counseling where both partners attend sessions to learn communication skills. Sometimes sex therapy, an adult version of high school sex education, is in order. These classes teach you everything you want to know about sex and desire, including how, why, and when sexual desire waxes and wanes, how an emotional problem, like depression interferes with libido, and how physical illness affects one's love life. A busy routine that barely leaves room for alone time robs many people of not only desire, but the longing to be intimate with a partner.

Low sex drive is also a sign of poor health. People who are healthy tend to have higher sex drives because they feel well. And a well-adjusted sex life is good for your health. If your sexual vitality is lagging, take the following makeover steps.

Know Your Sex Drive Cycle

The first step to achieving sexual vitality is to realize that libido is not a fixed feeling. Sex drive for both men and women waxes and wanes depending on mood, health, and time.

Female libidos are particularly affected by the monthly or menstrual cycle during which sex hormones like estrogen and progesterone peak and then decline. Some women, for instance, find that during ovulation—a couple of weeks after menstruation—arousal increases. This is the most fertile time for women; enhanced libido is Mother Nature's way of ensuring procreation of the species.

A man's sex drive is also affected by changing hormone levels. For example, testosterone in the blood of men peaks between 6 A.M. and 8 A.M., and hits a low 12 hours later.[1] It's also been shown that human sexuality operates on a yearly basis. Sperm count, for one, is highest on average between February and March and lowest during September.[2] These facts explain the appeal of morning sex, and why some couples might find it easier to get pregnant in the springtime.

Since overall health also alters on a daily, monthly, and yearly trend, it makes sense that libido is similarly affected depending on how well you feel. If your mood changes with the seasons, stress, or weather—winter blues being one example—shouldn't your desire for lovemaking also fluctuate?

Sandy and Tom Learn to Give Their Sex Life a Break

Newly married Sandy and Tom didn't know what was wrong. According to surveys they'd read, they should be having sex three times a week. But that wasn't happening, and the young couple was worried that their love and desire for each other was dying a quick death.

Finally, they decided to visit with a marriage counselor who discovered that Sandy and Tom were under a considerable amount of strain. Not only had they both just graduated from college and had no money, but they were brand new parents as well. Sandy was exhausted from waking with the baby at night and Tom was worried about finding a job to support his family. It was a great relief for both Tom and Sandy when the counselor told them a low sex drive, due to fatigue and tension, was perfectly normal. She said that with time their desire for each other would return, and told them to remember there's no such thing as "normal." Each couple has its own unique relationship, and as long as they were happy with each other, nothing else mattered.

Sleep Away the Sexual Blues

The next step to boosting desire is sleep. Without adequate sleep—eight hours nightly for most adults—our bodies are unable to refresh and rejuvenate. Signs of sleep deprivation include declining libido ("not tonight, dear, I'm too tired"), lack of mental concentration, loss of judgment, and decreased resistance to illness.

Spend the next week on sleep therapy. This means establishing a regular bedtime routine. One hour before lights go out, get ready for bed, put on your pajamas, put away work, turn off the TV, and do something relaxing. Try having a hot bath (romantic in itself); sip a cup of soothing herb tea or read a light non-work-related book. Turn the lights out on time, and sleep for at least eight hours.

Laura Finds Sensuality in Rest

Laura, a 26-year-old waitress, was a go-getter. Besides her full-time job, she enjoyed attending aerobics class, biking, reading, and pursuing several hobbies. She also had a tendency to stay up late, either visiting with friends or talking on the phone. The only trouble spot in Laura's life was relations with her husband. George complained that frequently when he asked Laura to make love, she turned him down, saying she was too tired.

Finally, after a couple of months of rejection, George stormed out of the house. Laura was stunned. She hadn't realized how much her busy life and lack of sleep were affecting her relationship with her husband. When George finally returned, Laura vowed to cut down on her activities and concentrate, instead, on catching up on sleep. After four days of eight-hour nights, Laura was pleasantly surprised to discover her flame for George burning brightly. Not only that, but her normally short temper and her body aches disappeared as well.

Alcohol—A Sexual Downer

Thirty years ago, movies treated liquor as sexy. Just think of Dean Martin, Frank Sinatra, and the rest of the Rat Pack, and you'll understand. While alcohol can let down inhibitions, it can also remove some of your sexual edge both directly and indirectly. For starters, alcohol robs you of vital nutrients needed for sexual and other bodily functions by causing inflammation of the stomach, pancreas, and intestines.[3] It also impairs immunity, and contributes to osteoporosis and some cancers.

Closer to reproductive home, excessive or long-term drinking can cripple the liver and its ability to metabolize hormones. Alcohol's tendency to rattle the hormonal cart is described in many studies on women. Judith Gavaler and her research associates from the University of Pittsburgh found that downing less than one drink per week was enough to disturb a postmenopausal woman's normal hormonal levels.[4] Similarly, experts report that many women with PMS have a hard time handling alcohol. They not only seem to become inebriated more easily immediately prior to their periods, but actually crave alcohol.[5]

Men, of course, are not immune to alcohol's effects. In addition to liquor's adverse health influences, men who drink every day or drink more than 20 ounces a week are more likely to experience impotence.[6]

■ *Makeover Hint #49—The Alcohol Substitute*

A glass of wine is very relaxing, and can help you get into the mood. However, it can also break the mood when you drink too much, not to mention its long-term side effects. Try these "mood enhancers" instead:

- Give each other a slow sensuous massage.
- Read love poetry to your loved one.
- Play romantic music and slow dance in your living room.
- Caress your partner's feet with a luxuriously scented oil.
- Sneak a love letter into your loved one's pocket early in the day for love later that night.
- Tell each other secrets.
- Go for a long walk with your arms around one another.

Smoking Isn't Sexy

Lighting up after love-making, according to the movies, seems a natural conclusion to passion. But if you smoke, you could be puffing away your sexuality. Like alcohol, tobacco adds to impotency for men.[6] Smoking also increases your risk for heart and blood vessel disease; this means less circulation to your genitals and everywhere else. Smoking adds to your liver's load, so hormonal metabolism is shaken up. Smoking is neither healthy nor sexy.

The 10 Dietary Commandments for Sexual Vitality

Behind every great sex life is a healthy diet. A deficiency of some nutrients contributes to a lagging sex drive. Wholesome eating also ensures better overall health, which, in turn, boosts sexual function and desire. Follow these 10 dietary commandments to regain sexual vitality.

1. Eat plenty of dark green leafy vegetables and fruits (not citrus) for their boron content. Boron has been found to boost estrogen and testosterone levels in postmenopausal women.[7] Skimping on potassium, abundant in produce, can lead to that dragged-out feeling.[8]

2. Include whole grains, like brown rice, millet, and barley, for B-vitamins to soothe jangled nerves. Whole grains are also high in zinc, a mineral that aids sexual development in both girls and boys.

3. Stay hydrated with at least one quart of pure water daily. This will help drive away fatigue.

4. Get adequate protein. Start with plant sources like beans, legumes, nuts, and seeds. If you enjoy meat, try fish, skinless organic poultry and lean cuts of beef or lamb. Too little protein can decrease testosterone levels in men, thus lowering sex drive.[9]

5. Cut down on caffeine. While a cup of coffee gives you a boost, in the long run it's hard on the adrenal glands—one source of sex hormones. That's not to mention its role in anxiety, headaches, insomnia, and PMS.

6. Try giving flowers instead of candy on Valentine's Day—or any other time. There's scientific evidence that too much sugar harms the liver's ability to deal with estrogen and other sex hormones.[10] In addition, sugar contributes to obesity, PMS, and lower resistance to disease.

7. Go easy on the salt. Water retention caused by excessive salt use is not healthy or attractive.

8. Buy organic foods when possible. Many pesticides act like estrogen, and ultimately upset your endocrine system.

9. Eat the right kinds of fats. Saturated fats (the type that harden at room temperature and are mainly from animal-based foods) are less desirable—stick with lean meats and mix them up with plant proteins. However, essential fatty acids (EFA) found in seeds, nuts, whole grains, and fish, are required for sex hormone production. Male and female infertility is one classic sign of EFA deficiency.[11] Whole grains, seeds, and nuts are also high in vitamin E, necessary for proper sexual function and a useful treatment for menopausal hot flashes and vaginal dryness.

10. Variety feeds vitality. Eat a wide assortment of fresh, whole, organic foods to ensure you're getting all the nutrients you need for reproductive function and overall health.

■ *Makeover Hint #50—A Romantic Meal*

The house is empty and you've both cleared your schedules for a night of love. Begin your night of amore with a romantic meal. Follow these guidelines.

- Prepare a simple meal in advance. Running back and forth from the kitchen disrupts the mood.

- Set a simple and attractive table complete with candlelight. Visual appeal not only heightens your appetite for food, but love as well.

- Choose light foods that won't weigh you down. Raw vegetables with a light dip, skinless chicken strips grilled with a tasty sauce, fancy breads.

- Pick healthy finger foods, like grapes, so you can feed and take care of each other.

- Select foods that will leave you with pleasant breath. This isn't the time for garlic and raw onions. For extra insurance, have a dish of breath-cleansing parsley nearby.

- Avoid foods that cause you or your partner digestive problems. Late-night gas does not add to an evening of love.

Vitamins and Minerals Help Sexuality

Vitamins, minerals, and other nutrients are necessary for hormone production and sexual function. Following the 10 Dietary Commandments outlined earlier as a starting point, the other step is to take a well-balanced, high-potency multiple vitamin and mineral pill. Below are examples of three of the dozens of vitamins and minerals needed for sexual vitality.

At the U.S. Department of Agriculture's research facility in Grand Forks, North Dakota, Forrest Nielsen, Ph.D. conducted studies on a relatively obscure mineral called boron. He found that estrogen levels rose to "levels found in women on estrogen replacement therapy" when postmenopausal women were fed supplemental boron each day.[12] Note: If you have a condition that is aggravated by high estrogen levels, such as estrogen-dependent breast cancer, don't take extra boron.

The antioxidant vitamin E is recognized as a nutrient for sexual ailments. Early studies found that animals couldn't reproduce and males' testicles shrunk without vitamin E in their diet.[11] Vitamin E, both by mouth and applied topically, is useful for menopausal women suffering from vaginal dryness.

The prostate gland contains high amounts of zinc. When zinc levels fall too low, the result is poor sperm production and reduced testosterone levels.[12] Zinc supplementation is also useful in some cases of male infertility.[13] Zinc deficiency can also cause sexual dysfunction in women, a condition that's reversible with supplementation according to Turkish physician Suleyman Dincer, M.D.[14] Ironically, synthetic estrogens used in birth control pills rob the body of zinc.

Exercises for Super Sex

Exercise is a wonderful thing. Not only does it decrease your risk of heart disease, high blood pressure, and osteoporosis, help control weight, and give you strength, but it also makes sex better. This is partly because you feel so good when you're physically fit. People who are physically active on a regular basis also have more life-giving oxygen flowing through their bodies.

See Chapter 9 for how to tone your muscles. In the meantime, take your partner for a romantic walk in the moonlight.

■ *Makeover Hint #51—The Arousal Exercise*

To enhance sexual arousal try Kegels. These exercises train your pubococcygeus or PC muscle, which spans your pubic bone in front to your tail bone. These exercises were originally developed by Dr. Arnold Kegel to help women who had problems controlling urination.

However, some women and men find that following a regular Kegel routine benefits the genital region by increasing circulation there and expanding awareness of feelings in that area. The great thing about Kegels is you can do them anywhere, anytime, and no one can tell. Here's what you do:

1. Identify your PC muscle by stopping the flow of urine next time you urinate. Do this without moving your legs. This is the muscle that shuts urine flow on and off.

2. Practice Slow Kegels by tightening your PC muscle, as if shutting off urine flow. Hold for three seconds and then relax.

3. Practice Fast Kegels by tightening and relaxing your PC muscle as fast as you can.

4. Do five each (one set) of the Slow and Fast Kegels before each meal. You can do more sets each day if you like. Increase the number of Kegels by five each week. So you're doing 10 Slow and 10 Fast Kegels during week two, 15 of each during week three, et cetera.

5. Keep in mind that these exercises may feel awkward or difficult to do at first, and the muscles might feel tired. This is to be expected, as it would be if you started moving any other sedentary muscle in your body. Breathing and patience will help you gain control and more sexual pleasure.

Not Tonight, Dear, I Have a Headache

Feeling bad is a valid, and too common, reason for sitting on the sexual sidelines. If none of the above works for you, ill health or medication could be the cause of decreased desire or pleasure. Any time you're rundown, hurting, or sick, libido is bound to fall.

Prostatitis in young men is a condition where urgent, burning urination invades the groin, scrotum, anus, lower back, abdomen, and legs and is accompanied by painful ejaculation. Such a condition can rob sexual pleasure. Hypothyroidism, an underactive thyroid gland, can drag desire down. Many chronic diseases, such as clogged arteries, affect overall health and slow blood circulation to the genital region.

Medicines can also cut down your sex life. Hypoglycemic agents, vasodilators, cardiovascular drugs, antihistamines, tranquilizers, antidepressants, hormone replacement, and other medications have this effect. Also beware of recreational drugs like cocaine, heroin, and marijuana.

The answer to this dilemma is a complete physical by your doctor, along with appropriate laboratory tests. If you're taking medicines, whether prescription or over-the-counter, find out if they're responsible for cheating you out of romance.

■ *Makeover Hint #52—Practice Safe Sex*

If you're not in a monogamous relationship with a longstanding partner, please, practice safe sex. This means using condoms for men; women, you might consider a diaphragm or cervical cap as added protection. Inquire about your partner's health history before engaging in lovemaking. AIDS, gonorrhea, herpes, genital warts, and a host of other sexually-transmitted diseases are just a few reasons not to make love unsafely.

Should I Take Herbal Aphrodisiacs?

Can herbs electrify your sex life? Probably not—at least not by themselves. Many of the herbs suggested for waning desire work as reproductive tonifiers, calming agents, or as overall health enhancers. What we think of as aphrodisiacs are often urinary tract and genital irritants. *Cantharis*, or Spanish fly, for instance, creates sexual desire in this way but is poisonous in large doses.

An herb that works as an aphrodisiac by promoting general health is Asian ginseng, or *Panax ginseng*. It works by helping the body use oxygen more efficiently, by maintaining blood sugar and cholesterol levels, and by helping manage stress via adrenal gland support. Some people find Asian ginseng overstimulates them to the point of insomnia. If this happens to you, cut down on your dose or stop using it. The safest way to take this herb is two weeks on, one week off. If you have high blood pressure, use ginseng cautiously and have your blood pressure checked regularly.

■ *Makeover Hint #53—Ginkgo Is Gold*

For impotence due to poor genital blood flow, *Ginkgo biloba* is a logical choice. Its leaves contain compounds so beneficial for circulatory and nervous system problems that it's among the most prescribed and well-researched herbal medicines in the world. Side effects are rare, and when present, mild—upset stomach and headaches.

One of the safest and most effective ways to take this plant is as a 24 percent ginkgo heterosides-standardized formula of ginkgo biloba extract (GBE); this form guarantees a specific amount of potency. Dosage begins at 40 mg three times daily and may take three months for results. Other herbalists prefer using the untouched, whole plant. If you're not certain what's causing your impotence, check with your doctor. If you plan to stay on this herb for a long time, consult an herbalist or other practitioner versed in botanicals.

Yohimbine: What's the Story?

The bark of the yohimbe tree has been hailed as an aphrodisiac for more than a century. Today, doctors prescribe yohimbine, an extract from that tree, to treat impotence. It is thought to energize a man's sexual response by stimulating select portions of his nervous system and increasing blood to erectile tissue. By some estimates, only one-fifth of impotent men completely recover after using yohimbine.[15]

The down side to using this herb-based drug is side effects such as increased blood pressure, racing heart rate, tremors, irritability, headaches, nausea or vomiting, sweating, dizziness, flushed skin and frequent urination. Some medications—like tranquilizers—can interact with yohimbine. Anyone with a heart condition, kidney disease, glaucoma or history of gastric or duodenal ulcers should avoid it because it elevates blood pressure and excites the central nervous system.

If you choose to use this substance, select the herbal form, yohimbe, over the pure extract. Combine it with other herbs like Siberian ginseng or saw palmetto to temper its effects, and to be perfectly safe, use it under the care of an herbal-wise practitioner.

Sexuality Makeover Check-Up

Congratulations! You've just completed another phase of your Natural Health Makeover. Here's a summary:

- Learned about the sex drive cycle.
- Got some more sleep.
- Was careful of alcohol—and tried a few alternates.
- Alerted to watch out for smoking.
- Learned the 10 sexual dietary commandments.
- Made sure your supplement had boron, zinc, and other sexual nutrients.
- Vowed to keep exercising.
- Tried Kegels.
- Had a physical exam and medication screening.
- Looked into herbs like ginkgo and ginseng, if needed.

For Related Problems, See

- Urinary Tract Infections
- Yeast Infection

Laboratory Tests Your Doctor Can Order

- Sex Hormone Profile
- DHEA or DHEA-Sulfate Levels

Chapter 11

Build Stronger Bones and Teeth

Your Supportive Skeleton

The skeleton is the framework that gives the body support and shape, like the wooden frame of a house. Not only that, but the hundreds of bones in the body are jointed to permit fluid, easy movement. Muscles attached to the end of bone joints are what make movement possible (see Chapter 9).

If you've ever seen one of those dolls on which you pull a cord and the arms and legs flop around, you get an idea of the skeleton's two main parts. The axial skeleton (skull, ribs, backbone, pelvis) is most rigid and provides the main support, in other words the doll's head and body; the appendicular skeleton are the doll's swinging limbs. What you don't see on floppy dolls are the three types of bones. There are flat bones, such as in the skull, breastbone, and pelvis, that protect delicate organs like the brain, lungs, and bladder. Long bones make up your arms and legs, and act as levers allowing you to pick up things and walk. Short small bones comprise the wrist and ankles, and lend strength to these areas. The thirty-three vertebrae stacked up in your backbone not only support most of your body's weight, but allow a wide range of motion from bending back and forward, side to side to twisting. In your mouth are 32 permanent teeth; 28 if wisdom teeth are missing.

But that's not all. Bones are not merely stick-like structures holding up other body parts. They're living, changing tissues that receive and require a wide range of nutrients from the blood vessels that infiltrate them. Most bone is made up of collagen fibers, which give it strength. Ground substance—a collection of chondroitin sulfate and hyaluronic acid—fills in the gaps. Calcium, phosphate and other bone salts like magnesium, sodium, potassium, and carbonate, reinforce this framework.

Teeth are built much like bones, only denser, with a meshwork of collagen fibers and mineral salts. Enamel covers a tooth and protects it against acids (in pop, by the way) and other corrosive substances. Unfortunately, once the very hard enamel is worn away, that's it. It doesn't reform. Nerves, blood vessels, and lymph vessels form the middle pulp of a tooth.

New bone is continually being laid down by special cells called osteoblasts, while osteoclasts—another specialized bone cell—absorb or take bone away. Under healthy circumstances this check and balance of bone give-and-take is equal so that total bone mass stays constant. Unlike bones, only a small portion of teeth contains these special remodeling cells. However, the mineral salts in teeth are constantly being replaced by new ones—though very slowly in the enamel.

Warning Signs of a Crumbling Frame

Several conditions can put your skeleton in jeopardy—rickets, osteomalacia, osteitis fibrosa cystica, hypoparathyroidism, and others. But the most common bone-stealing disease is osteoporosis, a progressive bone loss condition that threatens 24 million Americans[1] and costs them an estimated seven to 10 billion dollars annually in treatment.[2] The irony of osteoporosis is that everyone begins to lose bone at some time in their life. Osteoporosis (literally translated as "porous bone") is merely an exaggerated version of this naturally occurring aging process. Maximum bone density peaks in one's twenties. After that, both sexes begin to lose bone mass at a rate of about one percent per year.[3]

This process, however, is accelerated in women once they reach menopause. Very thin bones caused by menopausal changes, such as drops in estrogen and other hormones, is called postmenopausal osteoporosis. One third to one half of women who've gone through menopause are afflicted.[4] Although twice as many women suffer from fractures due to osteoporosis, this bone disease is an important and growing problem among men as well.[5] Other kinds of osteoporosis, labeled according to what age group they strike, include senile osteoporosis (a condition of the elderly), juvenile osteoporosis (seen in children and adolescents), and idiopathic osteoporosis, a form with unknown cause that strikes people under 40.

The most frightening feature of osteoporosis is its insidious nature. Very often there are no symptoms associated with the disease. It's one of those conditions where you need to do the right thing—lifestyle-wise—just because. Your bones aren't going to give you much feedback. Rather, thinning bones are usually discovered inadvertently on X-rays or as a person gradually shrinks in stature. There are tests available that can tell you current bone density and amount of bone lost over a specific time period. Ask your doctor about these, if you're interested.

Unfortunately, it's only later-stage osteoporosis that creates the most obvious subjective symptoms like mid-back pain or fractures of the hip or wrist. A history of "bad teeth" can be a sign of impending bone loss. There is no one known cause for the most common forms of osteoporosis. Instead this disease develops because of your genetic makeup, age, sex, race, weight, physical strength—and a few factors you can actually control. These are the things we're going to discuss here. If you're concerned about protecting your teeth, beware of bleeding or sore gums, bad breath, and frequent cavities. Below, learn about the steps you can take to make over your bones and teeth.

How to Stop the Calcium Robbers

Calcium is an important bone nutrient, so vital, in fact, that we're constantly reminded to take extra helpings. However, it's equally important to recognize those habits and foods that steal calcium away from bones and teeth. If you can stop calcium robbery, your current calcium supplementation will be more effective.

A good place to start is with caffeine, that stimulating substance found in coffee, black tea, soft drinks (also high in phosphorus, not good for bones), and chocolate. A very large six-year study involving almost 85,000 women discovered that caffeine, particularly coffee, increased the incidence of hip fractures—a sign that bones are weakening. Caffeine does its damage by prompting the body to spill extra calcium into the urine. This occurs on less than one cup of coffee per day.[6] Excessive salt can add to this problem, as can an overabundance of animal-based protein foods like red meat, chicken, eggs and dairy products.[1]

Putting aside soft drinks most of the time is a must for women. If you like pop mainly for the carbonation, try this healthy, tasty substitute.

Pour half a glass of orange juice or your favorite fruit juice.

Top off with seltzer (make sure it's sodium free).

Add ice and sip.

I began doing this 20 years ago as an alternate to cocktails and soda. Many of my friends and family members also love this refreshing drink.

Calcium Mysteries of the World

In this country, women are advised to ingest between 1000 and 1200 mg of calcium daily to protect their bones. Yet there are places in the world where calcium intake is much less—and osteoporosis is less frequent. The Bantu women of South Africa, for example, who live on reservations, consume only 220 to 440 mg of calcium per day and are virtually free of osteoporosis. South African women living in cities, on the other hand, have thinner bones and a calcium intake that is two to four times higher.

Why the difference?

Well, the rural-dwelling Bantus are primarily vegetarian, while the South African city women eat meat. Animal protein, say researchers, makes the urine more acidic and thus increases calcium loss from the body.[7] I'd wager that there's more to this puzzle than meat. Citified folk also tend to nibble on more refined foods, sugars, and salts. In *The Paleolithic Prescription*, S. Boyd Eaton, M.D. and his co-authors say osteoporosis was rare among the hunter-gatherers of long ago—these people *did* eat meat. However, they also dined on plenty of wild, calcium-rich vegetation and exercised every day.[8] So if you choose to eat meat, remember the principles of consuming a whole foods diet, and pay attention to the other food on your plate.

Calcium (and Other Mineral Deposits) to the Rescue

Taking calcium for stronger bones is a popular preventive step. Recommended dosage lies between 800 and 1000 mg daily, and increases to 1500 mg per day for high-risk individuals.[9] And for good reason! Calcium is stored mainly in your skeleton, and when your diet falls short of this mineral, it's drawn from bones. Of course the calcium-bone relationship is more complex than popping a pill, as we learned earlier. In addition, the age at which you begin calcium supplementation is also important. As adults, we gain the benefits of a little extra calcium; so do pre-adolescent children,[10] and women well past the age of menopause.[11] Women just entering menopause gain a small, but positive, effect from additional calcium.[12]

Calcium, of course, does not stand alone. Other minerals such as magnesium are required for strong bones. Not only is magnesium an integral part of bone, but it helps form new calcium crystals[13] and the conversion of vitamin D to its active form. Vitamin D aids calcium absorption.[14] Another mineral called boron strengthens bones by decreasing urinary excretion of calcium, magnesium, and phosphorus needed by the skeleton. Boron also keeps bones secure by increasing those hormones—estrogen and testosterone—that enhance bone health.[15]

Also on the bone mineral list are manganese, zinc, strontium, silicon, copper, and vanadium. Paul Saltman, a biologist at the University of California in San Diego, first became interested in manganese when well-known basketball player Bill Walton developed osteoporosis even though he was eating a healthy, macrobiotic diet. Saltman discovered there was no manganese in Walton's blood. After six weeks of changing his eating habits and taking mineral supplements including manganese, Walton was back in playing form although his osteoporosis was not completely corrected. When manganese drops, the cells which lay down new bone—osteoblasts—are less efficient.[16]

Zinc, low in many older folks with osteoporosis, works with vitamin A and D to create normal bone formation.[17] Strontium, not to be confused with the radioactive kind, is abundant in bones and teeth and increases retention of calcium. When osteoporotic patients were fed this mineral in one study, many noticed their bone pain was less.[18] Silicon, a trace element found in such plants as horsetail, seems to disrupt bone growth when too low. (This silicon is different from that used in breast implants.) Too little copper appears to have the same effect. Very low, but definite, amounts of vanadium also appear necessary for stable bones.[19]

Building a mineral-full diet is important. Equally vital is having a digestive system that easily absorbs these nutrients. As we age, stomach acid tends to decline.

■ *Makeover Hint #55—Where to Get Your Fresh Minerals*

The best, most body-friendly sources of minerals are food. Start with a balanced diet packed with these foods for healthy bones.

- Calcium: milk and other dairy foods, sardines, clams, oysters, tofu, canned salmon with bones, dark leafy green vegetables (Swiss chard, mustard greens, kale, collards, beet greens, dandelion greens), broccoli, okra, rhubarb.

- Magnesium: whole grains, nuts, meat, milk, green vegetables, legumes.

- Boron: fruits (not citrus), leafy green vegetables, nuts, legumes.

- Manganese: beet greens, blueberries, whole grains, nuts, legumes, fruit.

- Zinc: oysters, whole grains, meat, lima beans.

- Silicon: high-fiber whole grains, root vegetables.

- Copper: liver, shellfish, whole grains, cherries, legumes, kidney, poultry, oysters, chocolate, nuts.

- Vanadium: shellfish, mushrooms, parsley, dill seed, black pepper.

Vitamins for Healthy Bones and Teeth

We know that minerals, especially calcium, are mandatory for good bone health. What about vitamins? If you remember that bone and teeth are living tissues with nutritional needs similar to those of other organs, then feeding them vitamins only makes sense.

Vitamin D is needed so calcium can be absorbed in the digestive tract. Unfortunately, as we age vitamin D drops as appetites wane. Nutrient malabsorption and problems with vitamin D metabolism are also to blame. Older folks who are house-bound (and us younger stay-at-home ones) spend less time outside than we should; less sun means less fun and vitamin D. Getting enough vitamins, whether through foods or supplements, should begin in childhood. Children who consume adequate vitamin D tend to have harder bones. Still, it's never too late for good bone nutrition. Vitamin D supplementation helps increase calcium levels and reduce bone loss in those with osteoporosis, too.[20]

Another important bone nutrient is vitamin K. A special type of protein found in bone called osteocalcin relies on vitamin K to trap calcium in the skeleton and otherwise function. According to British researchers, people with osteoporosis have one-third the vitamin K they should.[21] When thinking healthy bones, don't forget vitamin B_6, folic acid and vitamin B_{12}. These members of the B-complex family aid in calcium and magnesium metabolism and strengthen connective tissue, a supportive structure for bone.[22] Vitamins C and A are other bone-friendly nutrients that should be included in your regular multiple vitamin/mineral supplement and foods.

■ *Makeover Hint #56—What to Look for in a Bone-Strengthening Pill*

We need many nutrients for strong bones. The place to start is with a wide range of super-nutrient foods. For insurance purposes, you can also take a multiple vitamin and mineral pill. This will not only ensure strong bones, but overall better health. Look for these bone-specific nutrients when you shop. Of course your supplement can contain other nutrients too.

Boron 3 mg
Calcium 1000 mg

Copper 1 mg

Magnesium 500 mg

Manganese 15 mg

Strontium 100 mg

Vanadium 10 mcg

Zinc 15 mg

Vitamin A 5000 IU

Vitamin C 1000 mg

Vitamin D 400 IU

Vitamin B_6 50 mg

Folic Acid 400 mcg

Vitamin B_{12} 400 mcg

Dr. Aesoph's Fabulous Baked Beans

Let me share my famous baked beans recipe with you. It's full of bone-fortifying nutrients. This is an adapted version of my mother's recipe.

Soak 1 1/2 cups dried beans in water overnight (use pinto as the base; feel free to add others: navy, lima, soy).

Next morning, drain soaking water and rinse beans.

Cover beans with fresh water. Bring to a boil, then simmer slowly for 1/2 hour or more, until tender. If you like, add a ham hock.

Drain water, and save. To cooked beans add:

3–5 cloves garlic, diced

1 tbsp. dried mustard

1/4 cup molasses

Enough bean water to mix and keep moist.

Add bean mixture to baking dish with cover.

Bake in low oven (250 degrees) for several hours. I usually make this in the morning, and let it cook until dinner. The longer it cooks, the better it tastes.

Check on beans frequently; add water as needed.

One hour before serving, mix in one can of tomato paste. Serve with corn muffins and a fresh green salad.

Remove Sugar to Save Your Teeth—and Bones

Having a sweet tooth can harm your teeth—no doubt about that. But overindulging in sugar is damaging to bones as well. English researchers at the Royal Naval Hospital in Haslar, Gosport proved that eating white sugar pulls calcium from the body into the urine for excretion.[23] A similar investigation was carried out at the Marquette Medical School and Milwaukee County General Hospital, both in Wisconsin. These researchers fed their subjects 100 grams of sugar—the equivalent of 24 ounces of cola. Not only did the sugar promote calcium loss, but it acted like a diuretic and increased urination. People who had a history of forming calcium-type kidney stones *and their relatives* were affected even more so.[24]

Want to keep your bones strong and hold on to calcium? Simple. Cut sugar, and foods containing sugar, down or out.

■ *Makeover Hint #57—How to Bust a Sweet Tooth*

If you're having troubles breaking the I-have-to-have-sugar cycle, try some of these sweet tooth-busting tips. (See Low Blood Sugar, Part Two, for more ideas.)

- Eat five to six *small* meals every two to three hours throughout the day.
- Include a complex carbohydrate (whole grain, vegetable) and protein food with each meal. For example, a bran muffin and peanut butter. A dish of plain yogurt and fresh fruit. Cheese and crackers.
- Avoid refined sugars (sweets, white flour, white rice), caffeine, and alcohol.
- Carry healthful food with you to avert a sweet tooth attack.
- Eat something sour, like a pickle.

Toss the Tobacco; Pass on the Bottle

Drinking and smoking hurt your bones—one more reason to curtail these habits.

In the past, alcohol abuse was associated with a higher incidence of fractures in drinkers. Lately, moderate alcohol use, less than one ounce daily, has also been a nagging contributor to increased bone breaks and osteoporosis risk. Researchers think this happens because of falls due to inebriation, and liquor reduces bone density over the long haul.[6]

Having a cigarette, with or without a drink, leads to thinner bones in women, likely due to upset estrogen metabolism[25]. This doesn't mean, however, that men are immune. A 16-year study revealed that men who both smoked more than a dozen cigarettes per day and had at least one drink lost bone mass twice as fast as those who smoked or drank less.[5] Both of these habits also deplete your body of folic acid—a bone-loving B-vitamin.[17]

■ *Makeover Hint #58—Acupuncture Helps You Quit Smoking*

Saying you'll quit smoking is one thing; doing it is entirely another. Many people quit cold turkey successfully. If you'd rather engage a little help for the withdrawal cravings from tobacco, consider having needles put in your ears. In other words, use auricular acupuncture.

Auricular acupuncture is a specialized form of acupuncture where several painless needles are placed strategically in your ear and left in for half an hour. Done daily over a 10-day period, this treatment can dampen cravings and smooth out jangled nerves. For information on auricular acupuncture specialists, contact the National Acupuncture Detoxification Association, 3220 N St. NW, Suite 275, Washington, DC 20007; or call (503) 222-1362.

Eat Brightly Colored Fruit to Strengthen Your Skeleton

Make food your medicine. This is particularly true when you feast on delicious cherries, raspberries, blueberries, and blackberries for the sake of your bones. These and other red, blue, and purple fruits contain pigments from the flavonoid family called anthocyanidins and proanthocyanidins. These compounds with the $1000 names brace your skeleton by securing the collagen fibers in bone, those very same strands that give strength to your body's framework.[26]

■ *Makeover Hint #59—Tease Your Palate with a Palette of Fruity Colors*

When berry season hits, feast on the following fruit salad. Also take advantage of fresh fruit in season by freezing as many raspberries, strawberries, blueberries, and blackberries as your freezer can hold.

THE ALL-AMERICAN SALAD

1 cup fresh blueberries

1 cup fresh raspberries

1 cup fresh pitted cherries

1 cup fresh blackberries

Pour all fruit into a large bowl. Gently mix together. To create a patriotic salad complete with reds, white, and blues—and get an extra helping of calcium—add a dollop of whipped cream on top and serve.

Bustling Makes Better Bones

Physical fitness is another key to healthier bones. The more you bustle, the better. Being bedridden, or merely a couch potato, causes calcium to leave the body in massive amounts through the urine. On the other hand, study after study extols exercise, especially early in life, as bones' protector. Even very mild activity among elderly persons slows bone loss and increases skeletal strength.[9]

What's the best exercise for bones? Any activity that increases the load on bone or stresses bone, like jogging or going nowhere on a stair master, builds skeletal power. Yet studies show that even routine walking—a daily 20- to 30-minute walk—builds denser bones, especially when you take your calcium everyday.[2, 10]

■ *Makeover Hint #60—Childproof Exercise*

Exercise sounds great. But how do you fit a regular physical fitness program into a life filled with work and children?

There are several solutions to this problem.

1. Give up and take your chances.
2. Leave the house and conduct your exercise program outside or at a health club—and take your chances (especially if the children are unsupervised).
3. Include the children in your exercise routine. This way you get a workout, and they learn the importance of physical fitness.
4. Get up earlier than everyone and work out alone, in peace and quiet.
5. Let your family know that Mommy and Daddy must exercise everyday or they will not be fit to live with. Stress that working out is not only good for you, but for the mental health of the entire family.

Avoid Stress, Avoid Cavities

Stress is known to cause or add to many health conditions, ranging from tension headaches to indigestion to cancer. But can stress cause holes in your teeth? According to P.R.N. Sutton of Melbourne, Australia, it can. In a 1990 article printed in *Medical Hypotheses,* Sutton discusses how mental stress can cause cavities in less than one month.[27]

It seems that the middle man in this interaction is the immune system. Stress can seriously shake up your defense system, as explained in Chapter 6. This includes the built-in immunity found in your teeth. When your dental defenses are down, bacteria attack without much of a battle. Teeth become unable to defend themselves against cavities.

Too Much Worry Puts Holes in Kelly's Teeth

Kelly discovered firsthand how very real is the connection between stress and cavities. For one whole year, the 35-year-old was working on a big project for her boss. The work involved long hours with little time for relaxation, exercise, or taking care of herself. Kelly knew that the looming deadline of her project, problems that seemed to crop up each day, and general wear and tear on her body were more stress than she was accustomed to handling.

Finally the project ended, and Kelly released a sigh of relief, glad to return to a manageable schedule. One of the first items she took care of was a visit to the dentist. She was shocked to learn that her usually healthy teeth were riddled with four cavities. While Kelly hadn't exercised much in the past 12 months, her usually sound diet hadn't changed. She hadn't indulged in sweets and was careful to floss and brush her teeth regularly. Was it stress that caused so many cavities? Perhaps.

Pick the Right Paste

This next step focuses on your teeth. Did you know that the toothpaste you're using could be undoing your other Bone and Teeth Makeover plans? According to several studies, sodium lauryl sulphate (SLS), the most widely used detergent in toothpastes, hurts the soft tissues in your mouth.[28, 29, 30] This sudsy ingredient does this by stripping away the outer protective covering on gums, increasing permeability here by penetrating the soft tissue surface,[30] and causing general irritation.[31] The higher the concentration of SLS in the toothpaste, the more prevalent are these effects.[31] Scientists found two things helped this situation: 1) using toothpastes containing anti-inflammatory ingredients as well, or 2) using SLS-free toothpaste. I recommend the latter.

Once you start reading labels, you'll find that it's nearly impossible to locate a SLS-free toothpaste. Health food stores carry some brands. The one I recommend is made by Weleda; these very tasty toothpastes come in several flavors. Ask your favorite pharmacy or health food store if it carries these products, or call 800-289-1969 to order them.

As an endnote, I'd like to point out a study that tested several popular mouthwashes. The authors say the "results indicate that the use of some mouth rinses could predispose to excessive tooth substance loss and dentine hypersensitivity, particularly if used prior to toothbrushing."[32] Maybe mouthwash isn't such a good idea either?

■ *Makeover Hint #61—Brush Up on Brushing*

Do you listen to your dentist and brush at least twice a day, and practice daily flossing? Proper brushing and flossing techniques are a critical component of tooth care. If you're too tired or busy at the end of the day to floss, pick another time during the day. I always floss and do my "good" brushing after breakfast when I have time and energy. Maybe this or another time works better for you than late evening.

The Silver Versus White Filling Debate

There's a raging debate going on in the alternative health care field about which is better: silver fillings or white. Rather than suggest to you what to do, I'm going to present this information and let you decide. Part of patient responsibility.

The traditional silver or amalgam fillings are composed of half mercury, as well as silver, tin, copper, and sometimes smaller amounts of indium, palladium, or zinc; white fillings are resin-based composites. Other filling alternatives include glass ionomer cements, ceramics, and gold. For more than 150 years, silver amalgams have been used in dentistry; they are still widely used and preferred over other types of fillings. Only costly gold has been used longer.

The advantage of amalgam over other filling types is mainly its longevity in teeth (eight to 12 years), and cost when compared to others. For instance, gold costs four to eight times more, while composite is about one and a half times more expensive. It's also argued that while composite or white fillings have improved considerably over the years, they don't tend to last as long as silver or gold, or aren't as sturdy in high-stress, chomping areas. Some people find that composite fillings temporarily increase sensitivity of the affected tooth; I can personally attest to this. On the other hand, with composites, your teeth look better (can't tell there's a filling there) and even if there's minimal risk having silver fillings, now you have none. Also, composites are better at conserving tooth structure than amalgams.

Now for the heat. Mercury-based amalgams have come under fire in recent years because of their possible adverse health effects. In their 1993 report, scientists and public health experts from the U.S. Public Health Service and Environmental Protection Agency state very clearly that "dental amalgam can release minute amounts of elemental mercury, a heavy metal whose toxicity at high intake levels (such as in industrial exposures) is well-established."[33] They go on to say that a fraction of the mercury in amalgams is absorbed by the body, and that people with silver fillings certainly have higher mercury concentrations in their blood, urine, kidneys and brain than those without these fillings. However, it is the consensus of these experts that while a small number of people respond with allergic reactions to mercury, there are too few studies and it's too difficult to ascertain whether or not mercury in fillings is harmful. Improvements due to removal of silver fillings are mainly anecdotal, they point out. "Although minute amounts of mercury are released from amalgam restorations," they say, "they do not cause demonstrable adverse effects of significance to the general public." Thus this government report concludes that dentists should continue using mercury-based amalgams, and discourages the removal and replacement of silver fillings with other types.[33]

Let's travel to the other side of the world for a different opinion. In Sweden, a similar group—the Department of Environmental Hygiene Karolinska Institute and the National Institute of Environmental Medicine in Stockholm—also researched the amalgam phenomenon. They used autopsies to assess the impact of mercury fillings on health. These scientists found that the more mercury fillings a person had, the higher the concentration of mercury there was in that individual's brain and kidneys.[34] The researchers admit that foods eaten, especially mercury-contaminated fish, smoking, and alcohol can influence these results. However, even taking that into account, they feel their results are valid. Results like these have persuaded the Swedish government to ban mercury fillings in pregnant women and children; it plans to phase out all other silver fillings over the next few years.[35]

Whether or not to use amalgams seems to hinge on how you interpret results. For the Americans, the cup is half full; the Swedes consider it half empty.

Amalgam Removal Proof

Robert L. Siblerud, M.S. from Fort Collins, Colorado wanted to see if silver fillings had an impact on people's happiness. First he sought out volunteers with and without mercury amalgams, and then checked to see if there was evidence of mercury in their bodies. Indeed, he found that urine samples of the amalgam subjects contained 201 percent more mercury than the amalgam-free group. He also found that the amalgam bunch reported more emotional distress; when these individuals had their amalgams removed, 80 percent said they felt better.[36]

Bone-Robbing Medications

The last step to saving your bones is to watch the medicines you take. There are members of both the over-the-counter and prescription medication crowd that actually steal valuable mass from your skeleton. Aspirin, acetaminophen, ibuprofen, and other non-steroidal anti-inflammatory drugs (NSAIDs) interfere with bone repair and cartilage metabolism.[37] This is a frightening thought when you consider how cavalier many are about popping an aspirin or other pain pill for headaches, fevers, or other discomforts. Those with arthritis often take a dozen or more of these pills daily for pain and inflammation. Other medicines linked to osteoporosis risk, particularly when taken long-term, include anticonvulsant drugs, heparin, thyroid hormone, methotrexate, steroids and cortisone, tetracycline, and furosemide.[38]

Bone and Teeth Makeover Checkup

Are your teeth glistening and bones ever so strong? Great! This is what you just completed:

- Ousted some of the calcium robbers—sugar, salt, caffeine, alcohol.
- Incorporated calcium and other important minerals into your diet; made sure they were in your vitamin pill.
- Added important vitamins like D and K.
- Cut down even more on sugar.

- Determined that smoking and alcohol are still on the list of no-nos.
- Discovered the wonder of brightly colored fruits, berries, and cherries.
- Established a regular exercise routine . . . puff, puff.
- Learned to control stress.
- Looked for a detergent-free toothpaste. Gave up mouthwash.
- Thought about and read more about silver fillings.
- Checked the medicine cabinet for drugs that hurt bones.

For Related Problems, See

- Backache
- Sprains and Strains

Laboratory Tests Your Doctor Can Order

- Dual x-ray absorptiometry or DEXA (confirms bone density)
- NTx Bone Loss Assay (indicates amount of bone being lost)

Chapter 12

Secrets of Beautiful Skin

Your Body's First Line of Defense

To many, skin is merely a canvas to decorate with make-up and clothing. But it is much more. This 20 pounds of body covering encases the rest of the body's tissues—holds everything together, if you will. It is also one of the primary detoxification organs. Fat-soluble poisons like heavy metals and DDT are excreted from the body in sweat. Skin is one of the first lines of defense against germs and poisons. Intact skin is impregnable to infectious agents, though its porous nature does allow outside poisons to enter. When skin is broken, special cells called histiocytes attack and devour intruders.

With the help of blood vessels, skin helps regulate body temperature. When you're too hot, heat is dispersed through sweating. When it cools down, the skin helps conserve heat by shivering.

Last but not least, the skin provides us with sensations like warmth, cold, pressure, touch, itchiness, wetness, tickling, softness, hardness and pain. Some of these feelings are purely pleasurable. Who doesn't enjoy a hug or caress, the soft feel of a pet's fur, the warmth of the sun on a summer's day? On the other hand, skin is also responsible for that itch that drives you crazy, and intolerable pain. Skin is not only a source of enjoyment, but a gauge to determine when something's wrong. If, for example, you had little sensation in your feet—as happens with some people with advanced diabetes—you could cut your feet and not even notice the harm. Pain is a signal that something's wrong, a sign to stop whatever is causing the injury and get help.

167

When your Skin Screams
for a Makeover

The skin constantly renews itself by shedding billions of cells each day. Still, there are times when a makeover is in order. Unlike other body systems, you can physically see when the skin is ready to be made over. As the canvas of the body, the skin displays its needs as an itchy rash, acne, eczema, psoriasis, hives, or other visible marks. Then there are times when the skin speaks to you in whispers about its wants. You may notice that cuts and wounds don't heal as quickly as they should. Perhaps unexplainable bruises appear. Little red spots, called petechiae, gradually show up on your skin. It could be dryness, oiliness, or paleness that calls your attention. Or maybe your mirror says it best with its waxen image.

That's not to say that these troubles are skin-related only. As you've learned by now, all parts of the body are connected in one way or another. So while you can make over your skin superficially with some results, you also need to make over those other organs that contribute to your skin's distress. These include the liver, digestive system, and other body parts.

If your skin changes after starting a new medication, consult with the prescribing physician. Also see your doctor if a skin rash or infection persists, if a mole changes shape, color, or becomes itchy or painful, or if a skin condition is particularly severe or is associated with other symptoms.

Sleep Away the Bags

Your skin, or to be more specific, bags under your eyes are a dead giveaway that you're not sleeping enough. Insufficient sleep also tends to make skin sallow-looking, pale, and generally unhealthy. We also know that during sleep, blood flow increases to your skin;[1] little sleep and it receives less of that nutrient-rich, garbage-removing circulation.

So, wake up when your skin speaks to you, and go to bed.

■ *Makeover Hint #62—Groom Yourself for Bed*

Most adults need eight hours of sleep per night, children even more. It's also important to have a regular bedtime routine that you follow an hour before turning the lights out. I call this grooming yourself for bed. For instance, read a relaxing book (no work), listen to music, have a cup of calming herbal tea or soak in a hot bath. Make sure your bedroom is pleasant. Do the decor and colors appeal to you? Is your bedroom cool enough to sleep comfortably, but not so cold that you stay awake? Would burning a scented candle make it more pleasing? Are your sleeping quarters dark?

Treat Your Skin to Natural Ingredients

Once you've slept away the bags, consider the cosmetics and other skin products you use. This goes for both women and men. As the outside covering for the body, the skin is like a wall upon which a sundry of pollutants, car exhaust, chlorine from treated water, and other airborne chemicals are thrown. That's not to mention what we voluntarily apply to our skin each day.

Make-up may be fine for a beauty makeover, but it could also be behind that acne you still have at 35. Check the ingredients in your cosmetics; use hypo-allergenic, naturally based products instead.

The same goes for soaps and creams. Regular soap removes protective oils and may aggravate sensitive skin. If you have a rash that won't go away, stop using soap for a week and use only warm (not hot) water and a face cloth followed by a cold water splash, and see what happens. Switch to a glycerine-based soap. If dryness is the problem, try a soap with vitamin E, aloe, or chamomile added. Again, check the other ingredients. Be as careful of creams and lotions as you are with soaps. Men, watch your shaving cream and after-shave lotion if skin troubles arise.

Consume Fiber for Clearer Skin

What can a heaping bowl of oatmeal or oat bran each morning do for your Skin Makeover? More than you know.

The skin is one of the major elimination organs. That means the skin helps take out your body's garbage. When internal elimination—the digestive tract, liver, and kidneys—are having problems, the skin's elimination duties increase. So an overwhelmed liver (see Chapter 3), poor digestion or absorption (see Chapter 4), or struggling kidneys (see Chapter 5) push more trash toward the skin. The evidence is in blemishes and other skin problems.

Faulty digestion not only slows the bowels, but leaves the skin looking grayish and aged. Extra oat bran and other fiber also reduce constipation and putrefied compounds made from slow-moving feces; your goal is to prevent these undesirables from being reabsorbed into circulation and out on to the skin.

■ *Makeover Hint #63—How to Make an Oatmeal Mask*

Oatmeal isn't just for eating. You can use it to make a facial mask too.

Puree 1/2 cup of dry, raw oatmeal in a blender or food processor until it's in powder form. Mix this with 1/4 cup of pure water until you have a creamy paste. Gently apply to your face and massage onto your nose, chin, forehead and cheeks using circular movements. Lie down (you might want a towel under your head), close your eyes, and relax for 15 minutes. Imagine your skin coming alive and looking luminous. End by rinsing your skin with lukewarm water. Pat dry.

Wash Your Insides to Help the Outside

Keep drinking that water for shimmering skin. Like fiber, water helps your other elimination organs—the kidneys and digestive tract— work more effectively so that your skin isn't in charge of the trash. Aim for two quarts of pure water daily. If you're not a water drinker, begin with a cup or two and work your way up, by half a glass a day. Clean, filtered water tastes much better than tap.

■ *Makeover Hint #64—How to Ensure You Have Clean Water*

Since water, and plenty of it, is so essential to clear skin and good health, it makes sense to drink the purest water possible. The cleanest water for your money comes from a reverse osmosis unit.

This filtration system is attached directly to your kitchen tap and removes most pollution and minerals. When combined with a carbon filter, almost all contaminants are extracted. If you don't have access to such a system, you can try:

- Bottled water. In most cases this is safe. To be absolutely sure, request a list of ingredients from the company you purchase water from most frequently.

- Distilled water. More expensive than reverse osmosis, but removes more contaminants. May taste flat due to mineral removal as well.

- Sediment filter. This screen removes larger particles like dirt, but not the finer ones that reverse osmosis does.

- Carbon filters. Good for taking out chlorine and organic chemicals. It doesn't, however, eliminate germs or toxic metals.

- Membrane and ceramic filters. These long-lasting filters remove parasites and bacteria.

- Redox filters. This chemical exchange system removes toxic metals, chlorine, and diminishes bacteria.[2]

Fatty Acids for Better Skin

I'm now going to tell you to eat more fat for your skin.

While most Americans are resisting fats of all types, there's a movement within natural health circles to increase essential fatty acids (EFA). It's true that too much of the wrong fats contributes to heart disease, high blood pressure, obesity, some cancers, high cholesterol, and a host of other unpleasant conditions. However, the body needs some fat to operate. Your body uses fat to make hormones, build cell membranes, keep your kidneys humming, govern nerve transmission, fuel your heart, keep inflammation at bay, transport oxygen throughout the body, and perform a host of other vital functions. The trick is to consume beneficial fats—essential fatty acids—and minimize those fats that do more harm than good. Saturated fats, found mainly in animal-based foods like meat, poultry skins, and dairy, and hydrogenated or partially hydrogenated fats, like margarine, are the fats to downplay.

While a shortage of EFAs can become obvious as constipation, aching joints, memory problems, and fatigue, your skin all but shouts its need for this essential nutrient. Dry flaky skin and hair, and cracking nails are also signs of an EFA deficiency.

Adopting a whole-foods diet brimming with whole grains, raw unsalted nuts and seeds, beans and legumes is the best way to go. In the meantime, add one to two tablespoons of flax seed oil to your daily menu (either in homemade salad dressing, or take straight. . . . gulp!). Or try the following Makeover Hint.

■ *Makeover Hint #65—Flax Appeal*

If you have a coffee grinder or blender, and a place to buy flax seeds, then you're ready for the best makeover hint ever. Every day, put one to two tablespoons of flax seeds into your grinder or blender and mash them up into flax meal. Scoop these into a bowl and place them on your kitchen table. Then throughout the day, sprinkle a generous portion of these EFA powerhouses onto your food—cereal, salad, sandwich, stew, casserole—it doesn't matter.

If you're worried about the taste, don't be. When our son's young friend spotted a mysterious bowl of flax meal on our table and asked what it was, my son, Adam, replied, "Oh, that's flax. It's great. And it doesn't taste like anything!" Kid tested; mother approved.

Clear Skin Needs Nutrients

Beautiful skin requires a make-up bag full of nutrients provided by the blood vessels that circulate through dermal tissues. The skin's texture turns first to "goose flesh," and then a dry, rough, scaly "toad skin" (known medically as follicular hyperkeratosis), when vitamin A is very low. EFA deficiency, low vitamin B or insufficient cleansing also add to this condition. Dry skin, or xeroderma, where a fine, dandruff-like layer spreads all over the skin, especially the legs, also results when vitamin A is down.[3] Instigate a vitamin A makeover by turning to foods like yellow, orange, and green vegetables, eggs, and cod liver oil.

Age spots, seen on the hands, are actually cellular debris caused in part by cells damaged by roaming free radical molecules. One way to combat age spots is to eat foods rich in antioxidant nutrients. The red, orange, yellow, and dark green vegetables and fruits like carrots, yams, squash, broccoli and lettuces, are full of antioxidant pigments called carotenoids. Taking a supplement with beta-carotene (just one of hundreds of known carotenoids) or a mixture of carotenoids can help. Vitamins C and E are two other well-known antioxidant vitamins found respectively in citrus fruits, cantaloupe and peppers, eggs and fresh, cold-pressed vegetable oils.

For mysterious bruises, poor healing skin, and funny little red spots called petechiae—these are pinpoint hemorrhages—try taking extra doses of vitamin C and bioflavonoids. In addition to eating all the right foods, pop 1000 mg of each nutrient per meal.

■ *Makeover Hint #66—Watch Your Vitamin A*

Unfortunately, one of the signs of too much vitamin A—dry skin—is similar to a symptom of vitamin A deficiency. Other vitamin A toxicity signs to watch for are brittle nails, hair loss, loss of appetite, fatigue, irritability, and gingivitis. In your zeal to feed your skin, don't take too many vitamin A pills. Concentrate, instead, on vitamin A-rich foods, or get your vitamin A from a well-balanced multiple vitamin/mineral pill. A reasonable daily dose is 5000 IU (equivalent to 1000 mg or RE). Some supplements offer only beta-carotene, the precursor of vitamin A. Make sure your supplement says "natural beta-carotene."

Is the Sun Your Friend or Foe?

The sun is bad for your skin—or is it? With all the warnings we're given about sun exposure, skin cancer, and aging, you'd think that God was playing a cruel trick on us by placing that large, warm, inviting ball in the sky. Actually, sunlight—in moderate, regular doses—is good and even mandatory for good health and healthy skin.

We need sunlight for several reasons. Sun helps the skin produce vitamin D and heightens its absorption. For these reasons, the
bones benefit. In Ayurvedic medicine, the healing tradition from
India, the sun's warm rays are a source of higher consciousness. A
15- to 20-minute daily walk outside—avoid the most intense times
from noon to 3 P.M.—is actually a recommended treatment for some
skin conditions like acne and psoriasis.

For added protection under the sun, take advantage of fresh
fruits and vegetables rich in antioxidants, like carotenoids and
flavonoids, and high in potassium. Be sure to take vitamins E and C,
and if you happen to burn, apply vitamin E oil directly to your skin.
It's been shown to reduce the redness and inflammation caused by
the sun.[4] Other natural ways to cool burning skin include applying
aloe vera juice, zinc oxide, and vitamin A oil.

If you've been inside all winter, begin exposure gradually with
half an hour per day for a week and work up slowly. Remember,
sunburn is your body's warning that you've had too much. Guard
young children with both limited exposure and by placing a hat on
both them and you. (You'll look younger for it.) Be wary if near
water, snow, or metal, as these reflect and absorb rays that cause a
burn more quickly. You can burn just as easily on a gloomy day as
on a sunny one. Take extra care if you have moles, a history of skin
cancer, burn easily, or are taking medication that increases sensitivity to the sun.

Does Sunscreen Increase Your Risk of Skin Cancer?

In a shocking and controversial California study, Drs. Cedric
and Frank Garland report that using—not avoiding—suntan lotions
might be responsible for the rise in skin cancers. The reason, they
state, is because sunscreen interferes with the skin's production of
vitamin D, a nutrient that helps guard against melanoma and other
skin cancers. Also, sunscreens prevent sunburn, our warning that
we've had enough sun. The Garland research team also states that
there's been a direct link between sunscreen sales and skin cancer
incidence.[5]

No Wrinkles? No Smoking!

Here's one more reason to avoid tobacco. It ages you! Female and male smokers age 40 and older are two to three times more likely to have moderate to severe wrinkling compared to nonsmokers.[6]

Sally's Puffing Speeds up Aging

Years ago I had the opportunity to renew an old friendship. A friend of mine from my hometown of Victoria, British Columbia, had moved to Calgary three years previous. During a trip to visit my sister, who also resided in the oil capital of Canada, I decided to look up Sally. I phoned her the day after I arrived in Calgary, and we agreed to meet for lunch.

I arrived at the restaurant first, happy and somewhat nervous to see my friend. Sally was older than me, 28 to my youthful 21, and I was proud of the fact that this mature woman would have me for her friend. Sally's petite frame and easygoing manner gave the impression she was much younger. However, when Sally finally arrived for our luncheon date, I saw that her youngish complexion had aged considerably. She was an avid smoker, and since our last meeting had developed several lines around her eyes and mouth. If ever I was tempted to take up puffing, that moment erased all allure.

Sweat it Out

Perspiration is how we stay cool in hot weather, and how toxins are tossed from the body through the skin. Natural health practitioners take advantage of this innate detoxification process by promoting perspiration. Movement or exercise that makes you perspire is one way to cleanse the body and clear the skin. Done daily in moderate doses, it not only tones muscles (see Chapter 9), but helps elimination.

Another method uses saunas. Finland is their homeland. Dr. J. Perasalo from the Finnish Student Health Service in Helsinki writes a convincing article on the many attributes of this steamy heat in the *Annals of Clinical Research*.[7] With 1.4 million saunas scattered throughout this small country, there's no doubt that the Finns adore this relaxing (and cleansing) pastime. For one, saunas promote perspiration which effectively clears the skin and its sweat glands of bacteria. This prevents pimples. Finns have also used saunas as a place for childbirth and as a spot to cure a variety of ailments; a sauna to these people is "a holy place."

■ *Makeover Hint #67—The Finnish-ing Touch*

A full hot bath, no longer than 20 minutes, is an easy-at-home way to induce sweating and cleanse the body. Sip on a cup of yarrow or peppermint tea to enhance perspiration as you soak; while you're at it, pour a cup in your bath. Adding catnip, chamomile or lime blossom tea to your bath makes it more relaxing. This method is also useful for relieving muscle spasms and aching joints. Be careful of hot bathing if you're very weak or anemic, tend to bleed, or have a serious illness. Don't offer this technique to very old or very young individuals without professional supervision.

Makeup Herbs

Besides being our original medicines, herbs were our first cosmetics. When you run out of beauty products, run to the kitchen or local herb shop for these Skin Makeover aids.

- *Cucumis sativus* or cucumber slices placed over the eyes relieve strain.
- *Achillea millefolium* is yarrow; when made into a tea, it can be used as a wash for oily skin.
- Fresh *Fragaria vesca*—strawberries—rubbed on the skin is refreshing. Fragaria shortcake anyone?
- Blackheads may disappear with a dab of *Lycopersicon esculentum*, or tomato.
- A wash of *Arctium lappa*, the common weed called burdock, fights pimples.
- Normal skin enjoys a wash of *Mentha piperita* (peppermint), *Salvia officinalis* (sage) and *Matricaria recutita* (chamomile).

■ *Makeover Hint #68—Oatmeal Bathing*

After you've lathered oatmeal all over your face (see Makeover Hint #63), add it to your bath water for all sorts of skin rashes or irritation. Here's how. Cook one pound of oatmeal in two quarts of water for half an hour on low. When done, strain off excess liquid, and add it to your bath.

If You're Happy and You Know It, Look at Your Skin

The skin is a blabbermouth when it comes to how you're feeling. For instance, itching and sweating are immediate signs that you're stressed; others break out in hives within a few minutes. Fear shows itself with a paling of the skin or goose bumps. Embarrassment may be displayed with blushing; anger can also appear as a reddening of the face. For those with an allergic tendency, the weepy, itchy rash of eczema can emerge. Other skin conditions set off with the pressures of life include herpes, acne, warts, and psoriasis.

If you're just plain happy (and healthy), look for a rosy, vibrant glow.

Skin Makeover Checkup

As you admire your radiant new skin, glance at how you got there:

- Got some sleep, sleep, and more sleep.
- Screened cosmetics and cleansers.
- Remembered again with the fiber.
- Remembered once more, again with the water.
- Added flax seed oil, and other fats.
- Checked food and supplements for skin-happy vitamins.
- Did some sunning—but not too much.
- Stopped smoking.
- Learned to sweat.

- Made some cosmetics in the kitchen.
- Smiled.

For Related Problems, See

- Acne
- Eczema
- Hives
- Psoriasis
- Varicose Veins

Chapter 13

The Keys to Keener Vision

The All-Seeing Eyes

Eyes are the cameras of the body. Through them we receive color photographs of the world, pictures that give us information, memories, and enjoyment. When the eyes fail or weaken, reading or driving can be difficult—both severe detriments in this culture. If sight becomes severely impaired, movement and everyday activities like making a cup of tea or watching television are troublesome, if not impossible. For these reasons alone, it's important to take every Vision Makeover step possible to preserve your precious sight.

The volume of blood that flows through the eye each day is extremely high, relatively speaking, when compared to other body parts. Blood provides nutrients that guard the eyeball from damage caused by sunlight and exposure to free radical molecules. The regular workings of the eye also need nourishment.

Structurally, only one-fifth of the round eyeball is visible; the other four-fifths is encased in the skull's orbital cavity. Tissue and fat pads cushion the very delicate eyeball within this bony socket. The eyelids and fringe of eyelashes protect the outer exposed eye, by automatically blinking whenever dust or other unexpected object lurks near. Watch what happens next time someone's hand gets too close to your face. The transparent cornea and the fibrous "whites" of your eyes also guard sight from injury. Lacrimal or tear glands continuously leak out tears that lubricate and wash away dirt from your eyes; a special enzyme in tears kills unwanted bacteria.

The muscular iris, that part that gives you brown, green, hazel, or baby blue eyes, has in its middle a circular opening called the pupil. Light shines through this pinhole, and then passes through the lens which focuses images onto the retina—like film in a camera—situated at the back of the eye. The macula or "yellow spot" is the central area of the retina where vision is most acute. Photoreceptors—specialized cells called rods and cones—cover the retina where light energy is converted into nerve impulses that travel to the visual areas in the brain so you can see.

At least eight small muscles let you blink, glance sideways, and roll your eyes in disgust. Busy blood vessels rush nutrients and oxygen in, and a complex network of nerves works alongside these muscles to make sight possible.

Protect Your Sight With These Makeover Steps

Like other parts of the body, age and the perils of modern living are wearing on eyes. Problems include eyestrain from squinting at a computer screen all day, to redness caused by pollution or too little sleep. These acute problems are usually solved with a few common-sense steps like taking regular computer breaks and getting enough sleep.

More difficult to treat are the most common eye diseases of old age: cataracts, glaucoma, and macular degeneration. Unfortunately, these conditions develop very slowly, often without notice. When they're apparent, there's often no treatment. So, it's important that you include in your Natural Health Makeover steps to guard your priceless eyesight.

The leading cause of blindness in adults 50 and older is a condition called macular degeneration; almost 20 percent of those over 65 are affected. The number of people with beginning signs of this eye-stealing disease is probably higher. Early symptoms of macular degeneration are subtle. They include decreased central vision—the macula, remember, is in the middle of the retina—difficulty adapting to changes in brightness whether going from dark to light, or vice versa. Someone may experience disturbances while reading, or when looking at color. Contrasts in shades and color might not be as sharp. Very often, a person waits up to 10 years before seeking help because hints that something's wrong are so vague.[1] As of this writing, conventional medicine offers no cure.

Four million Americans are affected by cataracts, another insidious eye problem. Here the normally crystal-clear lens gradually turns murky. Loss of eyesight is gradual and painless. Cataracts begin in middle age, and are egged on by trauma to the eyes, X-rays, systemic diseases like diabetes, or medicines such as steroids. Conventional treatment involves surgery, though special glasses can be worn while the cataract is developing.

The third eye demon to watch for is glaucoma. Here, pressure inside the eye builds to such a point that eyesight is either partially or totally lost. Two million Americans are afflicted, but one quarter of these cases are undetected. Like cataracts and macular degeneration, the chronic open-angle type of glaucoma is slow-moving. A gradual loss of peripheral vision is the first tip-off, though unsuspecting trouble starts much earlier. Unlike the other two eye conditions, there is a kind of glaucoma that is a medical emergency called acute angle-closure glaucoma. It is characterized by eye and head pain—usually one-sided—as well as fleeting visual loss and colorful halos around lights. If this happens to you, call your doctor or go to the nearest hospital immediately.

It's fortunate for us that ophthalmology has been at the forefront of nutrition, compared to other conventional medical specialties. Solid research points to a wholesome diet and lifestyle as prevention against macular degeneration, cataracts, and glaucoma. These same steps can sometimes slow or reverse such conditions. To ensure your eyes are fit, read on.

Smoke Gets in Your Eyes

There's no doubt that smoking, a major free radical promoter, hurts the eyes. Free radicals are volatile molecules that in large amounts age and sicken you. Ironically, the largest source of free radicals is your body, which uses them to neutralize toxins and disarm germs. However, pollution, pesticides, radiation, drugs, alcohol, rancid fats, too much sun, *and* smoking push free radical levels from the useful to the harmful side.

At Harvard Medical School, William Christen, Sc.D. found those who smoked a pack or more daily were two to three times more likely to lose their vision due to macular degeneration than people who never smoked.[2] Smoking not only boosts free radical load, but steals vitamin C[3] and other important free-radical-fighting antioxidant nutrients from the bloodstream. Puffing on a cigarette, pipe, or cigar also impedes blood flow, thus nutrient and oxygen delivery, to the eyes. Some experts consider smoking to be a marker of a generally poor lifestyle.[4]

So, the first step you must take to improve eyesight is to snuff out all tobacco products. If this task seems overwhelming, consider the consequences if you don't. Besides risking blindness later in life, you invite lung and other cancers, emphysema, and overall poor health. While suggestions on how to quit are beyond the scope of this book, begin by locating a natural health practitioner who specializes in addiction treatment. Useful therapies in this area include auricular acupuncture, dietary changes, nutrient supplementation, herbs, and, last but not least, counseling. Stop smoking tip: take extra doses of vitamin C and other antioxidants to replenish body stores.

The Dim Vision Study

American and Australian scientists joined forces to confirm whether smoking played a role in cataract formation. Cataracts are a condition where the normally clear and colorless lenses in your eyes turn cloudy. These researchers printed these results in the *Archives of Ophthalmology* (1995, vol 113): Smokers were more than twice as likely to develop significant opacities of the eyes' lenses as were non- or past smokers. The more they smoked, the worse the problem.[5]

Alcohol Gets in Your Eyes Too

Too much wine, beer, or hard liquor affects eyesight too, both directly and by decreasing nutrient absorption.[6] The National Cancer Institute published a report in the *American Journal of Clinical Nutrition* (1995) stating that lutein and zeaxanthin—compounds important for eye health—are lower among women who drink alcohol versus teetotalers.[7] As with smoking, there's also a direct relationship between the alcohol you consume and your chance of getting cataracts.[8]

Monitor your liquor. If you choose to drink, make it the exception, not the rule. If you feel you have a drinking problem, consult with a practitioner experienced in treating this kind of addiction—whether she uses conventional or natural methods.

Spinach to the Rescue

If you like spinach salad, you're in luck. Spinach is especially high in lutein, a yellow carotene that congregates in your eye's retina. Zeaxanthin, another carotene, is often found beside lutein in the foods you eat; it's also produced by your body from lutein. Steven Pratt, M.D., of Scripps Memorial Hospital in La Jolla, California, and assistant clinical professor of ophthalmology at the University of California-San Diego is sold on the importance of lutein in eye health. "I eat a spinach salad every day," he proudly states.

Dr. Pratt knows that a diet brimming with spinach and other lutein-rich vegetables and fruits pays off. When patients showing early signs of macular degeneration listen to his nutritional advice, Pratt says not only are most healthier within a year, but many are free of this eye condition. Research backs up his observations.[9]

"Lutein in the lens," explains Pratt, "acts as nature's own sunglasses. Lutein and zeaxanthin absorb blue light, the most dangerous type of light for the eye." Ultraviolet light is mostly filtered out by the cornea and lens; yet visible blue light still reaches the retina. As an antioxidant, lutein in the macula helps protect the eye from photochemical damage caused by UV light, high-energy visible light, and other free radical-producing events like smoking and alcohol.

Kale, collard greens, broccoli, and other dark green, leafy vegetables also contain appreciable amounts of this eye-loving nutrient. But there's more. Over 400 carotenes have been identified to date; better-known ones are beta-carotene, in carrots, and lycopene, high in tomatoes. Carotenes give fruits and vegetables—like cantaloupe, yams, and red peppers—their eye-pleasing red, orange, and yellow colors. Like lutein, these pigments please your eyes in other ways too, namely as eye-guarding antioxidants.

Researcher Susan Hankinson led a Harvard study group to watch what over 50,000 nurses ate for eight years. The women who consumed more carotene-rich foods, not just those high in lutein, developed fewer cataracts.[5]

The moral here is to remember your mother's words: Eat all your vegetables (and then some). Diet supplies all the nutrients we need, if we eat a wide variety of high-quality food.

It's said that rabbits never go blind because they eat lots of carrots. Now you can see that there's some truth in that. Use your hunger and this carrot cure to fend off poor eyesight.

Directly prior to dinner (or lunch), before the food's ready and you're starving, pull out the carrot sticks. You can peel and slice them right there, or prepare them ahead of time for those munchie moments. Or if this is too much, buy prepared "baby carrots," bagged and ready to eat. (Not as nutritious, but better than not eating any carrots.) Munch away on this original fat-free, nutrition-packed snack. Guilt not included.

Add Anthocyanidins for Healthy Eyes

If carotenes give fruits and vegetables their autumn colors, then anthocyanidins are the flavonoids that paint produce—cherries, blackberries, grapes—with reds, blues, and purples. Like carotenes, anthocyanidins are antioxidants, instrumental in deactivating eye-harming free radical molecules. However, they keep eyes healthy in other ways too: by raising vitamin C levels in cells and bolstering overall eye strength. The anthocyanidin flavonoids are renowned for reinforcing blood vessels, including those in and connected to the eyeballs. This, in turn, improves blood flow and the delivery of nutrients and oxygen to the eyes.

Bilberry, or *Vaccinium myrtillus*, has a reputation as a sightful remedy. Folk healers have relied on this delicious berry to treat eyes. During World War II, legend has it that British Royal Air Force pilots who spread bilberry jam on their bread saw better during nighttime missions. Modern day science confirms that nontoxic bilberry is high in anthocyanidins, and may ward off cataracts, macular degeneration and glaucoma[10].

For those unable to find bilberries, local favorites like purple grapes, blueberries, and black currants serve just as well.

Some experts claim blueberries contain more anthocyanidins than any other blue, purple, or red fruit. You can strengthen your eyes in the summer with fresh blueberries; add frozen berries to your cereal or yogurt in the winter. Or for a delicious, eye-popping treat, try this recipe for Blueberry Eye Pie.

CRUST

2 cups whole wheat pastry flour (for a lighter crust try 1 cup unbleached white and 1 cup whole wheat; you can also experiment with other flours, such as spelt and barley)

2/3 cup butter

cold water as needed

Sift flour(s) together into a bowl. Cut butter into mixture and crumble into flour with pastry blender or hands until thoroughly mixed. Gradually add water, stirring with a fork, only until you form a ball of dough—not too dry and not too sticky. Put dough in the fridge for 30 minutes. When ready to work with pastry, flour rolling board and rolling pin. Place half of pastry on board and sprinkle a small amount of flour on top to prevent sticking. Roll out to 1/8-inch thickness and place in pie pan. Trim edges. Roll out second piece of pastry; place on top of pie pan after blueberry filling is added to pan.

BLUEBERRY FILLING

4 1/2 cups fresh blueberries

1/2 to 2/3 cup of honey or other sweetener

2 tbsp. cornstarch or arrowroot; mix with 1/4 cup water

1 1/2 tbsp. lemon juice

Mix all above ingredients in a large bowl. Pour into pie crust and top with second sheet of pastry. Trim edges, and cut several one-inch vent holes in top. Bake at 450 degrees for 10 minutes; reduce the heat to 350 degrees and bake an additional 35 to 40 minutes or until golden brown.

Serve warm after a meal of spinach salad, and see how much clearer everything seems.

Use Eye Savers

Protecting your eyes with foods high in lutein—nature's sunglasses—is a good step. But you need to cut down on the sun's glare on the outside too. Steven Pratt, M.D., suggests wearing the wraparound style of sunglasses that fit closely to your face; the larger the lenses, the better. Choose the type that screens out the most harmful rays, in the 450 nm range. Add a wide-brimmed hat to your goggle-type glasses, and not only will you look rather fetching, but you'll reduce UV light by 50 percent. Protecting eyes with this get-up is not only for adults, but for children as well.

Take Vitamins for Clearer Vision

Time to pull your vitamin bottle out again, as the next step in your Vision Makeover. A deficiency of vitamin A can end in night blindness or eventual cataract development. Very severe vitamin A deficiency, common among small children in some parts of Asia, Africa, and South America, sometimes results in a blinding condition called xerophthalmia.[11] In the case of retinitis pigmentosa, a genetic degeneration of the retina, vitamin A treatment helps preserve the retina's rod and cone function, thus slowing visual deterioration.[12]

Vitamin C, known for its ability to strengthen various body tissues by promoting collagen synthesis, appears to strengthen the eyes too. This is especially important for those with glaucoma, though research results in this area are mixed.[13] Other scientific stories attest to vitamin C's ability to preclude the development of macular degeneration[9] and cataracts.[5] Chemical burns to the cornea have also been treated with vitamin C.[14]

The eye uses the mineral zinc as a cofactor in several enzymes necessary for proper visual function. In fact, zinc is the most abundant mineral in the eye, and second most prevalent trace element in the body. Unfortunately, zinc is commonly deficient in standard diets, particularly among the elderly. Simple supplementation can, according to a Louisiana State University Medical Center study, offset macular degeneration. David Newsome, M.D., gave 151 people with this sight-threatening condition either zinc pills or a placebo. Those who took zinc had significantly less visual loss after one to two years of treatment than the group on sugar tablets.[15] Foods high in zinc include pumpkin seeds, sunflower seeds, soybeans and meat.

There are, of course, many other nutrients that feed vision and help prevent the development of degenerative eye diseases. But you can start with the above.

■ *Makeover Hint #71—Take a Well-Rounded Pill*

After reading about individual nutrients, it's very tempting to run out, stock up and take those particular vitamins and minerals. Please, don't do this!

As eye insurance, take a high-potency supplement containing a complete assortment of all known vitamins and minerals. To do otherwise invites nutritional upset and potential problems. The nutrients we need work in tandem, and when one is very high or low it can affect the absorption or effectiveness of another. For instance, 250 to 500 mg of vitamin C daily was found to be sufficient to prevent cataracts over a 10-year period.[5] More than 15 mg of zinc each day on a regular basis is too much (to use without professional supervision), and should also be taken with copper. Vitamin A is ample at 5000 IU each day. Higher amounts are fine under special conditions; but to be absolutely safe, consult first with a professional versed in nutrition.

Get Rid of Those Meddling Metals

As eye lenses get older, concentration of heavy metals seems to increase. Heavy metals are those poisonous minerals like cadmium, mercury, nickel, and lead that tend to settle in the body and cause a variety of problems ranging from mental disturbances in children (lead) to fatigue and headaches. These poisons are more prevalent than you might think. Seafood and cosmetic powders may contain arsenic; leaded gasoline releases lead into the air that then settles in the soil. Cigarette smoke spews out cadmium. Anyone who works in a gas station, dentist's office, or as a printer, jeweler, or roofer is at highest risk of heavy metal contamination.

This is all unfortunate because there is a possible link between heavy metals—cadmium in particular—and cataract formation. It's speculated that cadmium pushes out zinc that is necessary for eye function, and/or is just plain toxic.[16]

■ *Makeover Hint #72—Lighten Up on Heavy Metals*

To lighten your load of heavy metals, begin here:

- Begin by avoiding those situations that expose you (see Chapters 3 and 5).
- If you suspect you've been overly exposed, ask your doctor about testing you for these metals with a hair analysis, urine sample, or blood—whatever is appropriate for your situation.
- Take a good, high-potency multiple vitamin and mineral supplement.
- Take some extra vitamin C (1000 mg three times daily).
- Eat lots of sulphur-based foods like garlic, onions, beans, and eggs.
- High-fiber foods like whole grains will help remove some of these toxins.
- Find a physician who performs chelation therapy, and ask if you're a suitable candidate.

Exercise Your Eyes

The small muscles that maneuver your eyeball are no different from the other muscles in your body; all need varied and daily movement to work properly. You might say, "But I move my eyes all day. I blink. I look from side to side. I look up and down." This is true, we do naturally move our eyes as needed throughout the day. But we also live in an age where concentrating on close work, be it paperwork, computers, or books, outweighs eye relaxation.

This combination of focusing in closely and tight eye muscles compromises vision and can cause eyestrain and headaches. The late William Bates, M.D., a New York ophthalmologist, advocated that this combination can be behind why some people need glasses. Glasses, he felt, were a crutch for a problem that could be corrected with certain steps. First, he suggested regular breaks every hour for hardworking eyes. Second, deep breathing improves blood and oxygen flow not only to eyes, but to the rest of your body (see

Makeover Hint #79—The Right Way to Breathe In and Out). Third, stretching exercises that release tension around your eyes, head, neck, and shoulders relieve eyestrain (see Chapter 9).

■ *Makeover Hint #73—Eyeball Push-Ups*

A simple way to give your eyes a workout is with what I call Eyeball Push-Ups. If you've been doing close, concentrated work, begin by staring off into space for a minute or so. This is like a pre-workout warm-up. Next comes the sweat.

- Find an interesting picture or object on a distant wall; hold your gaze for 15 seconds (like a push-up).

- Then focus back on something close, your hands for instance. Hold your gaze for another 15 seconds (like lowering yourself after a push-up).

- Continue doing your Eyeball Push-Ups four times or until your eyes feel relaxed.

Relief for the Dry Eye Blues

If your eyes feel unusually dry, your problem could be Dry Eye Syndrome. For those experiencing other symptoms, like joint pain or fatigue, dry eyes could be just one sign that your health is being affected by rheumatoid arthritis, lupus, Sjogren's syndrome, or some other systemic disease. If you suspect this is the case, visit with your doctor.

Dry Eye Syndrome is also a condition unto itself, caused in part by a "tear" defect. Tears aren't just for crying; they are part of a vital and dynamic structure that protects your delicate eyeball from the irritating and hostile world. Tears are made up of a tear film consisting of three main layers. The outermost layer is oily; it slows down tear evaporation and acts as a seal over the eye. The watery middle layer is what tears are mostly made of. When we cry or get something in our eyes, this watery layer expands and helps clean out our eyes (and emotions). This layer also contains a bacteria-killing protein called lysozyme to protect eyes from infection. Last is the mucous layer nestled up against the eyeball itself. Its stickiness captures dirt and other debris in the eye and pushes it toward the inner corner of the eye—the same place you wipe "sleep" away.[17]

When your not-so-simple tears wash away, due to decreased secretion or increased evaporation, dry eyes can be a problem. While infrequent blinking could be the cause (see Makeover Hint #74—Think and Blink), your dry eyes could also be caused by one of the following:

- Rubbing eyes
- Hay fever or other allergies that cause red, itchy, irritated eyes
- Daily soap use around the eyes (often the case when eyelids are also dry)
- Eye drop overuse
- Contact lenses (usually the hard kind)
- Previous eye surgery
- Any trauma to the surface of the eyeball (physical, chemical exposure, infections).

While there are no substantive cures for dry eyes, knowing the cause and correcting it can help. Avoiding those situations that can injure your eyes and possibly lead to this problem (as listed above) is also wise. Artificial tears can be used, but they come with their own set of problems. Unlike real tears, fake tears don't contain important substances like lysozymes; instead, when overused, they can make dry eyes worse and increase your chance of infection by washing away these protective compounds.

■ Makeover Hint #74—Think and Blink

During a visit to my ophthalmologist, I complained of eye strain and dryness. After ruling out other possible causes, the doctor placed a small amount of fluorescein dye in my eye, and had me blink fully several times. He then instructed me to keep my eyes open for several seconds while he determined how long it took for the tears protecting my eye to disperse. Normal dispersion, or as he called it "tear break-up time," is eight to 10 seconds. My eye dryness, he determined, was in part due to my eye's short dispersion time— five to six seconds.

Not too much we could do about this physiological oddity.

However, he told me that while using computers (something I do every day, hours on end), watching TV, or even reading, many people stare or squint and forget to blink. The average and most comfortable blinking time is every five seconds. So when your eyes feel strained, think, then slowly blink . . . one, two, three . . . times. This will help remoisten parched eyeballs, and relieve some of that achiness. Eye movements help spread tears around too.

Discover the Healing Secret of Ginkgo Biloba

Ginkgo biloba is a most interesting tree. It lives for as long as a millennium, and because its ancestry can be traced back 200 million years, it's been dubbed by some as the "living fossil." Most people are probably familiar with ginkgo trees as an ornamental addition to their garden. So what has this got to do with eyes?

Because of its ability to scavenge free radical molecules, stabilize the membranes of cells, promote blood circulation and nervous system function, ginkgo plays a significant role in preventing and possibly treating macular degeneration.

Hundreds of studies attest to the advantages of taking ginkgo for other conditions, such as inadequate blood flow to the brain (a risk for stroke), some types of depression, impotence, inner ear troubles like vertigo and ringing, multiple sclerosis, and vascular problems such as Raynaud's and intermittent claudication.[18]

Take this gingko step to better eye health if:

1. You're at risk or in the early stages of macular degeneration or diabetic retinopathy, or

2. If you're affected by one of the other conditions helped by ginkgo listed above.

When All Else Fails, Think Liver

In Traditional Chinese Medicine, how well your liver functions is directly tied to eyesight. Although it's foreign to Western thought to think of the liver affecting vision, when you consider that the liver both stores and filters blood, then the connection to eyes makes perfect sense. Remember, blood flow through the eyes is extremely high. Traditional Chinese healers also view the liver as a regulator of emotions and thoughts. So if you're overly stressed, your liver feels it as do your eyes.[19]

If your eyes feel poorly, take steps to heal your liver (see Chapter 3). This isn't as crazy as it might seem. Even though we're talking about your body in 12 different parts, it's still all joined together.

Vision Makeover Checkup

Doesn't the world seem clearer? This is what you've just done:

- Been reminded one last time of the health consequences of smoking and drinking.
- Feasted on spinach and carrots.
- Added more blueberries to your diet.
- Bought new sunglasses and a wide-brimmed hat.
- Checked that vitamin bottle again for eye nutrients.
- Made a checklist of heavy metals in your life.
- Learned eye exercises.
- Determined if you have dry eyes, and why.
- Were reminded of the importance of the liver.

For Related Problems, See

- Fatigue
- Headaches

Chapter 14

Supercharge
Your Brain

Keeping Your Nervous System
in Tone

We speak of the body-mind as if our head could be easily detached from the rest of us. The head, home to the brain, is very much a member of the body. Perhaps it's our highly developed cognitive abilities and emotions that encourage us to separate physical sensations, complaints, and illness from thoughts and feelings.

At any rate, the nervous system reminds us constantly that the brain is firmly and undeniably attached to the rest of the body. The nervous system is divided roughly into two segments: the sensory and motor portions. The sensory part links each body part to the sensory section in the brain and allows us to feel pain and pleasure, hot and cold, and other sensations. Similarly, the motor portions of the brain and nervous system provide stimuli for walking and keep our internal organs functioning. You understand now why spinal cord injuries are so traumatic and often result in paralysis.

The brain itself is a complex and not entirely charted entity. The largest part is called the cerebrum and is divided into two hemispheres, within which are several lobes. The occipital, or back, lobe is where the vision centers are. Hearing is controlled by the temporal lobe and speech on the far side of the frontal lobe. Also housed in the brain are the hypothalamus and pituitary gland. The hypothalamus has a hand in controlling moods and motivation, as well as endocrine function. The pituitary, or master, gland is divided into two sections: posterior and anterior. The former releases the hormones vasopressin and oxytocin. The larger anterior lobe is ruled by the hypothalamus; in turn, this part of the pituitary sends out special chemicals that tell endocrine glands when to release their hormones.

Making Over the Body-Mind Link

As mentioned in Chapter 6, there's a definite link between your emotions, thoughts, the nervous system, and the rest of your body. Much of this connection occurs by way of the endocrine and immunity systems. What does this mean? Well, unless you pay as much attention to how you feel and think as you do to physical symptoms and sensations, then your Natural Health Makeover will remain incomplete. By looking at all aspects of yourself—physical, mental, emotional, and spiritual—you are practicing whole-person health care.

So what are some signs that you need a Mind Makeover? They might include:

- Fatigue
- Insomnia
- Depression
- Anxiety
- Frustration
- Cloudy thinking
- Memory loss

Food for Thought

Brain food. That's the next topic for discussion. Your brain has a voracious appetite. If you don't feed it right—both quality and quantity of food—it doesn't function and neither do you. Hopefully you know what I'm talking about by now. That's right, fresh vegetables and fruits, whole grains and legumes, lean meats and fish, consumed with diversity in mind.

As the central operator of the body, this hungry organ has to be satisfied at all times. Allow me to explain. Although 100 billion cells comprise the brain, it represents only 1/50th of your total body weight. Yet those cells are extremely active, conducting body business and thinking, and eating up much of what you feed yourself.

For as metabolically active as the brain is, it has very few energy reserves. The brain needs fats, in particular essential fatty acids, for cellular upkeep. Amino acids—the building blocks of protein—provide raw material for neurotransmitters, the chemical messengers of the brain and nervous system. So it seems that you not only *are* what you eat, you also *think* what you eat. For example, eating carbohydrate-type foods increases serotonin, the neurotransmitter that calms and relaxes you.[1]

Besides this, insulin is no help at all. Your body converts most of the food you eat into glucose—a basic form of sugar. Insulin, a hormone secreted by the pancreas, helps most of the body's cells grasp and use glucose. Your brain can't do this. Instead, glucose passes without assistance into the brain and brain cells second-by-second. That's why it's important to keep blood glucose (sugar) levels even at all times. Under ideal dietary circumstances, the body maintains uniform blood sugar for hours on end (see Low Blood Sugar). When it does fall, irritability, headaches, and dizziness are your brain's reactions. In the most severe cases, fainting, convulsions and even coma can result.

■ Makeover Hint #75—Eat a Brainy Breakfast

When I tell patients they must eat breakfast, many turn pale. Breakfast? In the morning? You've got to be kidding, they say. Yet a good breakfast helps kids learn and adults work. Here are a few hints on how to turn your stomach on to morning food.

1. Don't eat anything after dinner.
2. Don't eat dinner later than 6pm.
3. Shower and dress *before* breakfast, not after.
4. Begin your morning repast with a glass of water flavored with a slice of lemon.
5. Take your breakfast to work and eat it during your coffee break.

6. Eat filling, not greasy, foods like oatmeal, whole grain toast and sugarless jam, fruit, whole grain pancakes topped with yogurt and blueberries. If you can stomach eggs, go ahead.

Cognition Nutrition

Now that you're regularly feeding your brain, be sure that all necessary vitamins and minerals are covered. You can use your multiple vitamin/mineral supplement for this in most cases. Certainly the brain cannot develop properly without a generous serving of nutrients each day[2]—that's why obstetricians recommend prenatal vitamins for their pregnant patients. It's also been shown in studies that children improve academically by taking nutritional supplements, especially if they're eating a poor diet.[3] Even adult minds benefit from sound nutrition.[4]

Of course the brain needs a wide assortment of nutrients to get through the day. Calcium, magnesium, and potassium are particularly nourishing minerals. However, it's the B-vitamins that everyone remembers when it comes to the brain. Besides facilitating memory, these nutrients help form neurotransmitters. Pyridoxal phosphate, a B_6 member, is pivotal in the synthesis of the neurotransmitters serotonin, dopamine and gamma-amino butyric acid. When thiamin (B1) is too low, the neurotransmitters glutamine and aspartate also decline. Choline, the vitamin-like cousin of the B-complex, is needed for acetylcholine. Other members of the B-complex family include riboflavin (B_2), niacin (B_3), pantothenic acid (B_5), B_{12}, folic acid, and biotin. Inositol is sometimes grouped here too.

As added protection against free-radical damage, look to the antioxidants like vitamins C and E, selenium, and the carotenoid compounds. (See Poisons to Watch For.)

■ *Makeover Hint #76—Eat Oats to Soothe Jangled Nerves*

Good old-fashioned oatmeal is a brain favorite and nervous system supporter. It's rich in magnesium, and provides some calcium and B-vitamins. Oats taken as a food or in medicinal herbal form are a traditional remedy for nervous debility and exhaustion associated with depression. They are often used during convalescence after a lengthy illness too. So eat a big bowl of oatmeal or oat bran for breakfast (or a snack) topped off with walnuts, raisins, and a scoop of yogurt. While you're at it, soak in an oatmeal bath and spread it on your face (see Chapter 12).

Rev Up Your Brain Power

Your mind needs to "flex its muscle" on a regular basis in order to stay sharp. And like your body, variety is important too. Marian Cleeves Diamond, Ph.D. demonstrated that it's possible to increase both the size and function of the brain through interesting and diverse mental activities. Using rats to make her point, Dr. Diamond showed that keeping her rodents' minds engaged not only enhanced the number and size of connections between brain cells and brain cell size (number wasn't affected), but also increased blood supply to the area.[5]

How you exercise your brain depends on personal taste. Formal education—college or university—certainly keeps the brain busy for at least four years. Some people might choose to continue this trend with night classes at a local community college. My sister Kim, who resides in remote Prince Rupert, British Columbia, used correspondence courses to keep her brain active while raising her two small children. After eight years of reading and writing, her mind was not only sharper but she graduated with a Bachelors degree in English. For others, it might be interesting to:

- Read about something new.
- Play trivia (not trivial) board games.
- Converse (TV must be off).
- Hold discussion groups on a specific topic. You can do this at the dinner table too.
- Do crossword puzzles.
- Play chess.
- Balance your checkbook without a calculator.
- Write letters instead of phoning distant friends.
- Start a new hobby.
- Watch *Jeopardy*.

- Look up words you don't know in the dictionary.
- Help your child with homework.
- Listen to educational tapes in the car.
- Learn all you can about natural health.

Set Aside Alone Time

Having time—just for you—is vital. This might mean several 15-minute breaks spaced liberally throughout the day. If you have young children at home, you might create a "quiet time" when everyone in the household is silently engaged in his or her own activity, like reading or doing a puzzle. As the parent, this gives you semi-alone time. I know many daycare providers in our area that use afternoon nap-time as their recharge time. Alone time could also be an evening alone, or an all-day event every couple of months. Some people even enjoy solo vacations.

While I can't tell you how to spend your alone time, I personally equate it with meditation. By that, I mean this singly spent spell is meant to refresh you mentally and emotionally—thus ultimately physically. Keeping this in mind, the following guidelines might help:

- Don't use this time for work.
- Don't use this time to worry.
- Before you turn on the television or radio, listen to the quiet.

Whatever or however you integrate hours just for you, make it a priority. Let me tell you why. Being alone provides you with:

- Relaxation time
- Thinking time
- Dreaming time
- Breathing time
- Stretching time (physically or mentally)
- Collapsing time
- Unscheduled time
- Responsibility-free time

- Selfish time
- Frivolous time
- Healing time.

■ *Makeover Hint #77—Take a Two-Minute Holiday*

For those times when you have to get away but can't, take two minutes and escape. Places to hide out might be the lunchroom, bathroom, storeroom, the car, or any quiet corner. When you get there, take a cleansing breath—and then another. Close your eyes; if you wish, put in ear plugs. Now indulge in your favorite daydream and smile.

Don't Fall Into the Too-Tired-To-Think Trap

Get at least eight hours of sleep each night. More if you're sick and embroiled in a stressful situation. Sleep is one of the top factors in maintaining well-being. Yet busy schedules and endless demands for our time shove sleep to the bottom of our priority list. If you want to make over and maintain health, however, you must find the time for eight hours of restful, uninterrupted sleep each and every day.

I know several people who brag about how little sleep they get. Knowing how important nighttime rest is, I really don't understand why this should be an admirable trait. One hundred years ago, people got on average nine hours of sleep each night. Now we try to get by with seven or less—and it shows. Sleep deprivation appears not only as fatigue, but also as body aches, impaired memory, decreased concentration, and increased susceptibility to illness. Those who squeeze by with less sleep are more accident-prone and less apt to think clearly. Children who go to bed too late don't do as well in school and their parents aren't as sharp at work.

It is true that some adults need less than eight hours, and some need more. Use these signs to determine your optimal sleeping time.

You may be sleep-deprived if:

- You nod off while sitting down during the day.
- You fall asleep as soon as your head hits the pillow at night.

- You're irritable.
- You have vague body aches, and even stomach upset, that go away after a full night's sleep.
- You have trouble remembering things.
- You can't concentrate.
- You're accident prone.
- You rely on coffee, black tea, soft drinks, or other caffeine beverages to stay alert.

■ *Makeover Hint #78—Six Ways to Recover Lost Sleep*

Didn't get your ZZZs last night? Try these tips to catch up.

1. Go to bed one hour early. If you can't sleep, stay there and read a relaxing book. Even if you do this only one night a week, you'll feel better for it.
2. Sleep in a little. Even an extra 15 minutes will help.
3. Take a 20-minute catnap.
4. If you're not sleeping due to worry, try a cup of valerian root tea half an hour before bedtime.
5. If jet lag has got you down, try a 3 mg capsule of melatonin 90 minutes before the lights go out.
6. If a sick or restless child is keeping you awake, ask your spouse to care for him just this one night—and wear ear plugs.

Air Out Your Brain

Breathe. That's your next task. I don't mean shallow little puffs. I want you to inhale purposefully and deeply. Flood your brain and body with the oxygen it needs. Your very busy brain uses up oxygen almost as fast as it does glucose. And when that lifeline of air is shut off for a short time, disaster can strike. Four to five minutes of circulatory arrest (all blood flow completely stops) causes permanent brain damage in half of all people, and most people after 10 minutes.[6] A dramatic example of this is a stroke. While there are several causes and physiological explanations why a stroke occurs, one is cerebral insufficiency due to transitory disruptions of blood flow to the brain. Atherosclerosis, or clogged arteries in the brain, are often behind this cutoff of oxygen. Symptoms—including neurological—vary depending on what part of the brain is affected. TIAs, or transient ischemic attacks, are mini-strokes and often portend a major stroke. These episodes last anywhere from 2 to 30 minutes with confusion, vertigo, slurred speech, weakness, and tingling as part of the picture.

Sticking to your low-saturated fat and high-fiber diet is a great stroke-preventer (see Chapter 8). You can also take the herb ginkgo to enhance oxygen and glucose usage by the brain.

■ *Makeover Hint #79—The Right Way to Breathe In and Out*

When you're feeling breath-less, use this simple 1-2-3 method to breathe easier and deeper.

1. Sit up straight, close your eyes, and place your hands on your abdomen.
2. Slowly inhale through your nose to the count of seven. Feel your breath fill your chest, rib cage, and expand your upper abdomen. Hold to the count of two.
3. Slowly exhale; gently push on your abdominal muscles to help push the air out. Rest to the count of two. Repeat 5 to 10 times. (Don't hyperventilate, now.)

Poisons to Watch For

Your brain is very susceptible to environmental toxins, be they solvents or heavy metals (poisons, not rock bands—though maybe I should include loud music too). As protector and owner of this delicate organ, you must ensure that you steer clear of harmful substances. See Chapter 3 for a complete discussion about how to "Wash Away the Poisons" at work and at home. Food allergies can also be at work; again see Chapter 3.

Specifically, be mindful of heavy metal contamination. Your best treatment is prevention. But if you suspect you've been overly exposed, visit with a physician who can test you through hair analysis, urine or blood samples. He can also treat you for toxicity problems.

Lead poisoning, supposedly one factor in the mental decline of the Roman Empire, could be our undoing too. Exposure to this heavy metal is commonplace and neurotoxic. When leaded paint, banned in 1978, crumbles and turns to dust, people can inhale it or consume it if touched. Children are especially susceptible. Drinking water tainted by lead in old plumbing is another hazard, as is breathing fumes from leaded gasoline, or exposure to soil contaminated with settled car fumes. Imported pottery, lead crystal glassware and ink on the outside of plastic bread bags are also sources of lead. Fatigue, reduced appetite, decreased intelligence, and neurological disorders are some signs of lead poisoning.

The world's most abundant metal, aluminum, is another brain poison we must look out for. It's in baking powder, antiperspirants, antacids, black tea, drinking water (drink filtered water), cookware, aluminum foil and cans, coffee, bleached flour and soil saturated with acid rain. Alzheimer's has been linked to aluminum toxicity, as has hyperactivity in children. Too little magnesium and calcium can increase its effects.

Cadmium, obtained from cigarettes, coffee, white flour, and zinc and copper smelters, is a toxic nerve-wrenching metal. Accumulation of mercury—in batteries, tuna and other fish, floor polishes, some cosmetics, silver fillings—is brain-unfriendly. Other toxic metals include antimony, arsenic, beryllium, bismuth, nickel, platinum, silver, thallium, thorium, tin, and uranium.

Jim Tosses Canning Pot and Clears his Mind

For over 10 years, Jim owned a very large silver-colored pot. Being an avid gardener, he and his wife relied on this two-gallon container to render down fruits and vegetables for canning. It was the ideal size. It also pleased Jim that such a useful item had come to them so cheaply—50 cents spent at a garage sale. Besides growing and canning his own food, 62-year-old Jim was an avid reader. A couple of years before the pot purchase, he had read about the potential hazards of aluminum. Not wanting to take any risks, Jim cleansed his life of aluminum products—antiperspirant and the like.

One afternoon while talking with his daughter, he described the latest garden harvest, and also mentioned how concerned he was about his failing memory. For several years, Jim's brain seemed to be growing less sharp than it once was. Out of the blue, his daughter asked if he owned any aluminum pots. Jim stopped for a moment; the big, silver, garage sale pot came to mind. Was it aluminum? Immediately following the conversation with his daughter, Jim removed the canning pot from his cupboard. A month or two later, his memory hadn't improved, but it wasn't getting worse either. Was it the big, garage sale pot that was affecting his memory? Possibly. Either way, Jim was happy to be truly aluminum-free.

Dream On

I add this step as part of your Mind Makeover because without it the rest of your makeover can seem empty. Work on turning your dreams into reality. I believe that unrealized goals drag us down emotionally; and as you know, negative feelings have a very definite impact on physical well-being. So I challenge you to mold your life into exactly what you want. It won't necessarily be quick or easy; I know this from experience. But I also know the satisfaction that comes from clarifying desires, then consciously pursuing them. Perhaps the following acronym will help.

D—Dream. You need to fantasize first so your hopes and goals can surface.

A—Acknowledge. Believe and affirm that you can and want to make your dreams come true.

R—Realize. Take steps to realize your dream no matter how small.

E—Envision success. This is vital. If you know in your heart that you'll triumph, you will.

Dare to dream.

■ *Makeover Hint #80—Create the Perfect Day*

Creating the perfect day is an easy and fun way to practice your dream realization. Begin by listing your favorite things. Then invite happiness into your life by planning "Perfect Days" for yourself on a regular basis. Here's how:

1. Pick a day (several months in advance if necessary), circle it on your calendar, and book it like you would any other important event.
2. Make arrangements so you're free—babysitter for the kids, spouse is notified, etc.
3. Save money if necessary.
4. On the day, start early. The hardest part is leaving your house and responsibilities behind. If it helps, go out of town.
5. Now, have fun.

The best Perfect Days are spontaneous when you do what you want as you desire it. Recently, on one of my Perfect Days I began with breakfast at my favorite bistro followed by clothes shopping. I then went for a long walk, and saw not one but two movies. My day ended with visiting a friend I don't see very often, and home—after the children were in bed.

Neil Quits His Job and Finds Happiness

Neil was miserable. At 36 he felt hopelessly trapped in his job as a mental health counselor for a large agency. When he first began, the work was enjoyable and challenging, and he found satisfaction helping the people that came to see him. But eight years of working with distressed people, in an agency that demanded he see 30 clients weekly had sent him reeling into burnout. Every day Neil came home to his wife with the same complaints: headaches, achy neck and shoulders, tight stomach, and exhaustion; many nights he was unable to sleep.

As these physical problems grew worse, Neil looked to his doctor for answers. The doctor prescribed pain medication for Neil's headaches and sleeping pills for nighttime. Next Neil saw a chiropractor who suggested neck exercises and scheduled weekly sessions for spinal manipulation. A holistically-oriented physician gave Neil vitamins and minerals. Another doctor recommended that he be evaluated for depression. While some of these ideas helped slightly, nothing solved all his troubles. Finally Neil's wife told him to quit his job. While Neil knew his counseling work was having a toll on his health and happiness, the thought of quitting—especially when his family needed his paycheck to live—was frightening.

Two years after his wife's suggestion, Neil finally did quit. He had no idea what he would do instead or where he would work. He'd never thought before about what work he'd really enjoy. So Neil decided that his new assignment for the next few months would be to search for his ideal career. As he began exploring the workplace, Neil noticed that all his bothersome symptoms evaporated one by one.

Mind you, both Neil and his wife lost numerous nights of sleep over money and the possibility of failure. This was a tremendous risk he was taking, and without his wife's blessing and a back-up financial plan he would not have attempted it. Timing was another critical consideration. For several years before he resigned, Neil thought of quitting but the time was never right. He waited, instead, until his wife's paycheck was substantial enough to support the family and the children were in school.

Neil's revival in his health and mental outlook not only made him feel better than he had in years, but fueled his creativity. Today, five years later, Neil has started his own business, and is healthier, wealthier, and happier than he's ever been before.

Mind Makeover Checkup

Does your brain feel beautiful? These are the final steps you took in your Natural Health Makeover:

- You now eat breakfast—like it or not.
- You have made another vitamin checkup, this time for brain nutrients.
- You want to be alone.
- You're sleeping so much, you rival Rip Van Winkle.

- You learned how to breathe (so that's how it's done!).
- You made one last sweep for poisons.
- You are reassessing your life, and looking for ways to reshape it.

For Related Problems, See

All conditions listed in Part Two are related to the mind. Specifically, see:

- Anxiety
- Fatigue
- Headaches
- Insomnia

Laboratory Tests Your Doctor Can Order

- Hair Analysis—heavy metals
- Urine Test—heavy metals

How Did You Do? Complete the Before-and-After Chart

Congratulations! You have completed your Natural Health Makeover and have taken a huge step toward better lifelong health. During the past few weeks, you've eaten well, exercised regularly, perhaps used nutrients and herbs, watched out for stress, slept more, discovered new ways of cooking, and learned the importance of taking control of your well-being.

Depending on where you started health-wise, you may feel enormous benefits from this 12-step makeover plan. Or the effects may be more subtle. This is where your Before-and-After Chart comes in. Flip back to Chapter 2, and glance at the initial responses you made regarding your health. Now fill out the After portion of this chart and compare your answers to the Before part. What has changed? Has there been improvement? Have you forgotten how bad you felt when you began?

Most people who complete the Natural Health Makeover will notice at least some positive changes in their health. However, it's been my experience that the longer one sticks with good health-promoting habits, the better one feels. A few weeks or months is often not sufficient to undo years of unhealthy living. For every year of aches and pains, count on it taking one month to recover. In fact, promise yourself that every year you'll devote a few weeks to a touchup, using whatever steps are required from your Natural Health Makeover plan. 'Tis only human to slip off the health wagon once in awhile. Some unhealthy habits are harder to break than others. If you tumble completely off, just dust yourself off and start all over again.

If you're suffering from a more serious ailment, you might require the services of a physician who can tailor treatments specifically for you. But finishing a Natural Health Makeover is a great beginning. Therapies, whether natural or conventional, work better when laid upon a foundation of healthy living.

part two

Natural Remedies for Over Thirty Common Ailments

Getting Started

Now that you've completed (or while you're working through) your Natural Health Makeover, you can use this section when you need practical answers to over thirty common ailments. This information will help you stock a brand-new medicine chest brimming with herbs and vitamins, instead of prescription and over-the-counter medications. Research continues to validate these methods, and every year we're learning what traditional healers have known for thousands of years—that herbs and sound lifestyle choices have a dramatic impact on health and illness.

I begin each part below by describing the condition, then move on with tips on how to prevent it. This is followed by nutritional advice, herbs you can try (listed according to actions), homeopathic remedies that might help (the italics highlight the main symptom to watch for) and lifestyle recommendations. See Appendix A for guidelines on how to use herbs, and when certain ones *should not* be taken. Please read about each herb you want to use before trying it. Appendix B describes the principles behind homeopathy and how to use these remedies effectively.

Where appropriate, I end each section with a Lookout Alert: a list of symptoms or situations that require your physician's attention. Please don't ignore this information. If any illness is ongoing or doesn't improve with the suggested treatments, call your doctor. For suggestions on natural health practitioners, see Appendix D. The nutrients, herbs, and homeopathic remedies I recommend can be found in most health food stores or even drugstores. If you're not sure how to use any of these natural substances, consult with a knowledgeable practitioner.

■ Makeover Hint #81—Try Natural First

For mild conditions that you normally self-treat with over-the-counter medicines, try natural treatments first. They are usually safer and often less expensive than most synthetic medications. If you find that natural treatments don't work the first time you try them, there could be many reasons why.

- The products you're using may be of poor quality. For example, packaged herbs vary widely in potency depending on how they were cultivated, harvested, manufactured, and packaged.

211

- Natural products (like medicines) must be used correctly, i.e. in adequate amounts at proper intervals, to be effective.

- Natural treatments often work more slowly and are more subtle than stronger medicines. Give them time.

- Natural (and conventional) medicines tend to work better when you build a firm foundation of health with proper diet, exercise, sleep, and stress control. (This is where your Natural Health Makeover comes in.)

- Natural medicines work best when the principles of natural health are adhered to (see Chapter 1).

- Each person is unique. This means that different herbs, nutrients, and lifestyle steps must be made to fit each individual's needs.

- Self-care is the first level of health care. But if you don't get better using the following suggestions, consult with your doctor or a natural health care professional.

ACNE

At the bottom of each hair follicle is a pouch called the sebaceous gland. When natural oils get trapped in that pouch and bacteria grow, a pimple is born—red and inflamed. Pimples occur mainly on the face, and occasionally on the back, chest and shoulders.

Many things cause this most common skin problem. Hormonal changes, such as during puberty (especially in boys), or just before a period or mid-cycle for women. Various chemicals and pollutants can also aggravate or create acne. Others break out from poor food selections, or a reaction to certain foods. Low levels of nutrients can also aggravate an acne problem. Also see Canker Sores, Eczema, Hives, Psoriasis; refer to Chapter 12 (skin).

How to Prevent Pimples

- Drink water. Make sure it's pure and plentiful.

- Avoid overwashing your face. Once in the morning and once before bed should be adequate.

- Pick plain-jane soaps. Avoid cleansers with perfumes, colorings, and other unnecessary ingredients. Glycerine soaps work well for many; or try a soap with the herb calendula added, or vitamins A or E.
- Take makeup breaks. Leave your face bare at night, on weekends, whenever you don't need to look stunning.
- Be choosy about your cosmetics. Like soap, choose makeup that's free of potentially allergenic materials. Look into natural cosmetics free of skin-annoying ingredients.
- Protect your skin from pollutants. Also look out for machine oils, coal tar derivatives, chlorinated hydrocarbons.
- Use filtered water to wash your face, particularly if your tap water smells like chlorine.

Food and Nutrition for Acne

- Sugar be gone! Also avoid other refined carbohydrates like white flour.
- Stick with whole grains such as whole wheat and brown rice.
- Be careful of fats. Keep saturated fat and overall fat intake down.
- No more margarine or any foods containing trans fatty acids or hydrogenated oils (read labels).
- Add good fats. Your skin does need essential fatty acids found in flax seed oil (take 1 tbsp daily—see Makeover Hint #65—Flax Appeal), raw, unsalted nuts and seeds, fish and whole grains.
- Keep carbohydrates to a dull roar. For some, too many carbohydrate foods (pastas, breads) make acne worse.
- Avoid commercial milk. The hormones added to commercial milk worsen some cases of acne. Drink organic milk instead, or a dairy substitute like soy or rice milk.
- Get enough protein. This means beans and legumes, organic poultry, fish, lean meats, nuts and seeds.
- Pass on the pop. High in sugar and additives, soft drinks do nothing to prevent pimples.
- Caffeine is a no-no, whether it's in pop, coffee, or black tea.
- Make sure your multiple vitamin and mineral supplement contains: vitamin C (1000 mg), vitamin E (400 IU), zinc (50 mg for two months, then 15 mg maintenance), chromium (200 mcg).

- Vitamin A. Very high amounts of this vitamin improve acne. However, if you'd like to try this nutrient, see your doctor for help as high doses taken for a long period are potentially toxic.

Herbal Treatment

- Acne lotion—calendula, chickweed, witch hazel
- Dry skin—burdock, cleavers
- Clear skin through better liver function—blue flag, dandelion
- General skin herbs—red clover, yellow dock

The Homeopathic Difference

Using homeopathic remedies alone will not solve an acne problem—especially if you're taking them in low potency, acute fashion. Most pimples require lifestyle changes. If you have a particularly resistant case of acne and want to try homeopathy, consult with a professional homeopath for constitutional prescribing. In the meantime, you can try one of these remedies for temporary and partial relief.

- Belladonna—*Acne rosacea.* When you think Belladonna, think red alternating with pale skin. Along with pustules, your face may feel dry, red, and hot. This remedy is specific for acne rosacea, a chronic inflammatory skin condition of the mid face that usually begins in middle age or later.

- Hepar sulphuris calcareum—*Teenage acne.* If you or your youngster has moist blemishes, the type prone to forming pus, this may help. Some might also feel a prickly-type pain; others find their acne bleeds easily. Cold, dry, and touching the skin make it worse.

- Ledum—*Forehead pimples.* For those blemishes on the forehead, try Ledum. Some find a sticking pain accompanies this type of acne. Cold makes it better.

- Sulphur—*Unwashable acne.* These blemishes are not only dry and itchy with pustules, but burning as well. There's an unhealthy look to the skin. Scratching the itch makes the acne worse as does washing. For some, these pimples appear after using a topical medication.

Lifestyle Link

- Sunshine. Aim for 15 to 20 minutes daily; avoid the most intense times from noon to 3pm.
- Soap alternatives. Regular soap can make acne worse. Try a calendula-based cleanser instead. For the very sensitive, wash with warm water and pat your skin dry.
- Try a Bentonite clay mask.
- Consider PMS. Acne directly before a menstrual period may be part of premenstrual syndrome. Try taking a B-complex with adequate vitamin B_6.
- Digestive woes. For some, poor digestion of food can aggravate acne. Adopt the eating style recommended under Food and Nutrition. If this doesn't solve the problem, try using hydrochloric acid or digestive enzymes (See Chapter 4).

■ *Makeover Hint #82—Break Out the Tea Tree Oil*

Tea tree oil, also known as *Melaleuca alternifolia*, has bacteria-fighting properties. Apply this oil to acne-affected skin a couple of times each day. Some people are sensitive to full-strength tea tree oil, so dab a small amount on a sample skin area first. If the oil burns or irritates you, dilute it half and half in vegetable oil before applying.

ALLERGIES

See Hay fever.

ANXIETY

Unlike fear, which is directed at a specific person, thing, or situation, anxiety is vague. It's a physical, psychological, and behavioral response to stress. Many things contribute to anxiety: heredity, childhood experiences, health, and lifestyle. Our fast-paced lives—where quick adaptation to change is essential—create stress and anxiety. In addition, pollutants, chemicals, poor food choices and health habits allow anxiety to grow. For more information, see Fatigue, Headaches, Insomnia, Low Blood Sugar. Turn to Chapters 7 (adrenal glands), 8 (the heart), and 14 (the mind) for related topics.

How to Prevent Anxiety

- The balancing act. Try to divide your time equally between physical activity and mental exertion. This will relieve stress and prevent anxiety.

- Delegate. We get anxious when there's too much to do. You can't do it all, so learn what can be delegated (household chores, work duties), what you personally must do, and what activities are not essential and can be tossed.

- The right company. Associate with positive people, ones who will support you, not undermine or doubt you. While you're at it, stick with positive reading material, TV shows (even the news), and other forms of entertainment. (There's no rule that you *have* to watch violence even if everyone else is.)

- Exercise. Physical activity works off tension, floods your body with oxygen, and is generally invigorating.

- Relax. Easier said than done. Nevertheless, make a list of activities that truly calm you down, like walking, reading romance novels, planting flowers. Then take time to do them every day.

- Sleep. Fatigue magnifies most problems, both physical and emotional. So when you feel irritable, go to bed early.

- Chemical alert. The stressors that promote anxiety aren't just mental and emotional—they're also physical. Besides the above, reduce chemicals in your home and workplace, including household cleaners, solvents and pesticides. (See Makeover Hint #3—Less is More).

Food and Nutrition to Calm You

- Downsize caffeine. Caffeine, whether it's in coffee, black tea, chocolate, or soda pop, is a stimulant. It can create insomnia and robs your body of thiamin, vital for proper nervous system function.

- Sugar blues. Coffee's partner in crime is usually a glazed doughnut or other sweet delight. Refined sugar boosts blood sugar and mood temporarily. Soon afterward, both plummet leaving you crabby and anxious.

- Spare the salt. Too much salt depletes potassium, a mineral necessary for proper nerve functioning.

- Eat slowly and moderately. Reasonable portions eaten in a relaxed atmosphere will not only help digestion, but can calm and center you.

- Have a Papa-bowl of oatmeal for breakfast. Oats are well-known for nourishing the nervous system.

- B-complex. This family of vitamins (thiamin, riboflavin, niacin, B_6, folic acid, B_{12}) nourish the nervous system so they help you handle stress better, and keep anxiety down.

- Calcium and magnesium (1000 mg and 500 mg) taken daily are relaxing.

Herbal Treatment

- Calming—linden, oats, passion flower, skullcap, valerian
- Nervous digestion—chamomile, hops, peppermint
- Insomnia—lady's slipper, passion flower, valerian
- Muscle tension—skullcap, valerian

The Homeopathic Difference

- Arsenicum album—*Great fear and anxiety.* A restless nature accompanied by chilliness, fatigue, and weakness is the mark of someone who suits Arsenicum. This anxious type is also a clean freak, striving to control her environment. She's also possessive of things and people because of insecurity.

- Ignatia—*Changeable mood.* Ignatia is known as the grief remedy. It's often appropriate for someone who's suffering from grief or worry. Sighing and weeping are common signs, as are a tendency to be inward and non-communicative. Moods change quickly.

- Lycopodium—*Fear of rejection*. The anxious person who can't function in social gatherings because he worries about what others think fits the Lycopodium mold. A false air of bravado may be used to hide these insecurities, to the point of being overbearing. At the same time, he's afraid to try new things. Lycopodium-types like others around—but not too close.

- Rhus toxicodendron—*On the move*. A restless, anxious person fits the picture of Rhus tox. This need for movement continues on into bedtime, so much so that tossing and turning in bed makes it difficult to sleep. Even his mind won't stop moving when the lights are turned out.

Lifestyle Link

- Stop smoking. A recent study discovered that more women with panic disorders (an extreme form of anxiety) were smokers than were their anxiety-free sisters.[1]

- Eliminate drugs. Stimulating drugs like cocaine and amphetamines feed an anxious mood. If you can't stop on your own, seek help from an addictions expert.

- Take a snooze. While it may be difficult to fall asleep, dozing is imperative. Anxiety climbs when you are sleep-deprived.

- Other problems. If a past trauma or current situations are creating or aggravating your anxiety, seek the help of a counselor.

Lookout Alert

When anxiety grows beyond normal apprehension in intensity or duration and begins interfering with everyday life, it's termed a panic disorder. Here are some signs to watch for.

- Sense of terror for no rational reason
- Inability to catch your breath
- Racing heartbeat, irregular heartbeat, or sharp chest pains
- Trembling, sweating, or dizziness
- Anxiety accompanied by nausea and/or diarrhea
- Connection with reality lost

ARTHRITIS

See Gout.

BACKACHE

Most people suffer from back pain at one time or another. Very often tension underlies stiff or sore muscles. Other common aggravators include poor posture and gait, a "beer" belly, incorrect lifting techniques, and injuries—immediate or past. A herniated or ruptured disc, infection or fracture of the back bone or other more serious afflictions that require medical attention are possibilities too.

Seemingly unrelated conditions can also bring on back pain. Things like a bladder infection, uterine fibroids or cysts or infections, osteoporosis, osteoarthritis, menstrual cramps, and pregnancy can cause you to grasp your back and moan. Knowing exactly what's behind your aching back is important in solving this problem. Also be aware of whether this is an acute (immediate) problem, chronic (long-standing) trouble or a combination of both. Also see Anxiety, Headaches, Sprains & Strains, Urinary Tract Infections. Refer to Chapters 5 (kidneys), 9 (muscles), 11 (bones), and 14 (the mind) as well for more information.

How to Prevent Backaches

- Practice perfect posture. Stand up straight, tilt your pelvis in and your shoulders back. This may feel unnatural, but after awhile it'll become second nature.
- Sit up straight—for all of you who are chained to a desk.
- A gracious gait. When you move improperly, back troubles can arise.
- Lift and separate. When carrying heavy (or even light) objects, use common sense. Bend down with a straight back and lift.
- Help for the heavies. If a load is more than you can carry, ask for help.
- Be flexible. A supple, fluid spine has fewer problems. Use stretching or yoga to gain flexibility and iron out the kinks.
- Plain old exercise. Regular physical activity helps prevent back pain.

- Down with stress. Often backaches aren't so much physical as emotional and mental in origin. (After all, isn't that where most tension begins?) Learn to cope, and your back will love you for it.
- Breathe for your back. Deep and conscious breathing relaxes tension and increases oxygen flow to all your muscles (see Makeover Hint #79—The Right Way to Breathe In and Out).

Food and Nutrition for Healing

- Vitamin C and bioflavonoids. These nutrients, taken in equal amounts (1000 mg each daily), help strengthen connective tissue, and thus your back. If you're a smoker, quit, or at the very least take an extra 3000 mg spread throughout the day; smoking depletes vitamin C levels.
- Antioxidants. Besides vitamin C, add a general antioxidant supplement to your daily regimen, while healing.
- Bromelain or bust. This enzyme from the pineapple stem reduces pain and inflammation when taken between meals. Pancreatic enzymes can also be taken this way.
- Tackle inflammation. For back problems that are red, swollen, and hurting (signs of inflammation), avoid foods that promote swelling. These include saturated fats (in red meat, poultry skin, dairy fat) and turn instead to the essential fatty acids (flax seed oil, fish, nuts and seeds) that diminish inflammation.
- Drink water.
- Manganese. Take 50 to 100 mg of this mineral daily, in divided doses for two weeks.
- Extra calcium and magnesium. Load up on these minerals for awhile if muscle spasm is a problem. Include a dose (300 mg/150 mg) before bed with a snack if you can't sleep. Beware: too much magnesium can cause diarrhea.

Herbal Treatment

- Loosen muscles—skullcap, valerian
- Pain—black willow, Jamaican dogwood, St. John's wort, valerian

- Herbal liniment can include (don't use any of these on broken skin)—peppermint (oil), rosemary (oil), St. John's wort
- Help sleep—passion flower, valerian

■ *Makeover Hint #83—In a Pinch, Use a Pinch of These*

It's late, you've thrown your back out and the stores are closed. Here's a recipe for a homemade liniment.

1/4 tsp of *either* cayenne powder, ginger powder, or mustard powder

1 tsp of KY jelly or cream

Mix the two together and apply to back pain. Do not smear on sensitive or broken skin. And don't leave this mixture on too long. Watch for reddening of the skin or a warm feeling, then wipe off.

The Homeopathic Difference

- Calcarea fluorica—*Low back pain.* When your lower back gives you trouble, and eases up with a little stretching and walking about, think of Calcarea fluorica.
- Phosphorus—*Right between the shoulder blades.* Phosphorus addresses burning backaches, especially between the shoulder blades. Only sleeping in a dark room and lying on your right side feels good. Almost everything else makes it hurt: touch, warm food or drink, weather change, evening, climbing stairs, physical exertion . . . even thinking.
- Rhus toxicodendron—*Worse after a good night's rest.* You know those backaches that feel terrible after lying down for awhile? This is what you take for it. You'll probably find a little movement and heat will limber it up, though.
- Sabina—*I can't move.* This remedy offers help for a very specific type of trouble: paralytic pain in the small of the back. It feels worse with the smallest movement and heat, although cool fresh air brings some relief.

Lifestyle Link

- Ice it. The coolness of an ice pack helps reduce swelling for an acute backache. Do this for 24 hours, then alternate ice with a heating pad for a few days.

- Rest times four. For an immediate injury, don't overdo it and rest for at least four days. Use your pain as a gauge for your activity during the first week following an injury.

- Visit your local back specialist. This could be a massage therapist, chiropractor, osteopathic doctor, naturopathic physician, or physical therapist. The earlier you get help, the better your chances of recovery from an acute problem.

- Try acupuncture. This ancient Oriental art is wonderful for pain control; a series of treatments might help those with chronic back troubles.

- Uneven legs. Some people have one leg longer than the other. Ask your doctor about shoe lifts to correct this problem.

Lookout Alert

If muscular and stress control techniques don't help within a week, see your doctor for a diagnosis of your problem. If you experience these symptoms in addition to your back pain, seek professional help.

- Fever
- Flank pain
- Painful or burning urination
- Frequent or urgent urination, or frequent nighttime urination
- Sudden backache without known cause
- Severe back pain

BLADDER INFECTIONS

See Urinary Tract Infections.

BRONCHITIS (ACUTE)

This usual winter-time affliction is literally an inflammation of the bronchi found in the lungs. It often begins as a cold with runny nose, fever and chills, sore throat and achy muscles. Then it progresses into an upper respiratory infection where a cough develops—first dry and non-productive, then wetter with mucus. Some people experience difficulty breathing and chest pain as well. Pollution, fatigue, and stress, taxing the body with poor eating, and not enough exercise increase your susceptibility to this condition.

Like a cold, the body can heal bronchitis—a generally mild malady—without treatment (though suggestions below will hopefully help you recover more quickly or at least with fewer symptoms). However, older or debilitated people must be wary, or they might end up with pneumonia if not careful. Chronic bronchitis, not covered here, is often caused by smoking. Also see Colds and Flu, Coughing, Ear Infections, Fever, Sore Throat; refer to Chapter 6 (immunity).

How to Prevent Bronchitis

- Avoid bronchial infection by boosting immunity (see Chapter 7). This means get enough sleep, eat right, and avoid overdoing it.

- Prepare for winter. Harsh winters, like those we endure in South Dakota, are hard on everyone no matter how healthy. So I get ready by religiously taking my vitamins and minerals, loading up on vitamin C (1000 mg three times a day), drinking immune boosting teas like echinacea, and watching the sugar and exercise.

- Hibernate. Another resistance-building activity is snoozing. For those who live in colder climates, don't be alarmed if you find you need another hour's worth of sleep each night during winter.

- Avoid exposure to infected individuals.

- Don't smoke. And non-smokers, avoid exposure to second-hand smoke.

- Consider allergic possibilities. Ask your doctor if you can be tested for inhalant or food allergies. Avoid offending substances for at least one month and see what happens.

Food and Nutrition for Your Lungs

- Hot and spicy. Indulge in all your favorite spicy foods like jalapeno and other hot peppers, mustard, horseradish, garlic, and onions.

- Did I mention garlic and onions? These are natural bug slayers.

- No more mucus. Side-stepping sugar, dairy foods, starches, and eggs, as well as other potentially allergenic foods like citrus fruits and high-gluten grains (wheat, oats, barley, and rye) can diminish phlegm.

- Flood yourself with fluids. This means pure water, herbal teas, broths, and fresh vegetable juices. Avoid fruit juices, as the fruit sugar drags down immunity.

- Avoid sugar.

- Take your multi. Be sure it contains vitamin A, E, and zinc—all helpful for bronchitis.

- Don't take iron while sick. This mineral promotes bacterial growth.

- Extra vitamin C and bioflavonoids. Take 500 to 1000 mg of each every two hours. If you experience any gastric problems (diarrhea, gas, cramps), cut back.

Herbal Treatment

- Fight bugs—echinacea, elecampane, garlic, thyme
- Ease coughing—coltsfoot, elecampane, mullein, thyme
- Expectorants—elecampane, hyssop, thyme, white horehound
- Soothe bronchi—elecampane, marshmallow leaf

The Homeopathic Difference

See Coughing for other homeopathic suggestions.

- Antimonium tartaricum—*So much mucus, so little time.* The bronchi feel like they're overloaded with mucus, yet not much is coughed up. There's a rattling sound, too, when you cough, and a burning sensation in the chest. It all feels better sitting up, not so good lying down.

- Bryonia—*Deep chest cough*. This common cough remedy is for painful, dry coughs that have traveled into the chest. When you ask someone with this type of cough if it hurts, he'll reply, "Only when I breathe and move." Ironically, lying on the sore spot feels better. Those with a Bryonia-type cough are thirsty, tired, and irritable.

- Ipecac—*The cough that rattles*. This cough is deep, wet, and rattles because of all the mucus that has settled in the lungs. Breathing out is difficult, and much harder than taking air in. Coughing is so intense at times it may result in gagging or vomiting.

- Kali muriaticum—*Bronchial congestion that's stuck*. There's tenacious mucus in your bronchi, so thick and white that it's difficult to cough up. Like Ipecac, this bronchial cough rattles, but the cough is short and spasmodic, more like a whooping sound. Some hoarseness may result too, as well as a white or gray tongue.

Lifestyle Link

- Avoid smoky rooms. Tobacco fumes only make matters worse.
- Don't drink. Alcohol, caffeine, and pop, that is.
- Get your beauty (and health) sleep. Take naps, go to bed early, stay home from work and watch the soaps, whatever it takes to give your body time to heal.
- Inhale hot steam. Use a vaporizer at night and when you're resting. Add a few drops of eucalyptus oil to the water, or a dash of Vicks Vapor Rub™ (contains eucalyptus) for lung soothing steam.
- Soak in a hot tub. Add eucalyptus oil here too.
- Kick out the pets. If you also have allergies to cats and dogs, and heaven forbid, have one living with you, consider asking it to leave. At the very least, don't sleep with it. (I actually love animals, especially my two cats.)
- Watch for indoor pollution. New carpets, paint, homes, and cars emit poisonous fumes. If you're susceptible to bronchitis, or seem worse in a new home or new car, rethink how you live.

Lookout Alert

If your bronchitis or cough is ongoing and doesn't appear to be infectious, watch for other causes. Various dusts, fumes from strong acids or volatile solvents, cigarette or other smoke might be irritating your lungs and causing inflammation. Other signs to take note of are:

- Fever lasting a week or longer
- Any severe symptoms, or those lasting more than a couple of weeks
- Shortness of breath upon exertion
- A bluish tinge to your skin
- Recurrent bronchial infections
- Unintentional weight loss
- Persistent weakness
- Chronic wheezing that's worse upon lying down

CANKER SORES

Canker sores are small painful sores that range in size from a mere pinpoint to 1/2 inch and appear singly or in groups of two to 15. Doctors call these mini-mouth ulcers aphthous stomatitis or ulcerative stomatitis. While they usually clear up on their own in one to three weeks, they also tend to recur. One in five individuals is cursed, most of them women. These are different from cold sores, which are caused by the herpes virus.

While no one is entirely sure why canker sores develop, some theorize it's a localized immune reaction or possibly an autoimmune (the immune system attacking your mouth) reaction. For some, food sensitivities spark an outbreak. Others find stress a precipitating factor. Nutrient deficiencies have also been implicated. Read Chapter 6 (immunity) for more information.

How to Prevent Canker Sores

- Manage stress. When life becomes overwhelming, it not only breaks your spirit, but your immunity too. For those who are susceptible, canker sores are one way to express stress.

- Stay rested. Sleep deprivation sets some people up for a canker recurrence.
- Pick your dentist well. Dental trauma can lead to canker sores.
- Prepare for heat. Extreme heat—caused by weather, fevers, or exercise—spark canker sores in some.

Food and Nutrition for Your Mouth

- Nutrient deficiencies, especially of folic acid, pantothenic acid, vitamin B_{12}, iron, add to canker sores. Take these as part of a multiple vitamin and mineral pill.
- Fill up on vitamin C. This nutrient helps repair mouth tissue and, if allergies are present, acts as an antihistamine. Take 500 to 1000 mg three times each day.
- Zinc. Known for its wound-repairing abilities, zinc heals canker sores in some people. Try 25 mg (as zinc picolinate) for no longer than two months.
- Food sensitivities. Canker sores can be an allergic reaction to food (dairy, wheat, tomato, pineapple). Try eliminating these for a couple of weeks and see what happens.
- Help digestion. Take acidophilus before bed to help reestablish bowel bugs. (Important if you have a history of antibiotic use.) Also try digestive enzymes with meals.

Herbal Treatment

- Decrease stress—linden, oats, passion flower, skullcap, valerian
- Improve immunity—cleavers, echinacea
- Mouth wash (make a tea with these herbs, rinse and swallow)—chamomile, sage
- Nutritive herbs—alfalfa, dandelion, nettles, oats

■ *Makeover Hint #84—Chew on Licorice*

Herbal licorice (not the candy) has been proven to help heal canker sores. One of the most effective forms is deglycyrrhizinated licorice (DGL) in chewable tablets, best taken before meals.[2] You can find these at your local health food store.

The Homeopathic Difference

- Borax—*Bitter taste.* For canker sores that are hot and painful to the touch, and cause a bitter taste in your mouth, think Borax. These sores are so tender, they may bleed while eating. This remedy is fitting for those who have a concurrent thrush (mouth yeast) infection going on.

- Kali muriaticum—*A white, gray-coated tongue.* Like Borax, this type of canker sore can accompany thrush, as well as a coated tongue. Also look for swollen glands about the neck and jaw.

- Phosphorus—*Gums that bleed.* These canker sores are found in a mouth with bleeding gums; your mouth feels dry and thirsty, and you yearn for cold water. Like many canker sores, stress only makes Phosphorus sores worse, as does touching the painful area, and indulging in warm food and drink.

- Sulphuricum acidum—*Bad breath!* This canker sore remedy also includes gums that bleed easily, and possibly sores with pus. Poor digestion may be a contributing cause. No wonder your breath is bad.

Lifestyle Link

- Allergies. Possibly an allergic reaction . . . are you worse during pollen season or other times? Do you have other allergic reactions? Keep track of your outbreaks and see if you can pinpoint sores to a particular time, place, or exposure to, for example, pets or food.

Lookout Alert

- Sore that doesn't heal
- Severe pain
- Sores that are white, gray, yellowish, or brownish in color
- Persistent sores on the tongue
- Facial swelling
- Seek help if you're a long-term smoker

COLDS AND FLU

There is a respiratory tract condition that occurs so frequently, it's been dubbed the common cold. Most are familiar with its runny nose, sneezing, sore throat, headache, fever, and general ill feeling. Slightly less common, but still a winter regular, is influenza or the flu. It is often difficult to distinguish this illness from a cold, but it differs in its abrupt onset, shorter duration and more pronounced fever, chills, muscle aches, and fatigue. Also see Bronchitis, Coughing, Ear Infections, Fever, and Sore Throat. Read Chapter 6 (immunity).

How to Prevent a Cold or Flu

- Avoid exposure to infected individuals.
- Don't strain your brain. Mental fatigue, emotional distress, and physical exhaustion all invite colds and the flu.
- Get enough sleep. Eight hours per night on average; more if you need it. This is more important than you think.
- Eat plenty of fresh fruits and vegetables (this is your mother talking); don't forget whole grains.
- A daily dose of essential fatty acids (see Makeover Hint #65— Flax Appeal).
- If the air is dry where you live, use a humidifier.

Food and Nutrition for Colds and Flu

- Don't eat sugar. This means white sugar, brown sugar, maple syrup, honey, fructose and anything else masquerading as sugar. Ginger ale and 7-up are no-no's too. You can have some when you're better, but not when you're sick.
- Stay away from alcohol and caffeine (coffee, black tea, chocolate and cocoa, soft drinks).
- If you must drink fruit juices, dilute them half and half with water. Contrary to what we've been told, gallons of orange juice don't cure a cold—they make it worse.
- Drink lots of fluids like water, herbal teas, and homemade vegetable broth.

- Eat only to appetite. If you're not hungry, it's simple—don't eat. (Listen to your body.)

- Load up on vitamin C-packed foods such as broccoli, green peppers, tomatoes, and alfalfa sprouts. Or supplement with 1000 mg vitamin C every two hours. If you develop stomach cramps or diarrhea while taking vitamin C pills, cut back on the dosage. This vitamin C treatment is even more effective if taken with the same amount of bioflavonoids, also found in fresh fruits and vegetables.

- Avoid iron while ill.

- Go for the gold and orange and yellow and dark green vegetables—all packed with beta-carotene. Or use pills, about 200,000 IU daily while ill.

- Lace your breath with garlic and onions. So smelly, they keep the germs away.

■ Makeover Hint #85—Help From the Kitchen

Mix these common kitchen ingredients together in a mug to make a cold-fighting herbal tea or choose just one (up to 2–3 tsp. of total dried herb). Add boiling water, cover with a saucer, and steep for 15 minutes. Strain and drink.

1 tsp ginger (root or powder)

1 tsp sage (dried or powder)

1 bag of peppermint tea

Herbal Treatment

- Achy joints and headache—black willow, meadow sweet
- Coughing—elecampane, grindelia, mullein
- Fever—elder, feverfew, yarrow
- Runny nose—ephedra
- Bug battlers—astragalus, echinacea, goldenseal

The Homeopathic Difference

- Aconite—*Sudden symptoms.* If someone touches you, you're going to scream! Your head hurts, you're burning up, and bright red blood is seeping from your nose. You feel like a caged cat, restless and anxious. Use this remedy for the first 24 hours of your illness, particularly for that cold or flu that appears abruptly.

- Allium cepa—*A cold like an onion.* Those same symptoms caused by dicing an onion—burning eyes, nose, and lips, along with profuse, searing, clear discharge—is the Allium cold. Look for thirst, minimal fever, and symptoms that are better in the open air.

- Bryonia—*Chest cold.* You sound like a seal—dry, spasmodic, hacking cough. Everything seems to ache—your head, muscles and joints. What's left? To make matters worse, your mouth feels like the Sahara Desert; more water please! You "want to be alone" in the dark and feel cranky. All this feels worse when you move about.

- Gelsemium—*The three "Ds"—drowsy, droopy eyelids, dull.* You've had this type of downer cold before. It may start with a tickle in your throat and drop in energy. Pretty soon, moving, or even thinking, is asking too much. Your nose is running with watery stuff, but you don't feel like drinking anything. You feel chilly, stiff, and have a headache along your upper back and nape of the neck; all this sends you hibernating to the bedroom.

- Nux vomica—*Your cold is the fault of a cold, dry winter.* Aaaahhhhh. . . . choo!! You can't stop sneezing. And to make things worse, your nose can't make up its mind if it's stuffed up or running. Your throat is sore and raw with a feather-duster tickle of a cough. The light hurts your eyes, your tummy is queasy and you're constipated. You are definitely crabby. The morning is your worst time; eating doesn't help either.

- Pulsatilla—*Chilly crybaby.* Thick yellowish, green stuff is oozing from your nose—thank goodness it's bland, not burning. To top off your aching head is a case of diarrhea and nausea. You feel like a little baby, happy one minute, crying the next. Food and drink don't interest you.

Lifestyle Link

- Take naps—it's very European. Sleep longer at night too. Rest is vital to healing.

- Only exercise if you feel up to it. This is no time to train for a marathon; reserve your energy for getting better.

- Practice being lazy. Keep your work load to a minimum and delegate extra tasks so you can take it easy. Better yet, stay home and watch *Oprah*.

- Vaporize your air if coughing, a dry throat, or stuffed-up nose are keeping you awake. Add four drops of eucalyptus oil, a glob of Vicks™ or other chest rub containing eucalyptus to a vaporizer. Not only will the warm steam ease you, but the exotic smell of eucalyptus will help breathing (and announce to the rest of the household that you're sick).

Lookout Alert

- Yellow eyes or skin
- Very light-colored stools
- Dark looking urine
- Stiff neck, especially if it's painful upon bending
- Extremely painful headache
- Convulsions
- Severe symptoms, especially fatigue, weakness, irritability or confusion
- Extreme breathing problems, chest pain and wheezing (critical in infants)
- Sudden or unrelenting vomiting or diarrhea (most critical in children)
- If your illness lasts one week without noticeable improvement

CONSTIPATION

Constipation is a common problem, often due to poor food choices. Little or no roughage, provided by fruits, vegetables, and whole grains, slows food's trip through the intestines. The result is infrequent, incomplete bowel movements that are difficult to evacuate. Faulty health habits are the most frequent reasons for constipation, as well as a "sluggish" liver (see Chapter 3); other more critical conditions such as hypothyroidism or diverticulosis can also be the cause. In persons over 50, constipation lasting more than a week may be a sign of a more serious health problem. Also see Hemorrhoids and Indigestion; refer to Chapter 4 (digestion).

How to Prevent Constipation

Since most cases of constipation are caused by slips in diet and exercise, preventive measures are much the same as the Lifestyle Links it takes to correct this problem. Also consider . . .

- New medicines. If you become constipated after starting a new medication, mention it to your doctor. Many common medicines can plug up bowels. These include antipsychotics, muscle relaxants, antidepressants, and blood pressure medications.
- Beware of laxatives and enemas. How ironic that these very same medicines and techniques we use to correct constipation can eventually exacerbate the problem. This is because after a while the body relies on these aids, and is unable to go on its own.
- Plan for travel. Unfamiliar bathrooms are well-known constipation makers. Before a trip, remember to drink lots of water, eat lots of fiber, breathe frequently and, just to be safe, carry some herbal laxatives for temporary relief.

Food and Nutrition for Constipation

- Fluids, fluids, and more fluids. Water is your best bet here.
- Fill up on fiber. Once again, those foods are vegetables, fruit, whole grains, beans, and legumes.
- Is it your iron supplement? Some iron supplements (sulfate, gluconate) can plug up bowels. If you need extra iron (and most people don't), try iron picolinate, succinate, or fumarate.

Herbal Treatment

Just because a laxative is herbal and "natural" doesn't make it the solution to stalled bowels. I occasionally recommend herbal laxatives as a step toward normalizing bowel movements for patients who have used laxatives chronically. After switching to an herbal laxative tea, I have them gradually decrease the amount they drink (e.g., one cup daily the first week, 1/2 cup daily the second week) while making dietary and lifestyle changes.

- To bulk up stools—flax, oat bran, psyllium
- Laxatives—aloe, barberry, cascara, dandelion, rhubarb root, senna, yellow dock
- Liver/gallbladder help—barberry, blue flag, dandelion, milk thistle, yellow dock
- Tonify the colon—rhubarb root

The Homeopathic Difference

- Alumina—*Soft, sticky stools.* This remedy works best for hard and dry stools. There's no desire for a bowel movement, yet the rectum is sore, maybe bleeding and possibly itchy and burning. When you do go to the bathroom, great straining is involved.
- Bryonia—*The child's remedy.* For children who have great difficulty passing dry, dark stools.
- Graphites—*Large and smelly.* Graphites is for a type of constipation where stools are large, smelly, and made up of many lumps stuck together with mucus.
- Silicea—*Bashful stools.* The so-called bashful stools, those that may slip back when partially expelled, and in this case are large and hard, are best treated with Silicea.

Lifestyle Link

- Move that body. Regular physical activity helps move bowels too.
- Stress release. Tension, be it emotional or mental, creates tight intestines too.
- Intolerant foods. Food allergies can be the cause of chronic constipation.

- Leave laxatives alone. Reliance on these medicines (including herbs) can add to constipation problems.
- Correct digestion problems. Try taking acidophilus, 1/8 teaspoon two times daily, to re-seed the good bugs in your colon, especially if your problem began after antibiotic use.

Lookout Alert

- Constipation that alternates with diarrhea
- Blood in the stool
- Mucus or pus in the stool
- Black tarry stools
- Severe and/or unrelenting stomach pain or cramps
- Constipation that accompanies fatigue, cold intolerance, weight gain, and dry skin

COUGHING

To cough or not to cough is your body's way of cleaning out the lungs. The cough reflex is set off when something stimulates the airways. That something ranges from a virus to cigarette smoke.

If you wake up with a cough and fever, and your nose is running, no doubt your cough is due to a cold or other upper respiratory infection such as bronchitis. Smokers frequently wake in the morning hacking; long-term smokers develop "smoker's cough." Don't forget that living with a smoker, even if you don't indulge, can create a similar reaction.

Coughing in the absence of an infection or smoking may indicate an allergic reaction. If you cough only certain times of the year, this may be a reaction to pollen or other seasonal material. Watch if you only cough in particular environments, like at work—you may be reacting to noxious chemicals. Never ignore a persistent cough. It could indicate a more serious condition like emphysema or lung cancer. If your cough doesn't go away after using the following suggestions, visit your doctor. Also see Bronchitis, Colds and Flu, Ear Infections, Fever, Sore Throat; refer to Chapter 7 (immunity).

How to Prevent Coughing

- The reason is? To prevent a cough, you need to know what causes it.
- Avoid a cough due to infection by boosting immunity (see Chapter 7). This means get enough sleep, eat right, and avoid overdoing it.
- Avoid exposure to infected individuals.
- Don't smoke. Non-smokers, avoid exposure to second-hand smoke.
- Avoid or minimize exposure to toxic fumes. This means paints, solvents, and other poisonous chemicals. Use a face filter when exposure is unavoidable.
- Consider allergic possibilities. Ask your doctor if you can be tested for inhalant or food allergies. If possible, try avoiding the offending substance and see what happens.

Food and Nutrition for Coughs

- Drink water. Fluids like water, broth, and vegetable juices help break up lung congestion.
- No sugar.
- Avoid mucus-producing foods like milk and other dairy foods (cheese, butter, yogurt, ice cream), starches, eggs, and wheat.
- Aniseed, caraway, and fennel. These spices also have medicinal qualities, specifically, as expectorants and in calming respiratory spasms—in other words, cough. The pleasing taste of aniseed and fennel are also used to flavor cough medicines.
- Take time for thyme. Use this spice on food, make a tea, or take as an herbal remedy for irritating coughs.
- Food-based poultice. Applying different foods to the chest in order to help clear it out, or cause expectoration, is an old-time trick and one still used by naturopathic doctors. If you have mustard powder or horseradish in your cupboards, try making a poultice to relieve that nasty cough.
- Hot honey and lemon mixed together in a mug help soothe the throat and calm a cough.

- Avoid iron if cough is infectious.

■ *Makeover Hint #86—How to Make a Poultice*

A poultice is basically a pad, often containing healing ingredients, that is placed on an ailing body part. In this case, we're talking about a chest poultice specifically designed to open the airways for easier breathing and less coughing. Choose one of the following recipes for your cough. Do not use mustard or horseradish on very young children (under three) or those with sensitive skin.

MUSTARD POULTICE

3 Tbsp mustard powder

Water

Clean pillow case

Towel

Put mustard powder in a soup bowl. Add enough water to make a paste and stir. Spoon paste inside pillow case. Have patient lie down. Place pillow case on the patient's chest. Spread paste around inside case so it covers chest. (Note: Mustard paste is *inside* case, and not directly on patient's chest.) Place towel, and then blanket on top of the patient's pillow case poultice. Leave poultice on patient's chest until skin turns pink, or patient tells you that skin is warm. Be careful that the poultice doesn't burn the skin. Remove poultice. Patient may lean over edge of bed and expectorate into basin afterward.

HORSERADISH POULTICE

3 Tbsp horseradish

Clean pillow case

Towel

Follow same directions as for mustard poultice, but substitute horseradish for mustard powder paste. As with mustard poultice, don't leave horseradish on chest too long or skin will blister and burn.

■ *Makeover Hint #87—Homemade Cough Syrup*

1 large onion, cut up

3/4 cup honey

3 cloves garlic, diced

Mix onion, garlic, and honey in a large pot. Simmer over low heat for two to three hours. You can use a crockpot instead, if you like; cook for five to six hours on low. Take one teaspoon of onion/garlic syrup every hour or as needed for cough.

Herbal Treatment

Herbs work well for coughs, but you need to discover the underlying cause too. I suggest using herbal cough remedies only when your cough interferes with sleep or rest. Remember, a cough is your body's way of cleansing the lungs and healing. Also, don't ignore a cough that won't go away.

- Acute dry cough, soothing—marshmallow leaf, slippery elm
- Expectorant—angelica, coltsfoot, daisy, senega
- Bronchitis—mullein, pleurisy root, sundew, white horehound
- Catarrh—elecampane, elder flowers
- Pneumonia (See your doctor)—pleurisy root
- Respiratory relaxant—grindelia
- Whooping cough—mouse ear, sundew, white horehound
- General coughs; flavoring—licorice

The Homeopathic Difference

- Belladonna—*The crying cough*. When your throat is so red and raw that it makes you (or your child) weep when you cough, think of Belladonna.
- Bryonia—*Deep chest cough*. This common cough remedy is for painful, dry coughs that have traveled into the chest. When you ask someone with this type of cough if it hurts, he'll reply, "Only when I breathe and move." Ironically, lying on the sore

spot feels better. Those with a Bryonia-type cough are thirsty, tired, and irritable.

- Ipecac—*The cough that rattles*. This cough is deep, wet, and rattles because of all the mucus that has settled in the lungs. Breathing out is difficult, and much harder than taking air in. Coughing is so intense at times it may result in gagging or vomiting.

- Lachesis—*Choking cough*. A characteristic of Lachesis is that the slightest constriction around the throat is intolerable; this same feature makes coughing worse. Even swallowing water is hard. That tickle in the throat that bursts forth into a short, dry cough is typical for this remedy. It's worse around or during sleep-time.

- Spongia—*Sounds like a saw blade*. This harsh, croupy cough is dry, and may wake the afflicted early in the evening. Drinking liquids that are not ice cold makes the cough better, though talking, excitement, lying down, and alcohol bring it on.

Lifestyle Link

- Cough up phlegm and blow your nose one nostril at a time. Doing this helps keep your lungs clean and clear. Remember, a cough is how your body cleans out the lungs.

- If the air is dry where you live, use a humidifier; if needed, use a vaporizer at night.

- Apply a hot water bottle or heating pad on your chest for 20 minutes. Then lie on a bed, and hang your head over a pan. Cough out any loose phlegm.

- Avoid respiratory irritants, smoke, dust, or chemicals.

- Avoid environments that are too hot or too cold. Stay in places that have Mama-Bear temperatures—just right.

Lookout Alert

- Lingering cough
- Coughing up blood
- Swallowing something that blocks your air passages
- Coughing up a gritty-like substance
- Chest pain.

- Problems breathing
- Cough getting progressively worse
- Painful cough
- Cough is consistently worse after exercise or cold exposure
- Sudden or marked wheezing, vomiting, headaches, weakness, seizures or neck stiffness
- Accompanying symptoms persist or are severe

DIARRHEA

One way the body expels germs, toxins, and other irritants is through diarrhea—loose, watery, frequent stools. Stomach flu or other intestinal infections are its most common causes, followed by food poisoning. Emotional distress also creates fast-moving bowels. Dehydration from diarrhea, especially among children, is a major risk. Also see Anxiety, Food Poisoning, Indigestion; refer to Chapter 4 (digestion).

How to Prevent Diarrhea

- Cut back on caffeine. Too much coffee can cause diarrhea.
- Stay calm. Nerves, for some people, cause diarrhea.
- Careful of the water. When you travel or camp, carry bottled water with you.

Food and Nutrition for Digestion

- Eat yogurt. The culture, or good bugs, in this food can help tame infectious diarrhea.
- Alternately, you can take a *Lactobacillus acidophilus* or probiotic pill after the diarrhea is done to replace bugs lost from your colon.
- Avoid milk. Those who are lactose intolerant may experience diarrhea when they drink milk.
- Cut out the diet pop. Artificial sweeteners, especially in large amounts, can create diarrhea in some.

- Drink plenty of fluids, especially liquids with electrolytes like fruit and vegetable juices.

- Avoid eating for a while.

- After the worst has past, dine on soft foods: soup, cooked fruit, and yogurt.

- Eat apples, bananas, tomatoes, potatoes, and carrots, which might stop the diarrhea.

- Are you taking too much C? Overdosing on vitamin C can cause diarrhea, gas, bloating, and abdominal cramps. If that happens, stop taking it for awhile, then take smaller amounts.

- Is it magnesium? Loading up on magnesium can also lead to diarrhea. More than 500 to 600 mg daily is the laxative point for many people.

- Gorging on fresh fruit? If it's summer and you've eaten one too many peaches or other fruit, that might be the cause.

- If ongoing or recurrent, ask your doctor to check out food allergies.

■ *Makeover Hint #88—Natural Fluid Replacement*

Try this to restore lost fluids and electrolytes after a bout of diarrhea: mix equal amounts of tomato juice and cabbage juice together, and sip.

Herbal Treatment

- Astringent—agrimony, American cranesbill, greater plantain
- Chronic diarrhea (see your doctor)—black catechu
- Healing—agrimony, greater plantain
- Infectious—golden seal, Oregon grape
- In children—agrimony, meadow sweet, thyme
- Nervous diarrhea—tormentil

The Homeopathic Difference

A study conducted by Seattle physician and homeopath Jennifer Jacobs, M.D., M.P.H., proved once and for all that homeopathy helps diarrhea. She treated several children from Nicaragua, ages six months to five years, suffering from acute diarrhea. Each remedy was prescribed based on individual symptoms; a second group of children was given fake pills. After five days, the homeopathically treated children improved noticeably more than the others.[3] You too can use homeopathic remedies to ease diarrhea.

- Gelsemium—*Nervous diarrhea*. If you've ever had diarrhea because of fear, anxiety, or worry, this is the remedy for you. It'll help calm both you and your bowels.

- Phosphorus—*For that empty feeling*. When copious amounts of green stool leave you weak and empty-feeling—no pain, though—and keep you awake at night, think of Phosphorus.

- Podophyllum—*Painful and profuse*. Try this remedy for diarrhea involving a colicky pain and bad-smelling, watery green or yellow stools. This gushing and profuse diarrhea may alternate with a headache and is worse after eating, drinking, or moving about.

Lifestyle Link

- Rest.

Lookout Alert

- Diarrhea lasting more than a few days
- Alternates with constipation
- Fever, stomach cramps, blood or mucus in stool
- If person not drinking or eating (can lead to dehydration)
- Be particularly cautious in young children (they dehydrate more quickly)

EAR INFECTIONS

Many parents think ear infections during childhood are to be expected. It ain't necessarily so. The most common ear illness among kids three months to three years is acute otitis media, a bacterial or viral infection of the middle ear. This ailment often begins as a chest cold, though the first sign will probably be your child complaining of an earache. Very young children are often irritable or pull at their affected ear—which may look red. Nausea, vomiting, fever, and even diarrhea are other symptoms to watch for. Some kids suffer from temporary hearing loss.

A child's very anatomy contributes to this condition. That is, his winding ear tube allows mucus and germs to congregate and multiply—a perfect infection setup. According to Chinese Medicine, young children are natural mucus producers, hence those chronic runny noses you're forever wiping. However, like adults, we must look at a child's lifestyle, too, for causative clues. Food sensitivities and poor diet certainly contribute to chronic ear infections. Babies who are fed mother's milk versus formula are less apt to be affected. Exposure to second-hand smoke also increases a child's susceptibility to illness. Be especially aware of these factors if your child (or you) suffers from chronic or recurrent infections. Antibiotics and surgery (ear tubes) are not the only solutions.

Although adults do get ear infections and can use the following treatments, I'm focusing my suggestions on children since they're the most frequent victims. Also see Bronchitis, Colds and Flu, Coughing, Fever, Sore Throat; refer to Chapter 6 (immunity).

How to Prevent Ear Infections

- Breast feed. Nursing your infant exclusively until she's at least six months old is one of the best ways I know to avoid ear infections. Mother's milk is full of infection-fighting compounds, prevents food allergies from developing (one cause of ear infections), and is the perfect food for a new baby's developing gut.

- Stay away from the bottle. Babies fed formula in a bottle are at higher risk of ear infections than breast-fed children. If you do use a bottle, it's best to sit with your baby and hold him so his head is slightly elevated; don't lay him on his back with a propped bottle.

- Introducing baby to food. The premature introduction (before five or six months) of solid foods can damage a child's intestinal lining. The result is an increased risk of developing food allergies—which can contribute to ear infections.

- Delay certain foods. Introducing foods high on the allergy scale (wheat, dairy, corn, soy, tomatoes, citrus fruits, eggs, chocolate, peanuts) prematurely can create health problems later on . . . like ear infections.

- Groom defenses. Follow general immune-boosting ideas as outlined in Chapter 6.

Food and Nutrition for Earaches

- Sugar ban. All types of sugar (white, brown, honey—also glucose, dextrose, corn syrup, maltose). Read labels if you're not sure what has sugar.

- Dodge fruit juice. Young children often live on this sweet liquid. However, the fruit sugars in juice not only kill appetite for other foods and contribute to obesity, but can diminish your child's immunity. Avoid during illness (it really makes a difference); use as a treat other times. Best bet is to dilute fruit juice half and half with water.

- Boost fluids. Teach your children to love water. Also broths and fresh vegetable juices are fine.

- Push the veggies. A child does better with plenty of fresh vegetables and fruits, and whole grains. The younger they are when you offer them these foods, the more likely they are to eat them.

- Phase out fatty foods. Kids' fast food is often laden with fat. Cut this out, and their ears might feel better.

- Food sensitivities. During an acute infection, eliminate dairy foods. If there's no improvement, also cut out wheat, corn, and oranges. When the child is better, have a food allergy panel done by your doctor if ear infections keep coming back.

- Vitamin C. Decide the dose by multiplying their age × 100 mg up to 1000 mg; give every two hours while ill. Discontinue if child experiences diarrhea. (See Diarrhea)

- Beef up on carotenes. This is the orange-yellow-dark green color in vegetables. Eat extra servings, and take a supplement.
- Children's multi. During and as a precaution, give your child a multiple vitamin/mineral pill.
- Push probiotics. If you or your child has used antibiotics, or relied on them extensively in the past, supplement with acidophilus and other "probiotics" to replenish the good bacteria in the colon.
- Too little, too late. Specific nutrient deficiencies have been implicated in recurrent ear infections. If the above measures don't work, consult a knowledgeable nutritionist or naturopathic doctor on how to supplement. Nutrients to watch for include vitamin A, zinc, and iron. Note: iron shouldn't be given during an infection.

Herbal Treatment

- Ear drops (put in ear only; don't take by mouth)—aconite, garlic, golden seal, mullein, pasque flower, pennywort
- Bug killers—echinacea, garlic, golden seal, wild indigo
- Immune builders—echinacea, garlic, golden seal
- Increase circulation around ear—ginkgo
- Sleeping aids—chamomile, passion flower, skullcap, valerian

The Homeopathic Difference

- Belladonna—*Throbbing hot ear.* This is a great remedy for acute ear infections in children. The child might be sensitive to loud noises and touch, and cry out in her sleep from pain. The earache is worse in the afternoon and from lying down.
- Chamomila—*Whining and aching.* Another great child's remedy, Chamomile, fits children whose sore ears are ringing. Ears might feel stopped up, sometimes with a stitching pain. These earaches make the child hot and thirsty. The guiding symptom for this remedy is irritability that only a hug can calm.
- Kali muriaticum—*Chronic ear infection.* This remedy is most suitable for chronic conditions of the middle ear. Often the glands around the ear are also swollen, and the child hears snapping noises. Eating fatty foods makes it worse.

- Pulsatilla—*Stuffed-up ears*. Pulsatilla ears are red on the out-side, and feel full on the inside. A thick, smelly discharge might leak from the ears. The pain is worse at night, and when your child doesn't answer you it's probably because he can't hear.

Lifestyle Link

- Antibiotic myth. Studies show that antibiotics have been overused for children's ear infections.[4] Work with your doctor, and ask if you can try natural methods first with his guidance. If antibiotics are needed, see if you can decrease the dose and/or duration of treatment. (Be sure to follow up with pro-biotics. See Food and Nutrition for Earaches.)
- Hot and cold. Hydrotherapy, or water treatment, is an old-fashioned but effective natural therapy. For ear infections, place a comfortably hot washcloth to your child's sore ear for about five minutes. Alternate this with a comfortably cold cloth for a minute or so. Repeat this three times.
- Sleep and rest.
- Cover those ears. Especially when outside on cold winter days, wear a hat or scarf.

Lookout Alert

Most ear infections heal without complications. However, if your child displays any of the following signs, seek help from your physician. Also, if you suspect your child's hearing has declined and not returned after the infection clears, be sure to have her checked. This is critical for very small children, under the age of one.

- Sudden profound hearing loss
- Vertigo
- Chills and fever
- Headache
- Ear drainage
- Stiff neck
- Persistent vomiting or diarrhea
- Other ongoing and/or severe symptoms

ECZEMA

It's difficult to stop scratching and rubbing this very itchy skin rash called eczema. If you take a close look, you'll notice your skin is red, dry, and swollen with little blisters that eventually pop and ooze. Areas that are scratched become scaly and crusty, with thicker than normal skin. Elbow and knee creases are often affected, although other areas like the eyelids, neck, and wrists are also stricken. Doctors call this rash atopic dermatitis; atopic refers to eczema's allergic tendency. That is, people with this chronic rash often have a family history of allergies including eczema, hay fever, and asthma. About one out of every 20 people has it, and for many it begins in childhood and comes and goes throughout life. See related topics, Acne and Psoriasis. Read Chapter 12 (skin).

How to Prevent Eczema

- Pick the right parents. Those with eczema usually have a family history of this or other allergic-type conditions. You can't do anything about the genetics, but you can use natural treatments to minimize their effects.

- Moisturize skin. Especially in winter months, drink plenty of water and use moisturizing creams.

- Avoid skin irritants. This includes harsh soaps, household cleaners, and chemicals. I had one young patient whose eczema got considerably worse if her father didn't filter out the chlorine in her bath water.

- Eat right. See below.

Food and Nutrition for the Skin

- Eliminate allergic foods. Cow's milk, eggs, wheat, and tomatoes most commonly aggravate eczema—start by avoiding these for a month.

- Get rid of food additives. Shun foods with artificial colorings, flavorings, and preservatives. This is best done by sticking with whole, natural foods.

- Face the fats. Use essential fatty acids that quiet inflammation, rather than feed it. Begin with evening primrose oil (EPO), 1000 mg three times daily (for an adult) for at least two months. Then try switching to less expensive flax seed oil (1–2 Tbsp daily).

- Rub EPO directly on the sore spots.
- Eat fish. The fat in fish works as an anti-inflammatory.
- Kick out the steak and wine. Red meat and alcohol tend to make eczema worse by promoting inflammation.
- Zinc. This mineral is often low in those with eczema, a critical loss since it helps decrease inflammation and aids healing of the skin. Try 30 mg daily for a month, then switch to a more moderate 15 mg dose.
- Itch attack. For symptomatic relief, apply zinc oxide cream (see Zinc above).
- Multiple. Make sure your daily supplement contains vitamins A and E.

Herbal Treatment

- Skin cream—aloe, calendula, chamomile, chickweed, golden seal, St. John's wort
- Dry eczema—burdock, cleavers
- In children—nettles, red clover
- Itching (also see skin cream)—figwort
- Nervous eczema—nettles

■ *Makeover Hint #89—A Weedy Wash*

Can't stand that itch anymore? Look no farther than your backyard for an herb that'll help—chickweed. Pick the flowers and leaves, cut up and steep 1 Tbsp in a cup of hot water. Let sit until lukewarm, then wash your itchy skin with it. Repeat as needed.

The Homeopathic Difference

- Calcarea sulphurica—*Dry eczema*. For eczema with those yellow scabs that sometimes ooze a pus-like discharge, think Calc sulphurica. If your child has this, the eczema is more likely dry.

- Ledum—*Facial eczema.* If you have this kind of eczema, and it's itchy at night in bed, try Ledum.
- Lycopodium—*Heated eczema.* This extremely itchy form of eczema bleeds easily when scratched. The skin may look thick, and frequently has cracks or fissures. Heat from a warm room or bed can bring it on; it feels much better when cold.
- Sulphur—*Settles in skin folds.* Itchy! Burning! Dry! Scaly! That describes the Sulphur-brand of eczema. Scratching makes it ooze, and you may find it settles in skin folds. The itchiness gets even itchier with dampness, like wet weather or bathing.

Lifestyle Link
- Control stress. (See Chapter 7).
- Wash clothes with mild detergents. Eczematous skin is sensitive skin that is easily irritated from chemicals or soaps.
- Avoid rough-feeling clothes, like wool.
- Apply a hot compress to the affected area.
- Seek counseling for unresolved issues. If you find certain situations trigger an outbreak, it may be time to talk to a counselor for help dealing with it.

Lookout Alert
- Fuzzy vision. People with long-standing eczema may develop cataracts in their 20s and 30s. Have your eyes checked regularly.
- High fever during an outbreak.
- Unrelenting or severe rash.

FATIGUE

Because fatigue is a symptom and not a disease, there are many causes. Like constipation, persistent tiredness is best resolved by first determining the reason. Inadequate sleep is the number one cause of fatigue in this country. Stress, lack of exercise, and even poor eating habits also contribute to feeling wrung out. There are, of course, medical reasons too. A chronic, undetected infection anywhere in the body can make you tired, as well as anemia, cancer, heart disease, or an array of other ailments. If taking the following simple steps don't wake you up, enlist your doctor's help in rooting out the cause of your fatigue. If standard laboratory tests are unsuccessful, consider visiting with a naturopathic physician to explore less conventional reasons like Chronic Fatigue Syndrome, food allergies, digestive disorders, environmental sensitivities, or subclinical hypothyroidism (also called Wilson's Syndrome). Look up Anxiety and Insomnia, and refer to Chapter 7 (adrenals) for more information.

How to Prevent Fatigue

- Get enough sleep.
- Stay well. In other words, use healthy practices to avoid chronic infections and other illnesses that drain energy.

Food and Nutrition for Exhaustion

- No caffeine. This pick-me-up eventually lets you down. Used chronically or in large amounts, caffeine can wear your adrenal glands down (see Chapter 7).
- Beware of sugar. Like caffeine, sweet foods give you a burst of energy—only to let you down a short time later. Consider eliminating sugar altogether. (Note: The first two to seven sugar-free days will be draining.)
- Slow down on fat. Fat takes time to digest, making you feel sluggish.
- Drink water by the quart.
- Nutrient shortage. Whether due to insufficient intake, malabsorption, or an inability to utilize vitamins and minerals, this is a definite fatigue-promoter.
- Watch your weight. Carrying extra pounds can be tiring.
- Iron-deficiency anemia. Have your blood checked. Low vitamin B_{12}, chronic disease, and other causes can also lead to anemia or "tired blood."
- Food allergies. Have them checked.

Herbal Treatment

There are many herbs that can be used to combat fatigue—depending on the cause. Below I offer a short list of plants useful for mainly anxiety-provoked fatigue, insomnia, and infections.

- Relax—linden, oats, passion flower, skullcap, valerian
- Promote sleep—lady's slipper, passion flower, valerian
- Untie knotty muscles—skullcap, valerian
- Fight infection—echinacea, garlic, golden seal

The Homeopathic Difference

- Arsenicum album—*Fearful fatigue*. Have you ever been worn out from worrying or being scared? If so, think of Arsenicum. Other signs that point to this remedy are exhaustion from the slightest effort, restless pacing, and for some, despair. Many are also chilly and feel better with fresh air.
- Echinacea—*Achy tired*. For that profound prostration that makes you ache, this homeopathic version of the herb echinacea is worth a try. Some also feel dizzy, confused, or depressed.
- Gelsemium—*A kind of daze*. This fatigue is best described as apathetic or listless. Not only does this remedy fit someone who is dull and drowsy, but also lacks coordination and wants to be alone. Bad news and excitement make this type of fatigue worse, or may bring it on.
- Phosphorus—*Tired brain*. When you feel low and your memory is shot, think of Phosphorus. It's not so much that your body's tired, it's your brain. A tendency to fidget and become easily startled also describe this remedy.

Lifestyle Link

- Aim for eight. Hours of sleep nightly, that is. Without sleep, immunity suffers.
- Snooze for stress. When times are tough—mental, emotional or physical—take time for extra sleep; you need it.

- Delegate. A fast-paced life can be energizing, but like caffeine has a let-down aftereffect.
- Medicine check. For some people, fatigue is a side effect of medication, like Accutane®, Prozac®, and Zoloft®. If you suspect this is your case, check with your doctor.
- Allergic to the world? Environmental sensitivity is becoming more frequent. If you react to a number of chemicals (in addition to being tired), seek the help of a doctor skilled in this area.
- Depressed? If you've experienced past or current psychological trauma, ask for professional help.

Lookout Alert

- Incapacitating fatigue
- Continuous fatigue (even after following above guidelines)
- High fever
- Other symptoms too, like flank pain, painful urination, earache, sore throat, aching muscles

FEVER

When your body temperature rises above 100 degrees F, you officially have a fever. The fever symptom is usually a reaction to an infection from a virus or bacteria, though it's your body that actually creates the fever. When white blood cells detect germs, they release a special protein called a pyrogen which tells the brain's temperature control center to crank it up. It's speculated that high temperatures help activate the immune system, decrease bacterial growth, decrease iron levels (needed by bugs to grow) and shift the body from running on glucose (another favorite bacterial food) over to fat and protein instead.[5]

Chills help increase a fever and can indicate a more hardy infection like the flu or pneumonia; taking aspirin or other anti-fever medicines can also spark the chills. If you have sweats, it means your fever is dropping. Night sweats occur in the early morning as your body temperature (and fever) is on its natural downward slope.

Many bodily functions, including temperature, follow a daily pattern. Fever (and body temperature), for instance, are highest in the late afternoon into early evening. Know too that fevers tend to be higher in childhood (perfectly normal), and decline with age.

Other fever promoters include adverse reaction, to medication, certain non-infectious illnesses like rheumatoid arthritis, heart attacks, cancer. Heatstroke can also bring on a fever; and sometimes we don't know why a fever appears. See related topics: Bronchitis, Colds and Flu, Ear Infections, Food Poisoning, Sore Throats, and Urinary Tract Infections. Read Chapter 6 (immunity) for more information.

How to Prevent Fevers

- Infections. Stay healthy. See Chapter 6 for tips.

- Use medications cautiously. Discuss side effects with your doctor before taking.

- Have fun in the sun—but be careful. Heatstroke is serious. Use sense when outside on a sunny day; drink plenty of fluids (including juices if you're perspiring), wear a hat, and if possible, go inside periodically.

Food and Nutrition for Fever

- A cup of tea. Both peppermint and ginger teas are natural fever fighters. They reduce hot brows by promoting perspiration.

- Treat the cause. If it's infection that's warming you up, take measures to enhance immunity and fight the responsible bug rather than reduce temperature.

- Drink fluids. Replace lost fluid with water, herbal teas, diluted fruit juice, and vegetable juices.

Herbal Treatment

(Also see Bronchitis, Colds and Flu, Ear Infections, Food Poisoning, UTIs)

In general, if anyone is experiencing a "safe" fever (see Lookout Alert below), then reducing a fever is unnecessary and may, in fact, hamper immunity. However, for comfort's sake, you can try one of the following herbs if you wish.

- Cool off with perspiration promoters—boneset, catnip, cayenne, chamomile, elder (flowers or berries), ginger, linden, vervain, yarrow
- Infection erasers—echinacea, garlic, golden seal, peppermint
- Reduce fever (these herbs contain aspirin-like compounds)—black willow, meadow sweet

■ *Makeover Hint #90—Horseradish Tea*

This stimulating herb is an old-time remedy for fevers and the flu. In a pinch, make your own medicine using horseradish root.

1 tsp powdered or chopped horseradish root

Steep in one cup of boiling water for five minutes.

Sip on this brew several times in a day while burning up with a fever.

The Homeopathic Difference

- Belladonna—*Burning desire.* Belladonna is for that fever that burns so hot that every little noise, motion, and light makes you cringe. The odd part of this remedy is that even with all that heat, you're not thirsty.
- Eupatorium perfoliatum—*Fevers AND the chills.* People with this type of fever are typically thirsty before it hits. The muscles in their arms and legs hurt, and they alternate between a fever and the chills.
- Ferrum phosphoricum—*Pale face.* Ferrum phos works well for the beginning stages of a fever, especially one that brings on exhaustion and a pale appearance.
- Gelsemium—*I ache all over.* When a fever makes you tremble with weakness, feel dull with fatigue, and ache all over, think of Gelsemium.

Lifestyle Link

- Rest.
- Cool down with cool compresses. Apply these to your brow or chest.
- Peppermint breath. Inhale the cool fragrance of peppermint oil (placed in warm water or a bath) to both cool a hot fever, or raise a low one (works both ways).

■ *Makeover Hint #91—Keep a Fever, Stop a Cold*

Contrary to conventional medical wisdom, natural health physicians won't tell you to take pills (or herbs) to decrease a fever. A fever, like many symptoms, is the way your body gets well. So if your fever is below 104 F, lasts less than three days, and isn't too uncomfortable, grin, sweat, and bear it. (Follow cautions below for very young children.)

Lookout Alert

- A fever over 104 F
- Any fever in a baby six months or younger
- A fever lasting more than three days or more than 24 hours in a child two years old or younger
- Fever that appears after extended time in the sun
- Fevers that occur after taking medication, especially if newly prescribed or purchased
- Fevers with unusual symptoms, like stiff joints

FOOD POISONING

If you've eaten bad food, you usually know it within a few hours. The symptoms, their severity, and onset vary depending on what you ate, how much, what bug infected your food, and how sensitive your digestive tract is. Symptoms occur anywhere from one to 48 hours after eating contaminated food. Many people mistakenly refer to food poisoning as the "24-hour flu." (There is no such thing.)

It often begins with nausea, gas, and bloating followed by vomiting, diarrhea, and stomach cramps. Your muscles might ache and your temperature can rise. You're weak and feel terrible. Ongoing vomiting and diarrhea can create dehydration and shock, if not remedied. *Staphylococcus* is the most common culprit, and likes to infiltrate custard, fish, and processed meat—especially when left out at room temperature.

Use clues to determine if you truly are suffering from food poisoning. Are others that you dined with also ill? Did you recently eat at a restaurant or did you consume questionable leftovers? Other circumstances mimic food poisoning—like travelers' diarrhea, immediate food allergies (versus delayed), ulcerative colitis, lactose intolerance, heavy metal poisoning, a drug reaction, and plant poisons (e.g., mushrooms). Also see Diarrhea, Fever, Heartburn, Indigestion, Motion Sickness; refer to Chapter 4 (digestion).

How to Prevent Food Poisoning

- Be meticulous about food storage. Don't let perishable food sit out for more than an hour.

- Cook poultry and eggs well.

- Give up sushi. This raw fish dish is a common cause of food poisoning.

- Toss questionable leftovers.

- Don't feed honey to children under one year old. Some honey contains *Botulism* spores, harmful to babies but not adults.

Food and Nutrition for Poisoning

- Careful of the water. When you travel or camp, carry bottled water with you.

- Eat yogurt. Once the worst of it is over, the good bugs in this food replace some of those lost.

- Alternately, you can take a *Lactobacillus acidophilus* or probiotic pill after the diarrhea is done to replace lost bugs from your colon.

- Drink fluids as able, especially liquids with electrolytes, like fruit and vegetable juices.

- Avoid eating for awhile.
- After the first stage is done, dine on soft foods: soup, cooked fruit, and yogurt. Avoid raw fruits and vegetables.
- Dine on garlic. This will help kill any offending bugs.

Herbal Treatment

During acute food poisoning, I would not recommend taking any herbs, except perhaps garlic and citrus seed extract. Instead rely on homeopathic remedies, and follow the above nutritional suggestions.

The Homeopathic Difference

The remedies under Diarrhea might also be useful.

- Arsenicum album—*Even the sight of food makes me sick.* This is a classic remedy for eating spoiled food. It comes complete with nausea, vomiting, and retching, not to mention burning pain in the pit of the stomach. Another sign to look for is great thirst that is quenched with tiny sips.
- Carbo vegetabilis—*Bloating and belching.* This is a remedy for distress after eating that's not quite as severe as Arsenicum. Sour burping (and some gas) is frequent and relieves the bloating and pain temporarily. Cramps that extend to the back and chest force one to bend over, and lying down doesn't help.
- Colchicum—*Cold stomach.* As is typical of food poisoning, this remedy helps with nausea (even to point of fainting, it's so bad) and vomiting up of food, bile, and mucus. Thirst is great, and though you may crave various foods, the very smell makes you sick. The peculiar sign to watch for with Colchicum is a burning or icy sensation in the abdomen.
- Ipecac—*Nausea and vomiting.* Although all the above remedies address the nausea and vomiting of food poisoning, Ipecac (yes, derived from the very same bottle you use in case of poisoning) is the star. Its guiding symptom is queasiness—the kind that is unrelenting. It differs, however, because the stomach feels relaxed, like it's hanging down, though the body is rigid. There's little thirst, and the pain is worst around the navel.

Lifestyle Link

- Take charcoal. That's right! Visit your local health food or drug store for these; take six to start, and then a couple every hour. They help soak up toxins. Don't be alarmed when your stools turn black.
- Bed rest.
- Check with fellow diners. If they're also sick, you might be able to track down the source of your poisoning.
- Throw out suspect food.
- Was it a restaurant? Once you're well, alert the restaurant and possibly the Department of Health so steps can be taken to prevent this from happening to others.

■ *Makeover Hint #92—Eat Burnt Toast*

When in a crunch (or should we say crust), and you're too sick to head out the door for charcoal pills, just burn some toast. The crispy bits are similar to charcoal and help sop up food poisons. (My mother used to make me eat burnt toast by saying it'd give me curly hair. Ha!)

Lookout Alert

- Diarrhea that lasts more than a few days
- If person not drinking or eating (can lead to dehydration)
- Be particularly cautious in young children (they dehydrate more quickly)
- Paralysis or weakness that travels down the body
- Dry mouth or visual disturbances
- Breathing problems
- Symptoms that appear after taking medication
- Symptoms that appear after eating "wild" mushrooms
- Symptoms that appear after eating home-canned food

GOUT

About one million Americans suffer from gout, a type of arthritis caused by high amounts of uric acid in the blood. When too many of these needle-like crystals form, they can settle in the kidneys, causing painful stones; joints, like the big toe, knees, and hips, are also affected. Gout is one of the most agonizing forms of arthritis, characterized by stabbing pain, inflammation, and occasionally scarring.

We've known about gout for over 2000 years, but it's only been since 1981 that we've understood exactly how this condition evolves. Gout develops when uric acid crystals flake off joints and float around the surrounding synovial fluid. The immune system sees these crystals as the enemy and sends out its battalion of white blood cells. The pain begins when the pointy edges of the uric acid crystals puncture large white blood cells called phagocytes. Powerful enzymes are released from the lysosome sacs in the phagocytes and inflammation begins. This inflammation, of course, is merely the body trying to heal itself. However, the end results are joints that are red, swollen, hot, and very, very tender.

This is a condition that tends to run in families, though typically gout hits overweight, sedentary men. A genetic inability to properly metabolize purines in food is one contributing factor. Another is overindulgence in rich meals and alcohol. Also see Backache, Fatigue, Sprains and Strains; read Chapters 4 (digestion) and 9 (muscles).

How to Prevent Gout

- Does Dad have it? If anyone in your family is gout-prone (especially the men), follow a gout-free diet.

- Stay on your toes. In other words, stay active.

- Watch what you eat. You don't necessarily have to avoid foods high in purines, but at the very least keep fatty foods down.

Food and Nutrition for Gout

- Purine foods. Since purines are what uric acid is made from, sticking to a low-purine diet helps immensely. Foods to avoid include anchovies, beef tongue, bouillon, brains, caviar, consomme, duck, goose, gravies, herring, kidneys, liver, mackerel, meat broth or soup, mussels, oysters, sardines, sausage, squab, and sweetbreads. Foods with a moderate amount of purine, and ones you can eat occasionally, are clams, pork, shellfish, and shrimp.

- Pour out the alcohol. Alcohol can increase uric acid production.
- Eat a bowl of cherries. According to the research of Dr. Ludwig N. Blair in the 1940s, eating half a pound or more of fresh cherries helps decrease uric acid levels. Cherry juice is another option.
- Coffee and sugar. Minimizing these foods seems to help; sugar increases uric acid.
- Drink plenty of clean water. This will flush out excess uric acid and decrease kidney stone risk.
- Eat plenty of fatty fish. The oils in fish act as natural anti-inflammatory agents. Warning: Avoid those fish that are high in purines (mackerel, herring, and sardines).

Herbal Treatment

- Reduce uric acid—bilberry, devil's claw
- Decrease pain—devil's claw, thuja
- Diminish inflammation—bilberry
- Keep water gain down—burdock root, celery seed, yarrow

The Homeopathic Difference

- Colchicum—*Red, hot, and swollen.* This is an easy gout remedy to remember because Colchicum (meadow saffron) is the plant that colchicine is made from: the medication used to treat gout. However, unlike colchicine, homeopathic Colchicum is without toxic side effects. Use this remedy for gout of the big toe and heel, especially when you can't bear touch or movement.
- Ledum—*For that shooting pain.* When gouty pains shoot throughout your small joints, especially in the foot and legs, and are hot, swollen and pale, this is your remedy. The soles of your feet are so painful, it's hard to walk. Placing your feet in cold water feels great; heat feels terrible.

- Lycopodium—*One foot hot, one foot cold.* For chronic gout where deposits have accumulated in the joints, this remedy could be the one. The heel is particularly painful, as if treading on a pebble. But most peculiar is that one foot feels cold, while the other one is hot.
- Urtica urens—*All in the family.* When joint pain is associated with a hives-like rash, particularly on the ankles and wrists, think of Urtica urens (see Hives). Sometimes the gout pain and hives will alternate. Coolness makes symptoms worse. This type of gout typically runs in the family.

Lifestyle Link

- Exercise that body for the health of your joints.
- Lose weight if needed. People with extra pounds tend to have higher uric acid levels than those who are svelte.
- Consider lead toxicity. If none of the above steps works, consider getting tested for lead toxicity. An unusual type of gout referred to as *saturnine gout* can occur because of too much lead in the body.[6]

Lookout Alert

- Don't take large amounts of vitamin C. This increases uric acid levels in some people.[7]
- Avoid large quantities of niacin, that is, more than 50 mg daily. Niacin competes with uric acid for excretion from the body—this in turn keeps uric acid levels high.[8]

HAY FEVER

This is an allergic condition that appears at a certain time each year. Those who react to tree pollens begin sneezing in the spring; the grass and weed pollens create summertime misery for some, and good ol' ragweed is sure to start autumn hay fever. The important thing to remember here is that hay fever frequency and severity all depend on where you live and what's floating in the air. Mold, animals, dust, and dust mites are also common culprits.

The symptoms are characteristic enough: first your nose begins to itch, then your eyes, even the roof of your mouth begins to itch and AACHOO!! You sneeze. And sneeze. Red, tearing, itchy eyes are part of the package, and for some, coughing and wheezing develop after a time. Depending on your symptoms, sleeping is difficult, eating impossible, headaches a bother, not to mention irritability (who wouldn't be), depression and fatigue. Because of the constant drain on immune reserves, many hay fever sufferers also find themselves victim to more colds and other upper respiratory infections. Remember, too, that hay fever is an immunity disorder unto its own. The body is pulling out all resources to fight nasty pollen; kind of like attacking an ant with a machine gun. For more information, turn to Bronchitis, Colds and Flu, Coughing, Ear Infections, Eczema, Fatigue, Headaches, Insomnia, and Sore Throat. See Chapters 6 (immunity) and 13 (eyes).

How to Prevent a Hay Fever Attack

- Pick the right parents. Hay fever is usually genetic.
- Move. Because this is an allergic response, often to outside influences like pollens and grasses, living in a different region might help (might not).
- Be a Felix. Keep your home clean to cut down on dust and dust mites.
- Cover up. Place hypoallergenic covers on your pillows and mattress to reduce contact with dust mites.
- Clean hidden allergy makers. This includes humidifiers, air conditioners, furnaces, the drip pans in refrigerators, and mildew anywhere in the house, especially around leaky windows.
- Be like a table. I explain the table analogy to allergic patients in this way: the four legs of the table are your habits of diet, exercise, sleep and stress control. When these are strong, like sturdy legs of a table, they support the load of allergies that sit on top of the table.

Using the following nutritional, herbal, and homeopathic advice a month or two before symptoms hit can lessen your hay fever misery.

Food and Nutrition for Hay Fever

- Eat well; skip the junk. See table analogy above.
- Can the sugar. This only adds to already diminished defenses during hay fever season.
- That goes for the caffeine and alcohol too.
- Keep water up. Hay fever is very dehydrating.
- Extra C. Take 500 to 1000 mg of vitamin C three times daily.
- Multiple protection. Take a high-potency vitamin and mineral pill with adequate vitamin A, B vitamins, calcium, potassium, and manganese.
- Eat cold water fish. They provide essential fats to battle nasal inflammation.
- EPO to the rescue. Evening primrose oil works for some. You can also try flax seed oil.

Herbal Treatment

- Decongestants—ephedra, nettles
- Eye soothers—eyebright
- Clear nasal passages—elder flowers, golden seal, licorice
- Immune builders—echinacea, golden seal

The Homeopathic Difference

- Allium cepa—*Symptoms like peeling an onion.* This remedy is derived from red onion, and is fitting for symptoms such as profuse tearing, red burning eyes, clear, irritating nasal discharge, frequent sneezing and thirst; worse in the evening and indoors.
- Euphrasia—*Onion's opposite.* Euphrasia's symptoms are the flip-side of Allium's: bland nasal discharge and burning tears, grogginess, and a sinus headache.
- Nux vomica—*Easily agitated.* Noise! Light! Odors! They all irritate you and make your maddening symptoms—watery nose that can't decide if it should run or keep you stuffed up—even worse.

- Sabadilla—*Non-stop sneezing.* Aaaaahhhh . . . choo!!! Aaaahhh. . . . The inside of your nose itches, and a copious, watery mucus drains from your nose. Even your red eyes are runny. Stepping outside into the open air eases symptoms a little.

Lifestyle Link

- Skin prick test. Get tested so you know your allergies, and are prepared to battle them.
- Pollen sufferers. Close your windows during pollen season, particularly in the morning (when pollen counts tend to be higher) and on windy days.
- Say good-bye to Rover. If cats, dogs, or other residential pets are causing you grief, consider saying farewell. At the very least, don't let them sleep on your bed.
- Raise the head of your bed. This allows for better breathing (and sleeping) at night.
- Investigate contributing allergies. Medications, foods, or other chemicals, including cigarette smoke or perfume, could be adding to the problem.
- Quit smoking.
- Try acupuncture. As a long-time hay fever sufferer, I know this works. It may require several sessions.

Lookout Alert

- Cough up blood.
- Chest pains.
- Severe or prolonged symptoms.

HEADACHES

A favorite teacher of mine in naturopathic medical school told us, "A headache is not an aspirin deficiency." What he meant by that was there are many reasons we get headaches and, although we regularly turn to aspirin and other painkillers for relief, there are safer and equally effective cures.

Headaches are so common we tend to dismiss them as annoyances rather than accept them as conditions that need treatment. A headache, like any pain, is the body's way of telling you something's wrong. It is a symptom of a larger problem.

Headaches occur for many reasons. Daily tension explains many aching temples; most of my suggestions here address this problem. I also include a few tips for migraines, a one-sided pounding, usually recurring headache that often annoys women in their 20s and 30s. A migraine is not merely a very bad headache, but rather a condition with very definite characteristics. Some see an aura—a veil of light—before the pain hits; others experience different visual disturbances as well as sweet cravings, weakness, depression, or slurred speech. Nausea, vomiting, abdominal distress, or even dizziness can be part of the headache package. Most migraine sufferers prefer to be alone in a dark, quiet room while the two-hour to days-long pain lasts.

Head injuries, infections such as the flu, sun exposure, secondhand tobacco smoke, breathing chemicals or pollutants, high blood pressure, low blood pressure, constipation, brain tumors, or conditions of the ears, nose or teeth can also lead to headaches. Menstrual headaches, especially among women with premenstrual syndrome (PMS), might accompany food cravings, fatigue, and dizziness. Or you can suffer from cluster headaches (intense, one-sided pain) that begin during sleep, causing the eye on the affected side to redden and tear. Also see Anxiety, Backache, Colds and Flu, Constipation, Ear Infections, Fatigue, Fever, Hay Fever, Low Blood Sugar; refer to Chapters 4 (digestion), 7 (adrenals), 9 (muscles), and 13 (eyes).

How to Prevent Headaches

- Rest. Fatigue is a common headache trigger. Get enough sleep every night; take extra care to rest and sleep when you're overtaxed emotionally, mentally, or physically.

- Relax every day. Contrary to what you've been told, rest breaks are a sign of health, not laziness. Spaced out during a busy day, they deter an aching head.

- A change is as good as a rest. Mixing your day up with physical movement and thinking reduces stress (and headaches).

- Even temperatures. Abrupt changes in temperature, for example going from an air-conditioned office out to a sweltering summer's afternoon, or from a snuggly warm home to a frostbitten winter's day, taxes your body and invites head pain.

Food and Nutrition for Headaches

- Stressed out on food. Stress isn't just emotional and mental; incorrect foods can put undue pressure on your body too. This is especially true for refined foods, caffeine, greasy meals, and sugary treats. Irregular meal times add to the strain.
- Focus on whole foods: vegetables, fruits, whole grains, nuts, seeds, and beans.
- Dine on fish, especially the fatty ones like salmon, halibut, and mackerel. Again, these essential fats help decrease inflammation, sometimes part of a headache.
- Flax instead of fish. If you live in fish-less country, turn to flax seed oil, raw nuts, and seeds.
- Add protein. If you get irritable between meals, low blood sugar or insulin resistance could be the cause of your headaches. Eat protein with each meal and snack.
- Drink water.
- Cayenne. The capsaicin in hot peppers decreases head pain by depleting the body's substance P, a chemical that creates pain.
- Food sensitivities. This is especially true for migraines, where studies indicate that 85 to 93 percent of the headache-prone recover by eliminating allergic foods.[9, 10] Most common causes are cow's milk, wheat, chocolate, eggs, and oranges.
- Good-bye chocolate. Some foods, like chocolate, alcohol, and cheese (all your favorites, wouldn't you know it?) contain chemicals that cause blood vessels in your head to constrict. This can lead to a migraine headache.
- Coffee headache. Those who drink coffee daily risk getting a caffeine withdrawal headache if they skip a day. This is one reason why many are reluctant to quit. When you do stop, do so gradually. If you end cold turkey, allow one week before withdrawal signs are done.

- Magnesium helps those headaches—including migraines— where the sufferer is low in this mineral.[11]
- Add vitamin C. 1000 mg three times daily acts as an antihista- mine, helpful if your headache is allergy-provoked.

Herbal Treatment

- Pain—black willow (this plant contains aspirin-like compounds good for pain; however, a headache is *not* a black willow defi- ciency); ginger; bromelain (take between meals)
- With digestive troubles—chamomile, peppermint, rue
- Menstrual headache—rue
- Migraines—chamomile, feverfew
- Tension headaches—chamomile, feverfew, passion flower, valerian

■ *Makeover Hint #93—Tiger in a Bottle*

An easy and natural treatment for any headache is tiger balm, that same smelly stuff you were rubbing on your aching muscles 20 years ago. A recent study found that this fragrant liniment mas- saged into temples every 30 minutes or so worked as well or better than Tylenol®.[12] I use the colorless form, and notice that the cam- phor, menthol, cajeput, and clove oils provide a warming sensation coupled with almost immediate relief. No need to wear perfume either.

The Homeopathic Difference

Acute homeopathic remedies are fine for mild to moderate headaches. However, if those headaches are an ongoing concern seek professional help (constitutional homeopathy may be appro- priate). If you know the cause, for instance stress, you need to take care of that. Essential oils like lavender, marjoram, or Tiger Balm are great headache fighters, but avoid them if you want to use one of these homeopathic remedies.

- Belladonna—*Throbbing headache.* For intense pounding pain that makes you sensitive to light, noise, touch, smell, and movement, this could help. These sorts of headaches hit you like a ton of bricks. They often settle in your forehead (though they can be anywhere), and your face feels flushed and hot. This headache feels better sitting up and with firm pressure applied to the painful area.

- Bryonia—*Don't move, it hurts.* This type of headache is aggravated by any movement. While a hug is fine for some, any touch is unwelcome for this person whose head aches constantly, left eye hurts, is nauseated or constipated, feels irritable and wants to be alone.

- Gelsemium—*Migraines.* This remedy fits many of the classic migraine signs such as pain preceded by dim vision or visual disturbances, and a worsening with light, noise, or jarring motion. What characterizes a Gelsemium headache is that it tends to be right-sided. If you (or someone you're helping) look dull and tired with droopy eyes, think of this remedy.

- Nux vomica—*Party now, suffer tomorrow.* This is a good remedy for hangover headaches, and other party activities—eating rich foods, taking drugs, staying up late. It involves an overall sick feeling, tummy upset, bitter taste in the mouth, nausea, and vomiting. (Aren't parties fun?)

- Pulsatilla—*Menstrual headache.* For throbbing headaches before or during a period that are one-sided or sit in the forehead, try Pulsatilla. The telltale sign for this remedy is emotional sensitivity where you crave company and cry easily, in this case from head pain.

■ *Makeover Hint #94—The Comfort Makeover*

Slight discomforts are a fact of life and easily dealt with. But too much heat, noise, or other annoyance is stressful. Listen to your body. When it complains, do spot checks on your environment. Are your clothes or shoes too tight? How are you sitting? Do you live or work in a place that's too noisy, cold, hot, bright, or dark? If so, make the necessary comfort changes.

Lifestyle Link

- Hot and cold. Try an ice pack on your head and put your feet in a tub of hot water. A quiet hot bath with a few drops of lavender oil added can be soothing too.

- Stress management. There are lots of ways to hold tension down. Take a brisk walk during lunch; trade neck and shoulder massages with a friend; listen to music or comedy tapes during rush hour. (See Chapter 7).

- Stand up straight! Check your posture.

- Visit the chiropractor. Manipulation of neck or spine (it's all connected) can relieve chronic headaches for some people.

- Get a massage. A soothing rub helps reduce overall tension, increases blood flow (full of oxygen and nutrients) and lymphatic flow (removes toxins).

- See your dentist. Headache and jaw pain could indicate a problem with your temporomandibular joint, a condition called TMJ. Other teeth problems cause more widespread head pain.

- Eye checkup. Straining eyes can lead to fatigue, nausea, and headache. (See Chapter 13).

- Acupuncture. This is a great pain fighter, and can address more body-wide problems.

Lookout Alert

There are many conditions, some extremely serious, that come with a headache. If your headache is associated with any of the following symptoms or conditions, see your doctor.

- Fever
- Stiff neck
- Convulsions
- Loss of consciousness
- Localized pain, for example in the eye or ear
- Visual problems
- Weakness on one part of your body

- Impaired speech
- Dizziness
- After head trauma
- After taking medicine (including herbs or vitamins)
- Long-lasting or unusual headache

HEARTBURN

Heartburn is just what it sounds like—a burning pain in the heart (mid-chest bone) area. In reality it's a digestive complaint where regurgitated stomach acid mimics heart pain that can radiate to the neck, throat, and even face. It usually happens after eating, and is worse upon lying down or at bedtime. The muscle that normally prevents stomach contents from reentering the esophagus, or tube that connects the mouth to the stomach, can weaken and is a common cause of this uncomfortable condition. Ulcers can also cause a heartburn-like pain. See Indigestion and Ulcers; read Chapters 4 (digestion) and 8 (heart).

How to Prevent Heartburn

- Establish regular meal times.
- Don't overeat.
- Eat slowly.
- Dine in peace.

Food and Nutrition for Heartburn

Many of the suggestions below are designed to minimize stomach acid output—cause of your heartburn—while other healing measures are put into play.

- Partake of Nature's bounty. Add those many fresh vegetables and fruits, whole grains, legumes, nuts and seeds to your meals.
- Eat when relaxed.

- Eat smaller meals.
- Don't eat directly before going to bed.
- Identify the acid provokers. These are alcohol, coffee, citrus fruits, tomato, chocolate, carbonated drinks like pop, spicy foods, black tea, peppers and onions.
- No more fat. Fried foods, whipping cream, milk shakes, and other delectable fatty drinks and foods make matters worse.
- Refrain from gassy foods. This could be individual items or combinations that cause you to belch.

Herbal Treatment

Note: Avoid carminative herbs like peppermint and spearmint. They make matters worse for some.

- Decrease acid—meadow sweet
- Healing—cabbage, comfrey, licorice root, marshmallow root
- Soothing herbs—marshmallow root, slippery elm

The Homeopathic Difference

- Cinchona officinalis—*Sour burps.* For that oh-so-bloated feeling, try Cinchona. Along with this acid, gassy stomach comes burping of bitter belches and liquid. Unfortunately they don't spell R-E-L-I-E-F. Only moving around helps.
- Echinacea angustifolia—*Just let me lie down.* Echinacea is a well-known herb, but homeopathically it also works for heartburn with nausea that feels worse in the cold air. This kind of heartburn makes you exhausted; lying down makes everything feel better.
- Nux vomica—*The workaholic.* Nux vomica is for the person who does everything in excess, including work. And when fatigue hits, he turns to coffee, drugs, or alcohol to keep going. These overindulgences in turn invite headaches, irritability, drowsiness, and *heartburn* that's usually worse in the morning.
- Pulsatilla—*Night-time pain.* For heartburn that strikes at night, Pulsatilla might ease your pain. A thick yellow or white tongue and queasiness that leaves your mouth tasting bad points to this remedy. Rich fatty foods aggravate this kind of heartburn.

Lifestyle Link

- Overdoing it. For those occasional times when you overindulge, don't lie down or bend over. This will surely create a heartburn episode.

- Prop your bed. To relieve nighttime burn, elevate the headboard side of your bed a few inches.

- Quit smoking. This habit relaxes the band of muscle separating the stomach and esophagus.

- Breathe. Many of my heartburn patients are worse during periods of stress. Learn to prepare for those times, or develop methods of handling tension to lessen or prevent a heartburn attack (see Chapter 7).

- Esophageal manipulation. Ask a chiropractor or osteopathic doctor you know about techniques that will help release tension in the area surrounding the esophagus.

Lookout Alert

Also see Ulcer.

- Chest pains not related to eating
- Chest pain that extends to the left arm, shoulders, or neck
- Shortness of breath—especially upon exertion
- Crushing sensation on the chest
- Nighttime pain accompanied by increased heart rate
- Nighttime pain accompanied by rapid breathing
- Intense or unrelenting symptoms

HEMORRHOIDS

Hemorrhoids are very common among the "civilized" in industrialized nations. In fact, half of those people age 50 and above have them, while one third of Americans have hemorrhoids to some degree. Simply stated, hemorrhoids, or piles, are like varicose veins, only in the anal region. There are many different versions: internal, external, combined internal and external.

The most frequent first sign of hemorrhoids is bright red blood on the toilet paper or in the toilet bowl. Other symptoms that can (but not always) indicate hemorrhoids are itching, burning, or irritation in the rectal region, seepage, or swelling. Hemorrhoids are usually painless. Some prolapse or sag outside of the anus and must be pushed back into the rectum after a bowel movement. Pregnancy can cause hemorrhoids. Among the non-pregnant, anything that increases congestion of blood in the anus is a contributory factor—things like straining to defecate (constipation), sneezing and coughing, physical exertion, prolonged standing or sitting. Also see Constipation, Varicose Veins; refer to Chapters 3 (liver) and 4 (digestion).

How to Prevent Hemorrhoids

- Move about. Standing or sitting for a long time invites hemorrhoids. So get up and move about (see Chapter 9).
- Fill up on fiber. Less roughage creates hard-to-pass stools. This means more straining during bowel movements, an ideal way to weaken veins in that region.
- Drink lots of water, at least one quart a day. This prevents constipation.
- Exercise regularly.

Food and Nutrition for Hemorrhoids

- Hurray for fiber. Concentrate on raw vegetables and fruits.
- Water, water, water.
- Flax seed oil. 1 tbsp. daily
- Citrus fruits. Here's where oranges and grapefruit are very helpful, especially the white rind; it contains tissue-healing bioflavonoids.
- Eat the red, purple, and blue. These deep-colored fruits (cherries, berries) contain special flavonoids called proanthocyanidins and anthocyanidins that strengthen veins.
- Take your supplements. Vitamins A, B-complex and E, and zinc aid recovery.

- Vitamin C plus bioflavonoids. An equal dose of each (500 mg to 3000 mg per day in divided doses) essential for tissue repair.
- Zinc oxide. Apply directly to affected region.
- Vitamin E oil. A good topical therapy.

Herbal Treatment

- Astringents—horse chestnut, witch hazel (topical)
- Circulation—ginkgo
- Constipation fighters—flax seed, psyllium seed
- Less swelling—Butcher's broom
- Soothing—aloe, slippery elm
- Tissue healers—aloe, comfrey, yarrow (topical)
- Vessel toners—Butcher's broom, gotu kola, horse chestnut, yarrow

■ *Makeover Hint #95—Direct Herbal Support*

Ointments, pads, or suppositories can offer a soothing and healing quality. However, if dietary and lifestyle changes aren't made these effects will most likely be temporary. Look for products containing one or more of these: witch hazel, aloe vera, plantain, St. John's wort, yarrow, golden seal, comfrey, vitamins A and E.

The Homeopathic Difference

- Aesculus hipposcastanum—*Sitting on pins and needles.* This is the homeopathic version of horse chestnut, and like many homeopathic remedies, it works for hemorrhoids just like the herbal form. This kind of hemorrhoid leaves the rectum feeling full. The area is dry, burning, and excoriating. It's like sitting on a pin cushion.
- Collinsonia canadensis—*And constipation too.* As one homeopathic textbook so graphically put it, these hemorrhoids have the "sensation of sharp sticks in the rectum." Bleeding, itching, aching, and obstinate constipation are also part of the picture. Heat makes it feel better, cold does not.

- Lachesis—*A choking sensation*. There's a throbbing pain and feeling of tightness in the anal region from this kind of hemorrhoids that actually feels better when the rectum bleeds. The hemorrhoids protrude and are purple in color. Sneezing and coughing increase pain, as does heat.
- Muriaticum acidum—*Hurts from toilet paper*. These hemorrhoids are swollen, itchy, dark blue, protruding, and very sensitive, so sensitive that even wiping oneself with toilet paper is agonizing. Women who get hemorrhoids during pregnancy are often helped by this remedy. One characteristic that separates Muriaticum from the others is that urination makes the itching and protrusion worse, and may even initiate involuntary stool evacuation.

Lifestyle Link

- Develop regular toilet habits. This means using the bathroom the same time each day to empty your bowels; avoid straining; give yourself enough time to have a bowel movement.
- Warm Sitz bath. Sit in a warm bath (bottom only), followed by a short cold one. Add witch hazel if you please.

Lookout Alert

- Black stools
- Blood in the stool. Bright red blood is often hemorrhoid related. However, any rectal blood should be investigated.
- Mucus or pus in the stool
- Alternating constipation and diarrhea

HIVES

If little red, swollen, intensely itchy circles (called wheals or welts) arise suddenly on your skin, you have urticaria—commonly known as hives. One in five people have them at one time or another, and because they're caused by so many things it's often impossible to track down their cause. Hives appear because of insect bites, the cold or the heat, physical exercise (usually after a heavy meal), rubbing, scratching or vibrating the skin, water or light, mental anguish or infection, penicillin or aspirin, food or food additives. They may happen once and last anywhere from hours to days, or they can be long-lasting. Also see Acne, Anxiety, Canker Sores, Eczema, Food Poisoning, Psoriasis, Yeast Infections; refer to Chapters 4 (digestion), 7 (adrenals), and 14 (the mind).

How to Prevent Hives

This is often a mysterious condition that comes once and disappears before its cause is known. Pretty hard to prevent, I'd say.

Food and Nutrition for Hives

- Vitamin C. This natural antihistamine may reduce hives.
- Subtract food additives. Choose foods without artificial colorings, flavorings, and other synthetic chemicals. (See Chapter 3.)
- Food allergies. Sensitivity to certain foods can create a host of problems, including hives. Check it out.
- Vasoactive amines. Those same foods that trigger migraine headaches can cause hives (see Headaches).

Herbal Treatment

- Bitters for better digestion—barberry, chamomile, gentian, golden seal
- Mellow out—chamomile, passion flower, skullcap, valerian

The Homeopathic Difference

- Apis mellifica—*Ouch, that stings!* To remember when Apis works, think of a hot, red, swollen bee sting—that's how your hives should feel. Cool compresses make it better, warm (and nighttime) worse. This kind of hives erupts when you sweat or get hot. If no other remedy sticks out, try Apis first.
- Rhus toxicodendron—*The unscratchable itch.* These welts form during cold or wet weather from scratching or perspiring, and are red, swollen, and very, very itchy. Walking makes these hives better, rest worse.

- Urtica urens—*A stinging nettles-type of hives.* If you've ever fallen into a patch of stinging nettles, you know what kind of hives is helped by Urtica urens—itchy, red, stinging, burning blotches. That's because Urtica is stinging nettles, or rather the homeopathic version. This type of hives often appears after vigorous exercise, bathing, or warmth, and feels better from lying down.

Lifestyle Link

Solving hives takes a detective. There are so many things that cause this itchy rash that to truly cure it, you need to figure out what caused it in the first place. If this is a one-time case, the hives might disappear before you figure it out. If hives keep pestering you, keep a diary of your dietary habits (see Chapter 4), activities, medicines and supplements, and emotional state, and see if you can find a correlation.

- Cold cloth. Like all swellings, hives feel better and improve slightly with a cold cloth applied to the area. (Unless, of course, the hives are caused by cold.)
- Feelings. For many, emotions play a part in hives.
- A dash of sun. For those who get hives from the cold, firmly touching the skin, after taking certain medicines, during a skin infection or other disorder, a daily 15-minute dose of sunlight might help.
- Lie back and relax. Practice daily relaxation techniques, like deep breathing, listening to soothing music or tapes with "relaxation talk," meditation, prayer—whatever it takes.
- Put oatmeal in your bath. See Makeover Hint #68.

Lookout Alert

Most cases of hives disappear before you know what caused them. But occasionally this swelling also includes the respiratory passages. When this allergic reaction is severe, the throat may be blocked and breathing difficult. If your throat feels tight or breathing is harder, call your doctor immediately or go to the nearest Emergency Room.

INDIGESTION

Indigestion is a general term for uncomfortable and gaseous feelings that occur in the abdomen after eating. It's caused by a variety of problems such as malabsorption, decreased stomach acid, or diminished digestive enzymes. Also see Anxiety, Constipation, Diarrhea, Food Poisoning, Heartburn, Ulcer. Read Chapters 3 (liver) and 4 (digestion).

How to Prevent Indigestion

- Chew your food. This is where digestion begins.
- Don't rush. Avoid eating in the car, while doing chores, or anything else. Instead, allow your body time to accept and properly digest the food you serve it.
- Laugh at dinner. Relaxed eating, prayer, and company also improve digestion.
- Regulate your repast. Predictable mealtimes let your digestive system work better.

Food and Nutrition for Digesting

See prevention tips above; also:

- Eliminate milk. You might be lactose intolerant.
- Keep eating wholesome. Fresh vegetables and fruits, whole grains, legumes, nuts and seeds.
- Don't eat refined. Processed foods lack enzymes that help you digest.
- Cut back on grains. For some, these foods cause problems.
- Stop at 6:30 P.M. Break the night-snack habit. If you must, some fruit or toast only.
- Simplify. Eat one to three different foods at a time only. Complex food mixtures make more work for your gut.
- Lemon tip. Sip on a glass of water spiked with a wedge of lemon before each meal.
- Green digestion. Eat a large, dark green salad with spinach, radicchio, endive, dandelion greens.

- Nibble. Dine on several small meals throughout the day, rather than three large squares.
- Liquids first, then food. For some people, it helps to drink beverages away from food. If you're used to sipping with meals, do so first, then eat. Or only drink what's required to eat comfortably.
- Digestive help. Try digestive enzymes and hydrochloric acid supplements; take throughout the meal.

Herbal Treatment

- Better bile—balmony, barberry, dandelion root, golden seal, wild yam
- Nervous stomach—chamomile, hops, skullcap, valerian
- No more gas—chamomile, ginger, peppermint
- Power-up digestion—barberry, chamomile, gentian root, golden seal

■ *Makeover Hint #96—Use Spices to Reduce Gas*

Many of our culinary herbs and spices are, interestingly enough, also helpful for digestion. Specifically, the following spices help curtail painful gas caused by eating: allspice, aniseed, caraway, cardamon, cayenne, cinnamon, coriander, dill, fennel, ginger.

The Homeopathic Difference

- Carbo vegetabilis—*The food just sits there.* When your stomach is heavy, full, and taut with gassy pain this remedy may help. You feel sleepy, yet the gas gets worse as evening nears and when you lie down. Sour burps and passing gas make it slightly better.
- Chamomilla—*Angry indigestion.* For a crampy, gassy indigestion that hits you after an angry outburst, Chamomilla might help. This remedy is useful for indigestion that leaves your cheeks flushed and a bitter taste in your mouth.
- Lycopodium—*There's a rumbly in my tumbly.* Weak digestion best describes the person who needs Lycopodium. Yet warm drinks and food do make it better. And there's a noticeable noise and rumbling in the stomach.

- Nux vomica—*I can't believe I ate the whole thing.* This is the remedy of overindulgence, be it food, alcohol, drugs, or work. Indigestion of this type makes you impatient and irascible. Flatulence is a problem, as are a bloated abdomen and stomach cramps.

Lifestyle Link

- Upset mood leads to an upset stomach. Avoid eating when you are distressed.

Lookout Alert

- Symptoms that worsen with exertion
- Alternating constipation and diarrhea
- Abdominal pain not related to eating
- Intense abdominal pain
- Bloody or tarry stools
- Mucus or pus in the stools
- Vomiting, especially blood or "coffee-ground" material
- Trouble swallowing
- Unusual weight loss
- Fever
- Jaundice (the whites of the eyes look yellowish)
- Change in symptoms
- Severe or unrelenting symptoms

INSOMNIA

If you have trouble falling asleep, wake up in the middle of the night and can't go back to sleep, or arise too early in the morning, you have insomnia. An astounding one third of Americans can't sleep on a regular basis. Daily pressures make sleeping difficult, as do other emotional difficulties. But how you live—caffeine intake for one— can also keep you awake long past bedtime. Refer to Anxiety, Fatigue, and Heartburn. See Chapters 7 (adrenals) and 14 (the mind).

How to Prevent Insomnia

- Calm down. Anxiety is a frequent cause of insomnia. (See Anxiety.)

- Caffeine be gone. This stimulant, found in coffee, black tea, chocolate, soft drinks, and some medications, creates sleeping problems in more than a few people. Decrease what you consume, or stop using it earlier in the day.

- Avoid alcohol. A glass of wine at the end of a busy day can unwind you, and then leave you wide-eyed later in bed.

- Short naps only. Too much daytime sleep may leave you wide awake at night. Nap for 20 minutes tops.

- Bedroom makeover. An uncomfortable bedroom, whether from temperature, noise, smell, or aesthetics, can rob you of zzz's. Make sure your sleeping chamber is pleasing and used only for sleep and sex—no working, no TV, no eating.

- Bedtime hygiene. Children go to bed better when they have a routine. Adults need a bedtime ritual too. Doctors call this sleeping hygiene. Start with a regular bedtime. Then one hour before that, follow a set routine—brush your teeth, make a cup of herbal tea, put on your PJs, read a happy book, and turn out the lights when sleepy.

■ *Makeover Hint #97—Create the Middle of the Night in the Middle of the Day*

You need to sleep during the day because you're working a graveyard shift or need to catch up on your rest. Your body is bone-tired, but the light streaming in from the window, yelling children, and insensitive lawnmowers are keeping you awake. Follow these ideas for more restful (and successful) slumber:

- Wear ear plugs. Get the snug-fitting kind that blocks most noise.

- Cover your eyes. Use a sleeping mask or T-shirt wrapped over your eyes.

- Keep the room cool. Turn off the heating vent (if winter), and crack the window open. Or if summer, use a fan or air conditioning.

- Do Not Disturb. Turn on the answering machine, take the children to a sitter, and take care of anything else that may interrupt your dozing.

Food and Nutrition for Sleeping

- Calcium/magnesium. These minerals have a soothing effect on your nervous system and muscles, especially if taken before bed with a snack or with your evening meal. (Always take calcium with food.)

- Skimp on nighttime snacks. If you must nibble before bed, keep your snack light and easy to digest. Pick fresh fruit or toast, not a ham sandwich.

- "Sweet" dreams. Avoid sugary foods prior to lights out. After a few hours, a sweet snack leaves your blood sugar low—a sure-fire wake-up call. (See Low Blood Sugar.) If no food before bed wakes you up, try a small, protein snack like yogurt.

- To B or not to B? Make sure you're getting adequate amounts of the B-complex vitamins in your multiple pill. Also dine on whole grains and dark, leafy greens.

■ *Makeover Hint #98—Be Still, Restless Legs*

A fairly common cause of insomnia is restless leg syndrome, a condition where you wake up from the irresistible urge to move your legs. Taking a calcium and magnesium supplement can help. Vitamin E, 400 IU twice daily, also works for some.

Herbal Treatment

Many different herbs with sedative actions are used for insomnia. They can be used alone, especially valerian or passion flower, or you may find them combined as teas or other herbal products. While these plants certainly don't carry the hazards of sleeping pills, use them only for occasional insomnia or as an adjunct to a more comprehensive sleeping program.

- Indigestion insomnia—chamomile, hops, peppermint
- Restless legs—ginkgo
- Sedatives—passion flower, skullcap, valerian

The Homeopathic Difference

- Coffea cruda—*Can't turn my mind off.* Think of how coffee makes you feel—nervous, agitated, restless—and you'll know when to use Coffea (or homeopathic coffee) for a sleepless night. Coffea is the remedy for a wide-awake mind, but a sleepy body.

- Ignatia—*Emotional insomnia.* If your emotions are keeping you awake, think of Ignatia. It might be shock, grief, sadness, or disappointment that prevents you from falling asleep. Sighing often accompanies this type of insomnia, and you probably don't feel like talking about it.

- Kali phosphoricum—*Nervous exhaustion; no sleep.* Anxiety and lethargy go hand in hand with this remedy. While you feel weak and tired, there's still a sense of irritability and "brain-fag" due to overwork, excitement, or worry.

- Nux vomica—*Early morning waking.* The person who fits this remedy can fall asleep all right, even feels sleepy after eating and early in the evening, but can't sleep after 3am. Waking this early makes the Nux person feel terrible. And even when he does sleep, his dreams are full of hustle and bustle.

Lifestyle Link

- Exercise. Regular activity not only improves overall health, but is a beautiful makeover step for sleeping. Hint: exercising three hours or less before bed has more of a wake-up than a good-night effect.

- Is your bedroom dark? Light filtering in from the street or other rooms disturbs sleep.

- Bathroom break. Don't turn on the light if you get up to urinate at night. It not only wakens you, but disrupts melatonin—the sleeping hormone.

- Avoid ibuprofen. This also interferes with melatonin.
- Low blood sugar. For those prone to low blood sugar, night-time awakenings may be a problem. When glucose drops too low, the brain gets hungry and you wake up.
- Sex. This is a wonderful, natural sleeping aid (see Chapter 10).
- Don't clock-watch. Looking at the time while falling asleep or during the night can make dozing difficult.
- Stay clear of drugs. Like alcohol, these can create sleeping problems.

Lookout Alert

- After starting new medication—prescription or over-the-counter. This includes herbs and vitamins.
- Accompanied by other symptoms, like aching joints.

LOW BLOOD SUGAR

This is a controversial condition. Medically speaking, there are two types of hypoglycemia (low blood sugar). There's spontaneous hypoglycemia, a rare kind of low blood sugar usually caused by severe disease like a tumor in the pancreas or liver. Reactive hypoglycemia, the other kind, is more common and occurs two to four hours after eating or in response to specific drugs like insulin. Low blood sugar is also common among pregnant women, after extended periods of exercise or during fever. For a select few, hypoglycemia is the first warning sign of impending diabetes.

The controversy among doctors and nutritionists surrounds low blood sugar that follows a meal, particularly one high in simple carbohydrates. People who claim to have this condition commonly complain of headaches, irritability, weakness, fatigue, trembling, poor vision, memory problems, and food cravings. Mid-afternoon is a common time for these symptoms to occur.

Jonathan Wright, M.D., calls this "refined carbohydrate disease," meaning it's the processed and refined foods we eat—low in fiber and nutrients—that create unstable blood sugar levels; caffeine and alcohol do the same. Past studies suggest that poor insulin response is responsible,[13] and is referred to as insulin resistance or hyper-insulinemia. Exhausted adrenal glands can also be at hand, as can a malfunctioning liver. Anna MacIntosh, Ph.D., N.D., proposes that we call this condition dysglycemia (literally bad blood sugar) rather than low blood sugar because many people have troubles regulating blood sugar, be it up or down.[14] Other names describing this condition include glucose intolerance, Syndrome X, and carbohydrate intolerance. There's even evidence that low blood sugar is related to high blood pressure.[15] So if other measures (dietary, nutrients, herbs, medication) don't help your hypertension, consider following a low blood sugar regimen.

If you suspect you're prone to this condition, follow the suggestions below. If they don't help, visit with your doctor for a more thorough evaluation. Related topics include Anxiety, Fatigue, Headaches, Indigestion. Also glance at Chapters 3 (liver), 4 (digestion), 7 (adrenals), and 14 (the mind).

How to Prevent Low Blood Sugar

- Steer clear of sugar. Sweet things and refined carbohydrates contribute to this state.
- Eat breakfast. This doesn't mean coffee and a Danish. Feast on oatmeal with fruit and nuts, or an egg alongside whole grain toast or bran muffin.
- Nutritious nibbling. After a wholesome breakfast, keep your body humming with more fiber-filled, nutritious foods.
- All in the family. If low blood sugar signs or alcoholism run in your family, you may be more prone. Take steps early to prevent greater troubles down the road.

Food and Nutrition for Low Blood Sugar

Follow prevention tips, as well as the ideas below.

- The more often you eat, the better you feel. Maintain even blood sugar levels with three small meals interjected with two to three snacks.
- Carry snacks. If it's difficult to stop and eat every couple of hours, carry a bag of raw almonds, walnuts, and raisins to munch on.

- Pour out the alcohol. This adds to the blood sugar roller coaster.
- Eat a little protein with every meal. Help prop up blood sugar with lean meats and poultry, beans, low-fat and cultured dairy, nuts and seeds at each seating.
- Get your chromium. This blood sugar-regulating mineral, in 200 to 300 mcg divided doses daily, helps those who are chromium-deficient.
- Other nutrients. The B vitamins, vitamin C, flavonoids, calcium, magnesium, and zinc are also important for pancreas and adrenal function. Begin with a good multivitamin/mineral.
- Lipotropics. If the liver's at fault, try liver-hungry nutrients (choline, folic acid, vitamin B_{12}, methionine, betaine and carnitine).
- The digestion connection. If gas, bloating, heartburn are also problems, consider indigestion as a factor. See Indigestion and Chapter 4.
- Consider food allergies. If the above steps don't help much, try avoiding suspected food allergies for one to two weeks and see if it helps.

Herbal Treatment

- Adrenal support—licorice
- Improve glucose tolerance—bitter melon, fenugreek, goat's rue, gymnema
- Liver help for more even blood sugar—dandelion, milk thistle

The Homeopathic Difference

A blood sugar dysfunction has such a strong lifestyle and dietary connection that I hesitate suggesting any homeopathic remedies for it. After all, using homeopathy in acute fashion is only a temporary fix. And blood sugar needs permanent nutritional and dietary attention. If you're having troubles getting your wild, modern ways under control, read up on Nux vomica (see Appendix B). This may help. Otherwise, seek the help of a practitioner expert in constitutional homeopathic prescribing. In the meantime, change your diet and see what happens.

Lifestyle Link

- Stop smoking. There's a strong link between cigarette smoking and malfunctioning insulin (called insulin resistance).[16]
- Testing. Ask your doctor for a Glucose-Insulin Tolerance Test if you want confirmation that hypoglycemia is causing you distress.

Lookout Alert

- If you're diabetic and have these symptoms
- If you're taking insulin
- Began a new medication prior to onset of symptoms
- Have a history of alcohol use or abuse
- Convulsion or loss of consciousness occurs
- Chest pain
- Chronic or severe symptoms

MOTION SICKNESS

That queasy feeling, and occasional vomiting, that come with travel is familiar to many. Cold sweats, sleepiness, hyperventilation, weakness, and a pale complexion, dizziness, headache, and fatigue can also occur. For unknown reasons, some of us are susceptible to movement whether by sea, air, car, or train. Some even become ill on a swing. We do know that motion sickness is the result of overstimulation of certain nerves, and that particular things like looking out the window (especially from the back seat), poor ventilation, cigarette smoke, fear and anxiety all make this miserable condition worse. Taking measures to prevent or minimize motion symptoms is much more effective than treating full-blown motion sickness. Refer to Anxiety, Fatigue, Headaches, Insomnia, Low Blood Sugar.

How to Prevent Motion Sickness

- Best seat in the house (or car). Whatever your mode of transportation, sit where you feel the least motion—usually in the middle—over the wings of an airplane, center seat in a car, or mid-ship if on a boat.

- Don't read while traveling.
- Lie down or semi-erect with your head stationary or braced.
- Don't watch the scenery go by; it only makes matters worse.
- Don't travel with smokers. Or ask them to extinguish their cigarettes.
- Get lots of fresh air.

Food and Nutrition for Motion Sickness

- Avoid eating. And drinking, if traveling a short distance.
- Eat lightly. Drink fresh lemon or lime juice, if going on an extended trip.
- Sip on green tea.
- Avoid alcohol.

Herbal Treatment

- Calm down with—passion flower, skullcap, valerian
- Nausea—ginger
- Nervous stomach—chamomile, peppermint (teas work well)

■ *Makeover Hint #99—The Three-Day Ginger Cure*

To avoid the nausea (and sometimes vomiting) of travel, begin sipping three cups of ginger tea three days before you depart. Continue drinking it on the day of your trip (every hour if possible. All this liquid also keeps you hydrated—good for plane rides). To make tea, purchase tea bags or brew this homemade version:

1 tsp powdered or chopped up ginger root

1 cup boiling water

Steep ginger in water for 10 minutes, strain (if needed) and drink.

If you prefer, take capsules: 1000 mg of ginger equals one cup of tea. This plan works well for extensive travel, like plane trips.

The Homeopathic Difference

- Cocculus indicus—*Oh so dizzy!* Nausea marks this motion sickness remedy, as well as an ache in the back of the head and eyes. Along with the vertigo is a weakness that makes it difficult to speak out. (In Dr. William Boericke's 1927 edition of *Materia Medica*, still a standard reference for homeopaths, he emphasizes that these symptoms are worse when riding in a carriage or by ship. I assume we can extrapolate and say this is also true for modern-day car and plane travelers.)

- Nux vomica—*A sensitive, dizzy type.* This remedy fits those who feel irritable and oversensitive with a pounding headache. Dizziness is part of the Nux picture; but the sign to watch for is nausea with dry heaves.

- Petroleum—*I feel like I'm inebriated.* This is another remedy that eases dizziness, especially when upon standing. Also, the back of the head feels very heavy and irritability is apparent. All of this feels better when lying back with the head held up. The sign to watch for most is a "drunk-like" feeling.

- Tabacum—*The moving vomit.* If you're traveling with a smoker, and the smell of tobacco makes your travel sickness worse, think of Tabacum—homeopathic tobacco. This nausea is incessant, and moving makes you vomit. A terrible sinking feeling lies in the pit of your stomach, and your head aches horribly. Open your eyes, and the room (or car) spins.

Lifestyle Link

- Breathe deeply. May help with the nausea and relax you at the same time.

- Fresh air versus stale fumes. Clean air certainly clears one's head and relieves nausea to a point. However, if you're traveling in the city during rush hour, roll up your window and keep auto exhaust out.

Lookout Alert

- Watch for dehydration if prolonged vomiting

PSORIASIS

This is a tough condition to treat both naturally and conventionally. It's fairly common, found in about three of every 100 Americans. All ages are affected, though it usually begins around age 10. Psoriasis tends to run in the family, and is caused by overzealous skin cell production. What results is thick, scaly, dry, sometimes reddish skin that has a silvery sheen to it and isn't itchy. Symptoms come and go. For some, psoriasis isn't too bad with only one or two rashes apparent, usually on the scalp, elbows, knees, back, and buttocks. More severe, widespread cases are also possible, with some people developing joint pain called psoriatic arthritis. Also see Acne and Eczema; read Chapters 3 (liver), 4 (digestion), 12 (skin), and 14 (the mind).

How to Prevent Psoriasis

- Reduce the rays. Moderate sunlight helps psoriasis, but avoid sunburn.
- Guard your skin. Local skin injuries can bring on psoriasis, as well as other irritations.
- Watch your health. Some people, particularly children, have an outbreak after a chest cold, bronchitis, or other upper respiratory infection.
- Avoid topical medications unless absolutely necessary.
- Be cautious of cortisone medications. Withdrawing from these medicines can also bring on psoriasis. If you need such medication, explore other alternatives with your doctor's help.

Food and Nutrition for the Skin

- Saturated fats. Step away from fatty animal-based foods like red meat and whole-fat dairy.
- Feast on fish. Eat plenty of fish like mackerel, halibut, and salmon.
- Eat up essentials. Ensure you're getting plenty of essential fatty acids from raw, unsalted nuts and seeds, whole grains and flax seed (or flax seed oil).
- Give caffeine the boot. Cut the coffee and other caffeine pleasures down or out.

- Eliminate alcohol, and see what happens.
- Enjoy fresh fruits and vegetables.
- Load up on whole grains. These are brown rice, barley, and whole wheat bread.
- Drink water.
- Use a high-potency multiple vitamin and mineral. Make sure it has at least 400 IU of vitamin E, as well as B-complex.
- Add some C. Extra vitamin C, 500 to 1000 mg thrice daily, might also help.
- Zinc. For three months, and no more, take 45 mg of this mineral. Then decrease to 15 mg daily.
- Digestive help. Try digestive enzymes or hydrochloric acid.
- Ask your doctor to test you for food allergies. If you suspect you're reacting to a food(s), eliminate it for one month. Wheat and citrus are common culprits.

■ *Makeover Hint #100—Give Up Pop*

Avoiding sugar is a common natural health suggestion for psoriasis. One afternoon, a fellow in his 50s came to visit me in my office wanting to know how to cure his psoriasis. I mentioned the above ideas, as well as the one about eliminating sugar. Turns out this gentleman drank two quarts of cola each day. "Ya know," he said to me, "when I was hospitalized a few years back, the nurses wouldn't let me have any soft drinks. Come to think of it, my psoriasis cleared up totally." Sounded to me like he already knew what to do, if he so chose.

Herbal Treatment

Many of the following herbs work best for psoriasis if taken long-term. Ask a skilled herbalist to guide you.

- Balancing/nutritive—burdock, nettles, sarsaparilla
- For irritation—sarsaparilla
- Less stress—linden, skullcap, valerian

- Reduce inflammation—licorice
- Scaly skin—burdock, cleavers

■ *Makeover Hint #101—Soothing Cream*

If you're searching for an herbal cream to ease psoriatic irritation, read labels and look for these ingredients: comfrey, chickweed, and marshmallow.

The Homeopathic Difference

- Arsenicum—*It burns.* Look for itchy, swollen, scaly, rough, dry skin, if you want to try Arsenicum. Often the right side is worse than the left, and a flare-up can make you restless. The odd thing about this remedy, though, is that the pain is burning, but cold makes it feel bad.
- Borax—*THE psoriasis remedy.* If confused, choose Borax for your psoriasis first. The back of finger joints are particularly affected, as well as the hands. Symptoms are often better in the evening and worse when the weather gets warm.
- Lycopodium—*Offensive odor.* For this type of psoriasis, there's violent itching and dry skin. Scratching makes the skin bleed, and any secretions—including perspiration—smell bad.
- Sulphur—*Don't wash.* This general skin remedy also helps when your psoriasis burns and itches. It's specific for psoriasis in the folds of skin, like elbow creases and behind the knees. But the distinguishing sign is that it's worse after bathing.

Lifestyle Link

- Move and sweat. Daily exercise is helpful, especially the type that makes you perspire (See Chapter 9).
- Breathe and relax every day (See Chapter 6).

Lookout Alert

- Sores that don't heal
- Accompanying joint pain

SORE THROAT

This is a common wintertime, cold-related symptom. Runny nose, fever, fatigue are some of the signs that a sore throat is infectious in nature. A virus is frequently responsible, though more serious *Streptococcus* (strep throat) can also be the villain. Besides throat pain, swallowing can be irksome. Tonsillitis, more often a bacterial—like strep—infection, has the added symptom of swallowing pain that shoots out to the ears, as well as high fever and vomiting. Laryngitis is key when your voice drops to a whisper. A sore throat is often a sign that an infection is on its way. This is your opportunity to take action and halt it in its tracks. Natural therapies tend to work better when used early.

Because a sore throat is a symptom and not a disease, there are many other causes. If you've been talking, screaming, or singing a lot, you might develop a pained throat. Allergies or inhaling irritating substances (including cigarette smoke) can hurt your throat. Tumors in that area (benign and cancerous) are unusual, but possible, causes. If the following suggestions don't help within a couple of days, see your doctor to rule out the possibility of strep throat. If your throat aches and doesn't seem to be part of a cold or infection, also seek help. See Bronchitis, Colds and Flu, Coughing, Hay Fever, and Heartburn; also refer to Chapter 6 (immunity).

How to Prevent a Sore Throat

- Guard your immunity to fight infection. (See Chapter 6.)
- Avoid cigarette smoke, your own and others'.
- Don't breathe paint. If working around any solvents, including house paint, wear a mask, make sure the area is well ventilated, and take frequent breaks.
- Protect your voice. Overuse can injure it.
- Change toothbrushes every month. Bacteria grow here and may contribute to an infection.

Food and Nutrition for the Throat

- Stay away from sweets. They keep an infection brewing.
- Drink up. The more fluids the better: water, herbal tea, soup, and fresh, raw vegetable juices are best.

- Avoid fruit juices. It's the fruit sugar.
- Homemade gargle. Add 1/4 tsp turmeric and a pinch of salt to warm water, gargle, and spit out.
- Lemon and honey mixed in warm water. Sip slowly.
- Suck on zinc lozenges. See Makeover Hint #102 following.
- Oh, say can you C? Take 500–1000 mg of vitamin C every two hours. Optional: add a similar amount of bioflavonoids.
- Extra carotenes.
- Consider food allergies. A chronic tickle that doesn't appear infectious might be food-related. Key question: if you're stuffed up, is the resulting mucus clear? If so, it's probably not infectious, but allergic.

Herbal Treatment

For teas made with the following herbs, gargle first, then swallow for maximum effectiveness.

- Drying herbs for mucus-filled throats—bayberry, sage, sumac
- Infection reducers—echinacea, garlic, golden seal, osha root, sage
- Soothing—slippery elm, marshmallow root

The Homeopathic Difference

- Belladonna—*Dry as the desert.* As is typical for Belladonna, this sore throat is red and dry. Your throat feels tight and even worse when you drink liquids.
- Drosera rotundifolia—*I can barely talk.* When spit seems to fill your mouth, yet your throat is dry and rough think Drosera. And you're so hoarse, the words don't come out right. Lying down makes your throat feel bad.
- Lachesis—*That choking feeling.* The most notable feature of this sore throat remedy is the sensation of constriction, especially when swallowing. The left side, for some reason, feels the worst.
- Lycopodium—*Better with a cup of tea.* This is a kind of moving sore throat; it may settle on the right, or hop back and forth from right to left. Warm beverages ease it a bit.

Lifestyle Link

A sore throat can be part of inhalant allergies. See Hay fever.

- Indulge in sleep.
- Don't overdo it.
- Give up smoking.
- Ditto for alcohol.
- Question antibiotics. If your doctor prescribes this medicine, first ask for a throat culture to confirm that you indeed have a bacterial infection. Viruses, which cause most sore throats, don't respond to antibiotics.

Lookout Alert

- Severe pain upon swallowing
- Pain that extends to the ear on the same side—especially if the only complaint
- Difficulty breathing
- Spitting up blood
- Pain with talking
- Hoarseness that lasts two weeks or more
- Severe or unrelenting symptoms

■ *Makeover Hint #102—Gargle With Killer Zinc*

According to studies,[17] zinc kills viruses on contact. This means if you want to attack the bugs that are causing your sore throat, you need to suck on a zinc lozenge, not merely swallow a zinc pill. If you can't find zinc lozenges at your local health food store, here's a quick health trick you can try.

Empty one capsule of zinc powder into half a cup of warm water.
Add 1/2 tsp of salt and mix.
Gargle and spit out.

The secret to this remedy is to gargle as often as humanly possible. (Warning, this mixture tastes like metallic dirt.)

SPRAINS AND STRAINS

The body's framework isn't just made up of bones and muscles. Ligaments act as the fasteners between neighboring bones, and tendons are the bridges across muscles and bones. All of these structures are prone to injury. More specifically, a strain occurs when a ligament or muscle is overstretched. Sprains, frequent in the ankle, are a slightly more serious injury where a ligament is either severely stretched or partially torn. Symptoms to watch for are pain (both on movement and at ease), swelling, redness, and heat in the affected joint—especially after a spill or accident. For related information, see Backache, and read Chapters 9 (muscles) and 11 (bones).

How to Prevent Sprains and Strains

- Ease in and out. Warm up before you exercise and cool down afterward.
- Don't overdo it. Especially for intense or prolonged exercise you're not used to.
- Be careful. If you're sick, tired, or recently injured, you're more likely to hurt yourself during these vulnerable times.
- Think before you move. Prior to an exercise regimen, consider your age, health, the environmental factors, your current fitness level. For instance, don't run a marathon if you've never run before.
- Visit with your doctor or a knowledgeable practitioner to help you determine an effective and safe exercise plan.
- Start slow and easy.

Food and Nutrition for Injuries

- Vitamin C and bioflavonoids. Repair damaged tendons and ligaments with these nutrients, taken in equal amounts (1000 mg each daily).

- Other antioxidants. In addition to vitamin C, take other antioxidant nutrients like E and glutathione—look for an antioxidant formula in one supplement.

- Fruit enzymes. Bromelain, made from the pineapple stem, douses pain and inflammation when taken between meals.

- Digestive enzymes. Take extra amounts of pancreatin (pancreatic enzymes) *between* meals to heal injuries. Note: If you experience stomach upset, cut the amount you're taking down or out.

- Eat to douse inflammation. Saturated fats (in red meat, poultry skin, dairy fat) may be swell, but they also enhance swelling. Avoid these while healing.

- Turn to essential fatty acids. Flax seed oil, fish, nuts and seeds, on the other hand, calm inflammation.

- Spice it up. Ginger and turmeric added liberally to food help combat swelling. (See Herbs below.)

- Extra calcium and magnesium. Load up on these minerals for awhile if muscle spasm is a problem. Include a dose (300 mg/150 mg) before bed with a small snack if you can't sleep.

- Manganese. Between 50 and 100 mg in divided doses for two weeks, followed by a maintenance amount (whatever is in your multiple).

■ *Makeover Hint #103—It's Thyme for a Bath*

Speed healing by immersing your injured body part into a hot bath (or basin) spiked with a tea made from dried thyme or rosemary (use one ounce of herb for every two cups of water). Not only will you feel better faster, but you'll also smell wonderful—lasagna anyone?

Herbal Treatment

- Healing—horsetail, nettles
- Pain—black willow, meadow sweet, tiger balm (see Headaches)
- Swelling—feverfew, ginger, turmeric

The Homeopathic Difference

Smelly, warming liniments that contain camphor and menthol, like Tiger Balm or eucalyptus, feel glorious on sore, stiff muscles. However, avoid these treatments if you plan to use homeopathic remedies. The two don't mix. In fact, such strong-smelling liniments will undo a remedy.

- Arnica—*First-line "owie" defense.* This remedy is designed for all types of injuries, be they sprains, strains, bruises, pain, swelling, and even shock. Known as a muscular tonic, Arnica should be taken by mouth and/or applied in cream form to the injured area immediately and continually for 24 hours.

- Bellis perennis—*For that deep, deep pain.* This is a remedy when you feel sore and bruised, and the strain you've just acquired is deep.

- Rhus toxicodendron—*The follow-up remedy.* After a day's worth of Arnica, switch to Rhus tox for achy sprains and strains that loosen up and feel better with a little motion.

- Ruta graveolens—*The pain keeps going and going.* For post-injury pain that *doesn't* abate with movement, try Ruta, a popular alternative to Rhus tox.

Lifestyle Link

Immediate first aid attention is imperative after an injury. Follow the RICE procedure for best results.

- R—Rest the limb or body part that's been hurt. This prevents additional injury.

- I—Ice the aching area. This reduces swelling.

- C—Compress the region with an elastic bandage. This calms swelling.

- E—Elevate the injured part above heart level. One more way to diminish fluid accumulation.

Lookout Alert

- Have an X-ray done for severe injuries to rule out fractures.
- Pinpoint pain.
- Swelling and pain that occurs without injury (see Gout).
- Injury with fever or other unusual symptom.

ULCERS

An ulcer is basically an open sore. It can pop up on many parts of the body—skin, mouth, eyelid, genitals—but the ones we're going to address are the peptic kind that infiltrate the digestive tract. The most common types occur in the first part of the small intestine, called the duodenum, and the stomach. These areas are bathed in enzymes and stomach acid, which serve to aggravate the situation when protective mucus thins and the underlying tissue is open to injury. Kind of like putting salt in a wound. Other vulnerable areas are the esophagus and further down the small intestine.

Some ulcers are silent and don't cause problems until something more dramatic develops, like bleeding. Others cause a burning, aching, soreness or gnawing-like pain that's steady and confined to one spot. Some ulcers feel better after eating, drinking milk, or taking antacids. Others might awaken you in the middle of the night with pain. Occasionally the pain disappears on its own, only to return.

No longer do we point a finger at stress as the cause of ulcer, although it does make matters worse. In 1983, gastroenterologist, Barry Marshall, from Royal Perth Hospital in Australia, and his colleague Robin Warren discovered that a bacteria called Helicobacter pylori is most likely behind many ulcers. They estimated that 70 percent of gastric (stomach) ulcers and 90 percent of peptic ulcers[18] were caused by this bug. This infection is easily detected with a simple blood test and the results confirmed by an X-ray or endoscopy. For related conditions see Constipation, Diarrhea, Food Poisoning, Heartburn, and Indigestion. Also scan Chapter 4 (digestion).

How to Prevent Ulcers

If you've had ulcers before, or the digestive tract is your weak point, be cautious about your diet, stress level, and other factors that invite ulcers. See suggestions below.

Food and Nutrition for Ulcers

- Avoid alcohol and caffeine.
- Pass on the spices. Cayenne and other spicy foods can aggravate an active ulcer. However, once an ulcer is healed, hot peppers may actually be preventive.
- Reduce saturated fats. These are found mainly in animal foods, like meat and dairy.
- Reduce acid. Pulverize cardamom, cinnamon, and cloves in a coffee grinder; mix 1 tsp in a cup of hot water, steep for 10 to 15 minutes, strain and sip.
- Eat bananas to speed healing.
- Dine on cabbage too.
- Check out food allergies.
- Eat more fiber.
- Increase essential fatty acids. Do this with flax seed oil (1 tbsp. daily in food) or flax meal.
- Check your multi for vitamins A and E, and zinc. These help with recuperation.

■ *Makeover Hint #105—A Little Cabbage with Your Tomato Juice?*

An old naturopathic cure for ulcers involves two common kitchen ingredients: tomato juice and cabbage or sauerkraut. Try it, you'll like it.

Herbal Treatment

- Antacid—meadow sweet
- Antibacterial—echinacea, golden seal

- Healing—cabbage, calendula, comfrey, licorice
- Relaxing—linden, passion flower, skullcap, valerian
- Soothing—comfrey, marshmallow root, slippery elm

The Homeopathic Difference

- Argenitum nitricum—*Radiating pain.* Ulcers of this kind often begin with a gnawing pain that shoots out to all abdominal parts. Belching and gas are other common signs that fit Argenitum. You might crave sweets (though they only make matters worse), as well as salt and cheese.

- Arsensicum album—*Raw stomach.* The burning, gnawing pain that comes with this ulcer may also be accompanied by vomiting of blood and/or bile. Your stomach is extremely raw and hurts from any food or drink; watch for acid-like belches. Your ulcer feels worse with cold foods like ice cream and drink such as ice water. A milk craving is possible.

- Kali bichromicum—*No more beer.* Although stomach pain stops after eating with this kind of ulcer, it feels like food just sits there. The upper left and right regions of your abdomen feel like stitches are running from there through to the backbone. And even though you yearn for beer, it only makes matters worse with nausea and vomiting.

- Uranium nitricum—*Boring pain.* This unusual remedy is specific for both gastric and duodenal ulcers. Excessive thirst and a ravenous appetite set it apart from other ulcer remedies. Other distinguishing signs to take note of are nausea, vomiting, burning in the stomach and a boring (not tedious) pain in a bloated abdomen.

Lifestyle Link

- Stop smoking.
- Avoid taking aspirin, especially if smoking.
- Eliminate antacids.
- Control stress.

Lookout Alert

- If no relief in three weeks
- Continuous nausea, headache and weakness
- Sweating and dizziness
- Fever
- Vomiting of fresh blood
- Vomiting of a "coffee ground" substance
- Blood in the stools
- Black, tarry stools
- Intense, persistent abdominal pain—especially if it extends beyond this area, for example, to the back
- Sudden, intense, steady pain that begins at the bottom of the breast bone. It might spread quickly, and extend to the right, lower section of the abdomen, and possibly to one or both shoulders. This is a MEDICAL EMERGENCY and suggests that the ulcer has perforated.

URINARY TRACT INFECTIONS (UTI)

Lower urinary tract infections (UTI) are very common, and are usually bacterial in origin. Women are hit with UTIs 10 times as often as men, though symptoms are similar: burning on urination, an urgent need to urinate, frequent urination, and getting up at night. Men with UTIs might notice the end of their penis is red and inflamed. Males 40 and older who notice these symptoms, without the burning or inflamed penis, but also with difficulty in starting and stopping urination and a weak urine stream, might have an enlarged prostate (have the doctor perform a prostate exam). When low back or lower abdominal pain accompany these symptoms, a bladder infection might be present. For conditions with similar symptoms, see Backache and Fatigue. Also refer to Chapter 5 (kidneys).

How to Prevent UTIs

These tips can also be used during UTI treatment.

- Women, wipe yourself from the front to the back. This prevents fecal material from contaminating the urinary tract opening (urethra).

- Urinate after intercourse.

- Drink plenty of filtered or bottled water, one to two quarts daily.

- Keep sugar intake down.

- Drink at least six ounces of unsweetened cranberry juice every day (especially if you're prone to UTIs or bladder infections).

- Do your Kegel exercises (see Makeover Hint #51).

Food and Nutrition for the Urinary Tract

- Cranberry juice. This hastens healing from infection. Drink 16 ounces of unsweetened juice each day until clear—usually two weeks; then decrease amount to six ounces daily.

- Blueberries or blueberry juice. Acts like cranberries, maybe even better.

- Vitamin C, 500–1000 mg every two hours during infection. If you experience bowel intolerance (diarrhea, gas, bloating, cramps) stop for the day, and resume taking C in smaller amounts.

- Eat plenty of garlic and onions. They fight the bugs.

- Beta-carotene (100,000 IU each day during infection), and yellow, orange, and dark green vegetables.

- Zinc it. Use 30 mg each day (total, including what's in your multi) until infection is finished, then resume with maintenance dose (15 mg) or what's in your daily multiple vitamin/mineral pills.

- Add good bugs. Take a probiotic supplement to reestablish the good germs in your system. This is vital if you're currently taking or have taken antibiotics to combat a UTI.

- Yogurt is a probiotic. If you like and can tolerate dairy, eat a cup of plain, culture-rich yogurt a day.

- Bladder irritants. Caffeine, artificial sweeteners, and tomatoes can do this.

Herbal Treatment

- Diuretic—cleavers, dandelion, uva ursi
- Soothing—corn silk, couchgrass, marshmallow leaf
- Infection fighters—echinacea, garlic, golden seal, uva ursi

The Homeopathic Difference

- Aconite—*Hot urine*. Urine is retained in the bladder with this type of UTI. You might feel a spasm in that region and fret about urinating because it's so painful and hot.
- Apis mellifica—*It stings*. Apis is suitable for infections where urination is frequent, and even involuntary. Your urine has a deep color, and it leaves you feeling burned, sore, and stung (like a bee invaded you there).
- Cantharis—*Want to, but can't*. This is homeopathic Spanish fly: the infamous aphrodisiac that excites by irritating both genital and urinary systems. If you have a constant urge to urinate or pain in that area—with little result—try Cantharis. Urine might burn, or be bloody.
- Equisetum—*A full bladder feeling*. If you're experiencing a dull, but intense, pain in the bladder, think of Equisetum. Some find incontinence a problem. Although you need to urinate often, it comes out in drips with extreme pain when done. The bladder feels full all the time—even after urination.

Lifestyle Link

- If you use a diaphragm, consider switching to a different form of birth control, as this type can contribute to UTI and bladder infections in some women.
- Kegel exercises (see Makeover Hint #51).
- No smoking.
- Rest. You need it; you're fighting an infection.

Lookout Alert

- Severe pain, especially higher up the back

- Flank or abdominal pain
- Chills, fever, nausea and/or vomiting (which may indicate a more serious kidney infection)
- Bloody urine
- Men: a whitish mucus-like discharge or pus from the penis
- Get a checkup, if you or your family has a history of kidney disease

VAGINITIS

See Yeast Infections.

VARICOSE VEINS

Unfortunately, varicose veins are usually the bane of women and half of those middle-aged because their veins are quite frail and, when the vein wall is hurt, it can balloon. In cases where the valves that control blood flow in the veins are injured, varicose veins result as blood pools. At first, there's a slight swelling or bulging where the vein is affected, but no visible vessel. That may be all, with no symptoms to speak of. Or you might feel more tired with achy, hot, tight legs, and the skin over the veins may swell and turn purple and red. Worst-case scenario—skin ulcers develop. They usually appear on the calves and along the inner leg, top and bottom. Also see Constipation, Fatigue, Hemorrhoids; refer to Chapters 3 (liver), 4 (digestion) and 9 (muscles).

How to Prevent Varicose Veins

Like a garden hose, your veins weaken with time. This, combined with increased pressure inside your veins, is what creates varicose veins. Obviously, the weaker your veins (caused, for example, by aging) and the more pressure exerted inside the veins, the greater the chance of trouble.

- Choose the right family. Varicose veins runs in families.
- Sit down. Excessive standing increases vein pressure—especially when accompanied by carrying heavy loads. So sit down and give your legs a rest.

- Exercise too. Sedentary lifestyle increases your chances of varicosities. So strike a balance between activity and rest.
- Be cautious about lifting. Increased vein pressure again.
- Support hose. Those elastic, tight fitting stockings or socks can ease tired legs. Fashionable too.
- Weight control. Obesity is another major risk factor.
- Toned muscles. As we age, muscle and vein tone drop. Biking, swimming, and walking keep your muscles (and veins) in shape, and push pooled blood back into circulation (see Chapter 9).

Food and Nutrition for Legs

- Roughage roundup. As for many conditions, a high-fiber diet is the most important step to prevent and treat varicose veins. The reason is that straining due to constipation increases the pressure inside your leg's veins. High-fiber foods, like vegetables and legumes, are also nutritional powerhouses.
- Berry up! All those wonderful red, blue, and purple berries you love—blackberries, blueberries, cherries—are full of vein-building flavonoids. Eating them helps treat and prevent varicose veins.
- Fill up on fish and other good fats too, like flaxseed oil, nuts and seeds.
- Keep that blood flowing and those veins healthy. This means cutting down on saturated animal fats, sugar, salt, alcohol, and refined carbohydrate foods.
- Vitamins and minerals. A good multiple containing vitamins A, B-complex, and E as well as zinc help nourish varicose-ridden legs.
- Vitamin C and collagen. This nutrient heals tissue like collagen in doses ranging from 500 mg to 3000 mg daily in divided doses; an equal amount of bioflavonoids helps too.

Herbal Treatment

- Bulk up—flax seed, oat bran or meal, psyllium seed
- Diuretics—hawthorn, horse tail, stone root

- Enhance blood flow—ginkgo, gotu kola
- Strengthen veins—gotu kola, hawthorn, horse chestnut
- Curb swelling (see Diuretics)—Butcher's broom, horse chestnut

■ *Makeover Hint #106—Topical Relief*

To ease aching legs, apply a cream, lotion, or ointment with these herbs: Butcher's broom, calendula, horse chestnut, and witch hazel.

The Homeopathic Difference

- Calcarea fluorica—*Start here*. Calcarea fluorica is considered *the* remedy for varicose veins, especially when vessels are bulging. To make sure this is for you, ask yourself this. Do your legs feel worse during rest and better with warmth? If so, Calcarea is a good fit.
- Hamamelis virginica—*Homeopathic witch hazel*. Here's a case where both the herb and its homeopathic cousin help the same condition. Hamamelis is homeopathic witch hazel, and is particularly good when legs feel tired, and muscles and joints are sore. Sometimes there's a chilliness too, that begins in the back or hips and travels down the legs.
- Pulsatilla—*Heavy and weary*. Another remedy for varicose veins is Pulsatilla, especially when they're restless, cold, and feel tired, in a heavy sort of way.
- Zincum—*Can't sit still*. Zincum works well for large varicose veins of the legs that feel weak, tremble, and twitch. You might find your soles are sensitive too. But most important, you're constantly moving your feet and legs. For women, menstruation makes it worse.

Lifestyle Link

- Menstrual period. For women, varicose veins can be worse during this time, so take extra care.
- Support hose. They ease tired, aching legs.

- Put your feet up. This gives varicose veins a rest.
- Get a leg massage. Rubbing your legs with fragrant almond oil is soothing and helps circulation. Add a little vitamin E oil if you like.

Lookout Alert

Superficial varicose veins arc generally harmless, though unsightly. It's when the deep veins are affected that potential problems occur—like blood clots in the lungs (pulmonary embolism), heart attack, and stroke. Watch for these signs:

- Painful skin ulcers or sores in the area of varicose veins
- Fever
- Reddish-brown veins

YEAST INFECTIONS

While they are normal residents in our bodies, when yeast grow beyond normal limits, an infection occurs. The most commonly known yeast infection happens in the genital area, especially among women. Itching and irritation, as well as a cheesy, white discharge are signs yeast has invaded. Men are often symptom-less, though genital irritation may be a complaint. Antibiotics, birth control pills, cortisone medication, pregnancy, and diabetes all contribute to this problem.

Another frequent, though less admitted, area prone to yeast infection is the gastrointestinal tract. Like genital yeast, increasing antibiotic use has made yeast infection an up-and-coming disease. The reason for this is simple. Normally, there is a happy existence between the bacteria and yeast that live in both the genital and digestive tracts. The job of antibiotics is to kill disease-causing bacteria. However, their action is not well directed and the "good" bacteria in our bodies that help keep yeast populations in check are also destroyed. The result is more room for yeast to grow and create an infection. In fact, it is not uncommon for patients taking antibiotics chronically to also be prescribed anti-yeast medicine. *Candida albicans* is one of the most common yeast found in infections, though others appear too.

Yeast infections spring up in other areas as well, such as the throat, skin, and less commonly, the bloodstream. Many of the treatments below are also used for GI yeast. Using this approach for vaginal yeast is more effective and will help prevent recurrence. For related topics see Constipation, Diarrhea, Eczema, Headaches, Indigestion, Low Blood Sugar, and Psoriasis; read Chapters 4 (digestion) and 6 (immunity).

How to Prevent Yeast (and its Recurrence)

- Avoid antibiotics unless absolutely necessary.
- Find alternatives to birth control pills, for example, natural family planning. (Read Toni Weschler's very comprehensive work, *Taking Charge of Your Fertility*, for more information.)
- Limit use of steroid hormone medication. For example, cortisone creams, prednisone.
- Find substitutes for ulcer medicines.
- Tame your sweet tooth. Lots of sugar over time can contribute to this problem.
- Get tested. Ask your doctor to run a stool culture for *Candida* and other yeast. Some women with vaginal yeast also have it in their GI tracts.

Food and Nutrition for Yeast

I'm giving you tips not only for fighting vaginal yeast, but intestinal yeast as well because sometimes both infections are present. I typically tell patients to initially avoid sugary foods, refined carbohydrates, and alcohol. If this doesn't work, follow a stricter diet as outlined below. Once the problem has cleared up, you can reintroduce some of these foods, but try to stick with a wholesome menu to prevent future troubles.

- Avoid sugars and foods high in them. This means table sugar, fructose, corn syrup. These are yeast's favorite foods.
- Eliminate refined carbohydrates. These are foods with white flour and refined grains.
- Don't drink. Liquor makes you sicker quicker.

- If the above three tips don't help, also stop eating milk (it contains lactose or milk sugar), starchy foods (potatoes), and fruits (berries, cherries, apples, and pears are OK).

- Take acidophilus and other probiotics. They contain the good bacteria you want.

- Douche with yogurt. Or insert an acidophilus capsule vaginally.

- Eat garlic.

- Nutrients to include (look to your multi first): Vitamins A, B complex, C and E, bioflavonoids.

- Topical E. Vitamin E oil or cream may relieve itching.

- Is it a yeast allergy? Many yeast diets recommend avoiding all foods with a high amount of yeast or fungi and mold like peanuts, cheese, dried fruit, bread, baked goods, vinegar, grapes, mushrooms, and alcohol. However, this may only be necessary if you have a sensitivity to yeast. Try eliminating these foods for one week, then reintroduce them one at a time. If you get worse, then yeast or mold may be at fault.

- Avoid other allergenic foods.

- There's nothing to eat! Feel free to munch on all vegetables (here's your chance to reach your goal of seven a day), beans and legumes, fish, poultry, lean meats and whole grains (wheat, barley, oats, rice, rye, etc.).

- Go organic. This is especially important for poultry, meats, and dairy, to avoid additional antibiotic exposure.

■ Makeover Hint #107—The Italian Dressing Douche

There are two ways to kill yeast. One, make their environment acidic; two, put a killer in their midst. Using common kitchen ingredients, you can make a vaginal douche with 2 tbsp. apple cider vinegar (the acid) and crushed garlic or liquid garlic (the yeast killer) mixed in one quart of water. The only side effect is smelling like a Caesar salad.

Herbal Treatment

These herbs are best used in a vaginal douche; however, the "yeast slayers" can also be taken orally.

- Yeast slayers—black walnut, calendula, echinacea, garlic, golden seal, pau d'arco, St. John's wort, tea tree
- Healing—calendula, comfrey
- Reduce redness—calendula, licorice
- Soothing—comfrey, self-heal

The Homeopathic Difference

- Natrum phosphoricum—*After antibiotics*. A creamy or honey-colored and sour-smelling discharge is apparent with this type of infection; sometimes it's watery. This (like Pulsatilla and Thuja) is a good remedy for yeast infections caused by antibiotic use.
- Pulsatilla—*Backache too*. A creamy white discharge that burns sets Pulsatilla apart from other yeast remedies. You may feel cold, tired, and have a backache.
- Sepia—*Bearing down sensation*. This remedy works for yellow or green discharge with plenty of itching. The vagina is very sore, particularly after intercourse. And there is a strange feeling as if the pelvis is being pulled down toward the vagina.
- Thuja—*Very sensitive*. Signs to look for when considering Thuja are a profuse, thick, white discharge (could be greenish too) and a very sensitive vagina. Symptoms increase at night while in bed and after drinking coffee or eating fatty foods.

Lifestyle Link

- Part of the relationship. If you have a genital yeast infection, have your partner checked and treated if indicated. Use condoms until both of your infections have cleared up.
- Avoid intercourse if possible. Besides decreasing chances of re-infection, this allows red, inflamed tissues to heal properly.
- Wear cotton underpants.

- Sit in a warm bath laced with Epsom salts (one cup).
- Wet basement syndrome. If moist places like damp basements make you feel worse, you may have a mold sensitivity. See above for yeast-containing foods to avoid while getting well.
- Other signs of yeast? Have your doctor check other areas, like the digestive tract, for a yeast infection.

Lookout Alert

The most serious form of yeast infection is systemic or body-wide. Usually this type of condition takes a long time to develop, and is more apt to appear in persons with limited reserves, for instance after radiation treatment, after using corticosteroids or immuno-supppressive medications, in people with diabetes, emphysema, tuberculosis, some types of cancer, severe burns, and AIDS. Also be aware of these circumstances:

- Foreign travel.
- Fever, chills, night sweats, loss of appetite, weight loss, malaise, and depression.
- Usual yeast symptoms don't respond to standard therapy.
- Symptoms are severe.

Appendix A

Over One Hundred Common Herbs and How to Use Them

Before using any of the herbs listed in this book, please read this section. Be a wise herbal consumer by following these steps:

- Know what you're taking. Before you take any herb, educate yourself about its actions on the body, and what it's usually used for.
- Know if there's any reason why you shouldn't take a certain herb. Since some herbs shouldn't be taken in particular situations, watch out for herbs that are contraindicated (shouldn't be taken):
  1. With some medications.
  2. If you have a particular health condition.
  3. If you have a history of a particular health condition.
  4. If you're pregnant. *As a precaution, never take any herbs unless prescribed by your midwife or obstetrician.*
  5. If you're nursing. *Most substances you ingest are passed along to your baby through breast milk.*
- Know why you're taking an herb. Don't take them just because. Whenever you take an herb in moderate to large amounts over a period of time, understand its actions and why it is indicated for your particular condition.
- Know the quality of the herbal products you're taking. Herbs are plants. As such, their potency changes according to when and where they're grown, when they're harvested, how they're prepared, and how long they're been sitting on the shelf. Quiz

your herbal vendor or call the herbal company directly with questions. Last, ask others what products work best and try them for yourself.

Herbal Preparation and Usage

Herbs come in a variety of forms—teas, tinctures or alcohol preparations, pills and others. For our purposes here, I'll describe how to prepare herbal tea. As a general rule, if you're taking a tincture 1/4 to 1 teaspoon three times per day should suffice. Many pill products have directions written on the bottle. For more information on exact dosing, refer to the following works:

The Complete Illustrated Holistic Herbal by David Hoffmann, Element Books, 1996.

Herbal Prescriptions for Better Health by Donald J. Brown, ND, Prima, 1996.

The Healing Power of Herbs by Michael T. Murray, ND, Prima, 1995.

A Field Guide to Medicinal Plants by Steven Foster & James A Duke, Ph.D., Houghton Mifflin Co., 1990.

The Green Pharmacy by James A. Duke, Ph.D., Rodale Press, 1997.

TEAS   If you ever drank a cup of herbal tea, you know how to make the medicinal version as well. There are two basic methods to preparing herbal teas. The first is called an infusion and is very much like making a cup of ordinary tea. Place the dried herb or tea bag in a mug, pour boiling water over it, cover with a small plate or plastic lid and let infuse (steep) for 10 to 15 minutes. This method works best when preparing soft parts of a plant such as the leaf or flower petals.

Decocting is the other way to create medicinal tea. This method is reserved for the hard parts of a plant, like the root, rhizome, nuts, seeds, bark, and stem. After all, it takes more time and heat to extract the healing qualities from these woody sections. To make a decoction simply place water and allocated herb in a pot. Slowly bring it to a boil, cover and let simmer for 15 to 30 minutes.

For those too busy or impatient to watch a simmering pot, or when you need to prepare a combination of soft and hard herbal parts, use the thermos method of decocting. Begin by powdering your herbs (both hard and soft portions) in a blender or coffee grinder. Place powder in a thermos, add boiling water and cap. Leave the mixture for 40 minutes. Strain the tea before drinking.

HOW MUCH, HOW OFTEN   As with tinctures, how much tea you take can vary according to what herb or herbs you choose. Again, here I offer general guidelines. If you experience any adverse reaction after taking an herb, stop immediately or consult with a professional trained in this area.

As a general rule, add 1 tbsp. of herb to 1 cup of water to make medicinal herbal tea; most tea bags contain 2 tsp. of dried herb. If you're treating yourself for an acute, short-term illness like a cold, drink one cup of tea every one to three hours. Do this for five to 10 days. If you need to repeat this cycle, take two to three days off, and start again.

For more chronic conditions like arthritis, or as a preventive measure, drink one cup of tea three times per day. Continue this trend for eight weeks, then take a two-week rest.

Be imaginative with your teas. Many can also be used in other ways. After preparing your tea using the above guidelines, try the following: add tea to a bath (two cups to a tub of water or sitz bath); as a douche for a vaginal infection; as a mouthwash for a gum condition or gargle for a sore throat; as a wash for a skin problem. Remember to adjust the temperature of the tea accordingly and don't burn yourself.

Herbal Glossary

Listed below are all the herbs mentioned in this book. They are presented in alphabetical order by common name; the scientific name follows in parentheses. For your information, I describe how each herb works. As a safety precaution, I also list situations where specific herbs should *not* be used.

Aconite (*Aconitum napellus*). Painkiller, sedative, decreases fevers. NOTE: THIS IS A VERY POISONOUS HERB; DO NOT TAKE BY MOUTH EXCEPT UNDER THE GUIDANCE OF A TRAINED PROFESSIONAL. This herb is often in ear drop medication, and can be safely used by consumers.

Agrimony (*Agrimonia eupatoria*). Heals wounds, helps the liver, promotes bile flow, diuretic, astringent, tonic.

Alfalfa (*Medicago sativa*). Stops bleeding, diuretic, estrogen-like, nutritious. NOTE: Avoid during pregnancy.

Aloe (*Aloe vera*). Heals wounds (internally and externally), soothing (external), enhances menstrual flow, helps the liver, kills worms, cathartic. NOTE: Avoid during pregnancy and during breast feeding; do not give to children internally.

American Cranesbill (*Geranium maculatum*). Astringent, stops bleeding (internally and externally), anti-inflammatory, heals wounds.

Angelica (*Angelica archangelica*). Controls gas, stimulates appetite, expectorant for coughs, eases spasms, induces perspiration. NOTE: Do not take large amounts without professional guidance.

Astragalus (*Astragalus membranaceus*). Antiviral activity, enhances immunity.

Balmony (*chelone glabra*). Helps the liver, promotes bile flow, mild laxative, general tonic for digestion, controls nausea and vomiting.

Barberry (*Berberis vulgaris*). Helps the liver, promotes bile flow, laxative, controls nausea and vomiting, bitter. NOTE: Avoid during pregnancy.

Bayberry (*Myrica cerifera*). Astringent, induces perspiration. NOTE: Large amounts may cause gas or nausea and vomiting.

Bilberry (*Vaccinium myrtillus*). Astringent, antiseptic, blood sugar lowering action, may improve vision (cataracts, macular degeneration, glaucoma), strengthens blood vessels.

Bitter Melon (*Momordica charantia*). Blood sugar lowering action.

Black Catechu (*Acacia catechu*). Astringent, antiseptic.

Black Walnut (*Juglans nigra*). Cathartic.

Black Willow (*Salix nigra*). Painkiller, lowers fever, anti-inflammatory, heals wounds, astringent.

Blue Flag (*Iris versicolor*). Helps the liver, promotes bile flow, laxative, diuretic, anti-inflammatory, promotes salivation. NOTE: Large amounts might cause nausea, vomiting, or facial neuralgias. Picking this plant might cause a rash.

Boneset (*Eupatorium perfoliatum*). Induces perspiration, clears respiratory mucus, eases spasms, bitter, diuretic.

Borage (*Borago officinalis*). Revives adrenal glands, anti-inflammatory, diuretic, induces perspiration, expectorant for coughs, stimulates breast milk.

Burdock (*Arctium lappa*). Bitter, laxative, diuretic, restores general health, heals wounds.

Butcher's Broom (*Ruscus aculeatus*). Lowers fevers, diuretic, constricts blood vessels. NOTE: Avoid if you have high blood pressure.

Cabbage (*Brassica spp*). Heals intestinal ulcers.

Calendula (*Calendula officinalis*). Heals wounds (externally and internally), anti-inflammatory, kills germs, astringent, promotes bile flow, brings on menstruation.

Cascara (*Cascara sagrada*). Laxative, purgative, appetite stimulant.

Catnip (*Nepeta cataria*). Controls gas, sedative, eases spasms, induces perspiration, astringent.

Cayenne (*Capsicum annum*). Kills germs, controls gas, promotes salivation, reduces respiratory mucus, controls nausea and vomiting, induces perspiration, reduces cholesterol and triglycerides, painkiller (externally in creams). NOTE: Do not apply cayenne cream to irritated or broken skin.

Celery Seed (*Apium graveolens*). Diuretic, controls gas, sedative.

Chamomile (*Chamaemelum nobile or Matricaria recutita*). Eases spasms, controls gas, anti-inflammatory, painkiller, heals wounds, sedative, induces perspiration.

Chickweed (*Stellaria media*). Heals wounds; soothing (externally) for wounds, itching, irritation, and arthritic joints.

Cleavers (*Galium aparine*). Diuretic, astringent, anti-inflammatory, helps the liver, laxative, heals wounds.

Coltsfoot (*Tussilago farfara*). Expectorant, controls coughs, soothing, tones the lungs, reduces respiratory mucus, anti-inflammatory, diuretic.

Comfrey (*Symphytum officinale*). Heals wounds (externally), soothing, astringent, expectorant. NOTE: Don't apply comfrey to very deep wounds as this can cause wound to heal over too quickly.

Corn Silk (*Zea mays*). Diuretic, soothing, prevents kidney stones.

Couchgrass (*Agropyron repens*). Diuretic, kills germs, soothing, prevents kidney stones.

Daisy (*Bellis perennis*). Heals wounds, expectorant, astringent.

Dandelion (*Taraxacum officinale*). Helps the liver, promotes bile flow, diuretic, laxative.

Devil's Claw (*Harpogophytum procumbens*). Anti-inflammatory, painkiller

Echinacea (*Echinacea spp*). Enhances immunity, kills germs.

Elder (*Sambucus nigra*). Induces perspiration (flowers, berries), diuretic (whole plant), laxative (berries), expectorant (leaves), heals wounds and soothing (externally—leaves). NOTE: Actions depend on part of plant used.

Elecampane (*Inula helenium*). Controls coughs, expectorant, induces perspiration, kills germs, controls respiratory mucus, helps the liver, heals wounds, bitter.

Ephedra (*Ephedra sinica*). Fights allergies, stimulates blood circulation, increases blood pressure, promotes weight loss, stimulating. NOTE: Due to its stimulating qualities, ephedra can cause anxiety, insomnia, irritability in susceptible people. Avoid taking if you are pregnant, have high blood pressure, heart disease, diabetes, thyroid troubles, trouble urinating due to an enlarged prostate, or if you take antidepressant or blood pressure medication.

Eyebright (*Euphrasia officinalis*). Eye conditions, astringent, anti-inflammatory, controls respiratory mucus, heals wounds.

Fenugreek (*Trigonella foenum-graecum*). Heals wounds, soothing, controls gas, expectorant, promotes milk production, promotes menstruation.

Feverfew (*Tanacetum parthenium*). Dilates blood vessels, anti-inflammatory, relaxing, bitter, stimulates uterus. NOTE: Avoid during pregnancy.

Figwort (*Scrophularia nodosa*). Restores health, diuretic, heart stimulant, laxative, heals wounds, blood sugar-lowering action. NOTE: Use only under professional supervision.

Flax (*Linum usitatissimum*). Laxative, soothing, controls coughs, heals wounds. NOTE: Flax seed oil can cause gas.

Garlic (*Allium sativum*). Kills germs, enhances immunity, lowers blood pressure, protects heart and blood vessels, anti-inflammatory, diuretic, blood sugar-lowering action, expectorant, promotes menstruation, controls gas.

Gentian (*Gentiana lutea*). Bitter, promotes salivation, promotes bile flow, gastrointestinal tonic, kills germs, helps the liver, promotes menstruation.

Ginger (*Zingiber officinale*). Controls gas, promotes salivation, enhances perspiration, anti-inflammatory, controls nausea and vomiting, decreases cholesterol, kills germs, anti-ulcer, painkiller.

Ginkgo (*Ginkgo biloba*). Helps the brain, nervous system, and blood vessels.

Ginseng (*Panax ginseng* or *Eleutherococcus senticosus*). These are actually two different species. *Panax:* Fights fatigue, anti-stress, blood sugar-lowering action, enhances immunity, helps the liver. *Eleuthero:* Supports and enhances adrenal function and immunity. NOTE: Avoid during pregnancy. Can cause a stimulant effect in some people; avoid taking late in the day. Women do better with Eleuthero.

Goat's Rue (*Galega officinalis*). Blood sugar-lowering action, induces perspiration, diuretic, promotes milk production.

Golden Seal (*Hydrastis canadensis*). Enhances immunity, kills germs, lowers fevers, bitter, laxative, astringent, promotes bile flow, helps the liver, heals wounds, promotes menstruation, expectorant. NOTE: Avoid during pregnancy.

Gotu Kola (*Centella asiatica*). Heals wounds (externally and internally), aids hair and nail growth, reduces cellulite, helps the liver, increases mental abilities, improves vein health.

Greater Plantain (*Plantago major*). Heals wounds, soothing, astringent, diuretic, expectorant.

Grindelia (*Grindelia camporum*). Eases spasms, expectorant, lowers blood pressure.

Gymnema (*Gymnema sylvestre*). Blood sugar-lowering actions (in diabetics), reduces sweet taste (when applied directly to tongue).

Hawthorn (*Crataegus laevigata* or *Crataegus oxycantha*). Heart tonic, lowers blood pressure, diuretic.

Hops (*Humulus lupulus*). Sedative, bitter, painkiller, astringent. NOTE: Avoid in cases of chronic or severe depression.

Horse Chestnut (*Aesculus hippocastanum*). Tones blood vessels, astringent—externally or internally. NOTE: USE HERB EXTERNALLY ONLY; TAKE INTERNALLY ONLY UNDER PROFESSIONAL SUPERVISION AS SEED IS POTENTIALLY POISONOUS.

Horsetail (*Equisetum arvense*). Heals wounds (externally), astringent, diuretic.

Hyssop (*Hyssopus officinalis*). Expectorant, eases spasms, induces perspiration, sedative, controls gas, heals wounds, helps the liver, controls respiratory mucus.

Jamaican Dogwood (*Piscidia piscipula*). Painkiller, sedative. NOTE: Do not take large amounts.

Lady's Slipper (*Cypripedium calceolus*). Sedative, painkiller, eases spasms. NOTE: Large doses can cause hallucinations.

Licorice (*Glycyrrhiza glabra*). Anti-inflammatory, aids adrenal glands, stimulates immunity, kills germs, helps the liver, estrogen-like action, anti-allergy, soothing, mild laxative, eases spasms, expectorant. Often used as a flavoring with other herbs. NOTE: Do not take for more than six weeks unless under care of professional. Avoid if you have high blood pressure, kidney problems, or take digitalis.

Linden or Lime Blossom (*Tilia x vulgaris*). Sedative, eases spasms, aids circulation, induces perspiration, diuretic.

Marshmallow (*Althea officinalis*). Root: soothing, heals wounds, diuretic; use this part of the marshmallow plant for the gastrointestinal tract. Leaf: soothing, diuretic, expectorant, reduces respiratory mucus; use this part of the marshmallow plant for all other ailments.

Mcadow Sweet (*Filipendula ulmaria*). Painkiller, lowers fevers, controls nausea and vomiting, anti-inflammatory, astringent, anti-rheumatic.

Milk Thistle (*Silybum marianum*). Helps/protects the liver, promotes bile flow, promotes milk production, soothing.

Mouse Ear (*Pilosella officinarum*). Heals wounds (externally), eases spasms, expectorant, reduces respiratory mucus, astringent.

Mullein (*Verbascum thapsus*). Expectorant, reduces respiratory mucus, soothing, tones the lungs, diuretic, sedative, heals wounds (externally).

Nettles or Stinging Nettles (*Urtica dioca*). Anti-allergy, astringent, diuretic, nutritious. NOTE: Touching the fresh plant can cause a rash.

Oats (*Avena sativa*). Supports the nervous system, soothing, heals wounds (external and internal), nutritious.

Oregon Grape (*Mahonia aquifolium*). Helps the liver, promotes bile flow, laxative, controls nausea and vomiting; used for skin conditions.

Osha root (*Ligusticum porteri*). Enhances immunity, kills germs.

Pasque Flower (*Pulsatilla vulgaris*). Sedative, painkiller, eases spasms, kills germs, promotes menstruation. NOTE: DO NOT USE THE FRESH PLANT.

Passion Flower (*Passiflora incarnata*). Sedative, sleeping aid, eases spasms, painkiller.

Pau D'Arco or Tahebo (*Tabebuia avellandae*). Anti-cancer (shrinks tumors and reduces pain).

Pennyroyal (*Mentha pulegium*). Promotes menstruation, controls gas, eases spasms. NOTE: Avoid during pregnancy or if you have kidney problems.

Peppermint (*Mentha piperita*). Controls gas, supports nervous system, eases spasms, controls nausea and vomiting, painkiller, kills germs. NOTE: Avoid peppermint oil internally during pregnancy or with children.

Pleurisy Root (*Asclepias tuberosa*). Expectorant, eases spasms, induces perspiration, controls gas. NOTE: Very large amounts can cause vomiting and diarrhea.

Psyllium (*Plantago psyllium*). Laxative, soothing.

Red Clover (*Trifolium pratense*). Skin conditions, expectorant, eases spasms, heals wounds, anti-cancer, sedative.

Rhubarb Root (*Rheum palmatum*). Laxative, bitter, astringent. NOTE: Taking this herb can make your urine appear yellow or red. Do not take if you have kidney stones.

Rosemary (*Rosmarinus officinalis*). Controls gas, eases spasms, anti-depressant, kills germs, astringent, supports nervous system, diuretic, promotes bile flow, repels insects (oil—externally). NOTE: Don't take oil internally. Avoid during pregnancy.

Rue (*Ruta graveolens*). Promotes menstruation, eases spasms, controls coughs, kills germs, bitter. NOTE: Avoid during pregnancy. Do not take oil internally. Do not take large amounts unless under professional supervision.

Sage (*Salvia officinalis*). Controls gas, anti-inflammatory, kills germs, astringent, promotes menstruation, reduces perspiration, decreases milk production. NOTE: Avoid during pregnancy.

Sarsaparilla (*Smilax sarsaparilla*). Promotes health, anti-gout, anti-rheumatic, "blood cleanser."

Senega (*Polygala senega*). Expectorant, induces perspiration, promotes salivation.

Senna (*Senna alexandrina*). Laxative.

Skullcap (*Scutellaria laterifolia*). Sedative, eases spasms, painkiller.

Slippery Elm (*Ulmus rubra*). Soothing, astringent, heals wounds (externally), nutritious.

St. John's Wort (*Hypericum perforatum*). Painkiller, antidepressant, sedative, anti-viral; externally—heals wounds, anti-inflammatory. NOTE: Makes susceptible people more sensitive to strong sunlight and tanning booths.

Stone Root (*Collinsonia canadensis*). Prevents kidney stones, diuretic, induces perspiration. Used for hemorrhoids in Europe where it's referred to as Pilewort.

Sumac (*Rhus aromatica*). Astringent.

Sundew (*Drosera rotundifolia*). Soothing, expectorant, eases spasms.

Tea Tree (*Melaleuca alternifolia*). Oil used externally: as a liniment, kills germs, repels insects. Tea taken internally: controls gas, eases spasms, expectorant. NOTE: Do not take the oil by mouth.

Thuja (*Thuja occidentalis*). Expectorant, astringent, diuretic, induces perspiration; kills worms, kills warts (externally). NOTE: Avoid during pregnancy. Do not take the oil by mouth.

Thyme (*Thymus vulgaris*). Controls gas, kills germs, astringent, controls respiratory mucus, induces perspiration; heals wounds (externally). NOTE: Do not take the oil by mouth.

Tormentil (*Potentilla erecta*). Astringent; heals wounds (externally). NOTE: THIS IS A STRONG HERB. USE CAUTIOUSLY BOTH INTERNALLY AND EXTERNALLY. DO NOT TAKE LARGE AMOUNTS FOR EXTENDED PERIODS OF TIME UNLESS UNDER PROFESSIONAL SUPERVISION.

Turmeric (*Curcuma longa*). Anti-inflammatory, helps the liver, kills germs, controls gas, supports the GI tract, lowers cholesterol. NOTE: At very high doses, can causes gastric ulcers.

Uva Ursi or Bearberry (*Arctostaphylos uva ursi*). Diuretic, astringent, soothing, prevents kidney stones, kills germs. NOTE: If used for extended periods, can cause constipation.

Valerian (*Valeriana officinalis*). Sedative, eases spasms, lowers blood pressure, controls gas, sleeping aid.

Vervain (*Verbena officinalis*). Sedative, eases spasms, painkiller, induces perspiration, expectorant, helps the liver; heals wounds (externally).

White Horehound (*Marrubium vulgare*). Expectorant, eases spasms, bitter, induces perspiration; heals wounds (externally).

Wild Indigo (*Baptisia tinctoria*). Kills germs, reduces fevers, reduces respiratory mucus, improves general health.

Witch Hazel (*Hamamelis virginiana*). Astringent, anti-inflammatory; heals wounds (externally).

Yarrow (*Achillea millefolium*). Induces perspiration, lowers blood pressure, diuretic, kills germs, astringent, stimulates digestion, supports blood vessels, helps the liver. NOTE: Large amounts can cause headaches and dizziness.

Yellow Dock (*Rumex crispus*). Laxative, helps the liver, promotes bile flow, astringent. NOTE: Large amounts can cause nausea.

Appendix B

Sixty Common Homeopathic Remedies and How to Use Them

This 200-year-old therapy has regained considerable popularity in the last 20 years due to its safety and effectiveness. Homeopathic remedies—of which there exist over 2000—are minute amounts of plant, mineral, or animal substances used to cure a wide variety of ailments. Remedies are diluted so few or no side effects occur. In fact, the more dilute a remedy, the more potent it is. It's believed that the vigorous shaking (called succussions) used to prepare these medicines help potentize them.

It's the principles of homeopathy that separate it from conventional medicine. One principle says "like cures like," meaning the compound used to treat a disease produces symptoms of that disease when given to a healthy person but cures that disease when given to an ill person. For example, *Coffea cruda* (homeopathic coffee) is ideal when used for restless insomnia.

In classical homeopathy, the law of the single remedy says medicines should be given one at a time based on current symptoms. Because the patient and the disease are each seen as ever-changing, the remedy is adjusted as symptoms change. Individual treatment requires careful documentation of physical symptoms, emotional and mental balance, food cravings and aversions, sleeping habits and other signs. These symptoms are then matched to one remedy at an appropriate dose.

Over-the-Counter Homeopathy

Most homeopathic remedies are used and sold for acute, short-term illnesses. Some practitioners call this acute homeopathic prescribing, versus constitutional homeopathy which requires an in-depth interview and expert diagnosis by a homeopathic practition-er. The second difference between acute and constitutional care is that acute remedies are typically used in lower potencies and are taken more frequently. Using the former is much simpler than the latter, and with a little practice, a homeopathic remedy kit or local health food store that carries these remedies, and a handy reference guide (see below), you'll be set.

Now that you're ready, be prepared to look at illness in a whole different way. With most over-the-counter medicines, you take the same pill for a particular illness, no matter what the quali-ty of the ailment. However, if you stop and think about it, no two colds, for example, are exactly the same. For instance, one time you might feel drowsy and dull and your eyelids droopy. Your nose is running with a watery discharge and you don't feel thirsty. Gelsemium would be a good choice here. Next cold might involve burning eyes, nose, and lips, along with profuse, searing, clear dis-charge, and thirst. Allium cepa is a better selection for this cold. So your job when picking a homeopathic remedy is to watch your symptoms: what do they feel like, when do they occur, where do they occur, how intense are they, what makes them better or worse, do they change with time of day, do your feelings or thinking abil-ity change, what is the quality of the symptom (is the pain stabbing or dull; is the discharge clear or green). As you become more famil-iar with homeopathy, you'll know what to look for. Ideally as symp-toms change, you'll pick a new and more appropriate remedy.

For an acute illness or injury, take three to five pills (or drops, if liquid) *under* your tongue. Let the substance dissolve for at least 30 seconds. You can take a remedy as often as every 15 minutes for an immediate problem, or three times a day for an ongoing condi-tion like a cold. Here are some other peculiarities of homeopathic remedies:

- Take 15 minutes away from food or drink.
- Do not take the remedy with anything else. For example, don't swallow pills with water or juice.
- *Avoid coffee and coffee products while taking a homeopathic remedy; they seem to erase the effects of this medicine. Black and herbal teas are fine.

- *Also steer clear of strong smells such as tea tree oil, eucalyptus, camphor (found in lip chaps, tiger balm, Vick's Vapor Rub™, liniments, cough drops, Noxema™, some cosmetics, some nail polish removers, some facial cleansers) Read labels. Also avoid mint products; read your toothpaste label. For alternatives to these products, visit the health food store.

- Avoid electric blankets. Water bed heaters are OK.

- Don't touch the remedy with your hands, mouth, or tongue. If you spill some, don't put it back in the bottle. (The best way to take a remedy is to pour a small amount on a clean spoon first.)

- Keep your open remedy container away from strong odors. Besides the above, this includes perfumes, cooking smells, and fresh paint.

- Store in a cool, dark place, but not the fridge.

* These steps are vital when taking constitutional remedies, but not as necessary for acute remedies. However, the more you follow these guidelines, the better your remedy will work.

For more detailed information on this fascinating field, refer to the following books:

Homeopathic Self-Care by Robert Ullman, ND & Judyth Reichenberg-Ullman, ND, Prima, 1997.

Everybody's Guide to Homeopathic Medicines by Stephen Cummings & Dana Ullman, Jeremy Tarcher, 1984.

Homeopathic Medicine at Home by Maesimund B Panos, MD & Jane Heimlich, JP Tacher, 1980.

Homeopathy: Medicine of the New Man by George Vithoulkas.

Homeopathic Glossary

Listed on the following pages are all the homeopathic remedies mentioned in this book. They are laid out in alphabetical order by name. Included by each are some of the keynote or peculiar symptoms that apply to that remedy; use these to make your selection.

Aconite or Aconitum napellus. This remedy is good for the first 24 hours of an illness. Symptoms come on suddenly. You might feel restless and anxious. Fear or shock might be the cause of your illness. Heat is key: hot feeling in the head, nasal discharge that's hot, fever, burning skin; thirst for cold beverages. Rest makes you better; cold makes you worse.

Aesculus hippocastanum. There's a feeling of fullness, especially in the lower bowel. The result can be hemorrhoids and backaches. Cool open air makes you better; walking makes you worse.

Allium cepa. This remedy is derived from the red onion, hence the profuse tearing, red burning eyes, clear, irritating nasal discharge, and frequent sneezing; also thirst. Not surprisingly you crave raw onions. Cool open air makes you better; worse in the evening and indoors.

Alumina. Skin and mucous membranes are dry. Bodily functions are sluggish and there's a general debility apparent. Spirits are low, though mood varies. Worse when you wake in the morning; better in the evening.

Antimonium tartaricum. Used often in lung conditions where mucous rattles, but not much comes up. You feel drowsy, irritable, dizzy, chilly, and run-down, and don't want to be touched. Muscles might hurt. Coughing phlegm or belching makes you better; lying down is worse.

Apis mellifica. This remedy from the honeybee is good for insect nips or bee stings. Also appropriate for any rash or allergic reaction that's red, hot, swollen, and stings. Your mind is "busy as a bee." Anything hot—room, bath, or drinks—makes you worse; coolness makes you better.

Argentum nitricum. The key characteristics for this remedy are nervous system complaints—uncoordinated, headaches, trembling, and a general feeling of being out of balance both physically and mentally—and inflammation of mucous membranes like the lungs and intestines; much gas and belching. Although you might crave sweets, eating them makes you feel worse. Cold makes you feel better.

Arnica. This is a key remedy for trauma—physical or mental (like shock). Anytime you bruise, bleed, bump, or turn black and blue, take Arnica. Can also be used before intentional trauma like surgery or dental work. As might be expected, you feel worse when overdoing it and better lying down.

Arsenicum album. Great anxiety and restlessness are key characteristics here, as well as searing pain, discharge, diarrhea, or other bodily afflictions. Regardless of this burning, you feel chilly. Thus cold food and beverages make you feel worse (even though you desire sips of cold drinks); heat and warm drinks make you better.

Belladonna. Think bright red, dry, and hot for Belladonna. This can mean a fever, headache, sore throat—often right-sided. Symptoms, as for Aconite, appear suddenly, and once there, make you very sensitive to movement, light, and sound. You feel better alone in a quiet and dark room.

Bellis perennis. This is homeopathic daisy. Yet this delicate flower is effective against deep tissue injuries, such as after surgery, or other trauma like bruises and sprains. Oddly enough, one old Materia Medica states that Bellis, or daisy, is good for gardeners. Not too much makes you feel better if you fit this remedy; however, hot and cold bathing and lying on your left side will surely make you worse.

Borax. This is a canker sore remedy especially when thrush (yeast in the mouth) is also present. It's most effective in children. As might be expected, spicy, salty or acid foods like fruit make these sores hurt.

Bryonia. Most important to look for here are symptoms—be it a cough, headache, or back pain—made worse with any movement. You'll find you yearn for cold beverages, and feel better pushing or lying on the hurting side.

Calcarea fluorica. Varicose veins are often helped with this remedy, as are any conditions where glands or veins are hard and stony, like a breast lump or goiter. Applying heat makes the lump feel better; rest makes it worse.

Calcarea sulphurica. Thick, yellow, pus-like discharges from the skin, eyes, nose, acne, or other body part best describe this remedy.

Cantharis. This is homeopathic Spanish fly, and is a key remedy for abruptly appearing bladder infections with a burning pain. Heightened libido can also be present. If you have this sort of urinary infection, urinating probably makes it worse, rest makes it better.

Carbo vegetabilis. This is homeopathy's version of charcoal, and is useful for abdominal complaints like gas, bloating, and indigestion. Even a small amount of food is not tolerated well. This remedy can also be used for fainting; the person often feels lethargic, yet irritable. Rich food and resting make things worse; moving air such as from a fan or draft makes you feel better.

Chamomilla. This is a great children's remedy for that whiny, restless baby or kid who wants to be held, yet is inconsolable. He might be fussy and crying because of great pain, like an ear infection, teething, colic, or general peevishness. Watch for green diarrhea, an intolerance to touch and a yen for cold beverages. His symptoms and behavior worsen at night (of course) and during teething; carrying the child makes him feel better.

Cinchona officinalis. After a long and debilitating illness, especially where vital fluids are lost, turn to Cinchona. You find that you feel apathetic and that gas and sour belches are a problem. When you eat, food just seems to sit there. Motion, a drafty room or touch makes you worse; pressing against the sore area makes it better.

Cocculus indicus. This is the motion sickness remedy where nausea, weakness, and dizziness reign. You don't want to eat anything. Women with morning sickness can also use this remedy. As might be expected, travel (and loss of sleep) make symptoms worse; sitting makes them better.

Coffea cruda. This is homeopathic coffee, and as such its symptoms are easy to remember. If you feel overstimulated, nervous and hyper, Coffea (not coffee) is the answer. Also think of insomnia and a racing heart for this remedy. Sleep makes you better; too much excitement, sound, or touch makes you worse.

Colchicum. This remedy is specific for gout, and also helps chronic afflictions of the muscles, joints, and related tissues. Watch for redness, heat and swelling and a tearing pain, as well as prostration. Evening and motion make symptoms worse.

Collinsonia canadensis. This remedy helps the rectal area, be it for constipation or hemorrhoids. Itching may be present as well as the "sensation of sharp sticks in (the) rectum." Heat makes it better, cold worse.

Drosera rotundifolia. This is a fine remedy for violent, dry and deep coughs that make you gag or even vomit. These annoying symptoms might make you angry though open air makes you feel better. Late at night, talking and lying down make things worse.

Echinacea. Like its herbal counterpart, homeopathic echinacea is helpful for acute infections. A general fatigue can be present, as well as chilliness and nausea. You can also apply homeopathic lotion or cream directly on infected areas.

Equisetum. This is a bladder remedy, good for both urinary or bladder infections and bedwetting. Watch for a full feeling, but once you urinate it only drips. At the close of urination, there is severe pain. The right side is often worse.

Eupatroium perfoliatum. This is homeopathic Boneset, and again, like the herb, it helps painful muscles and limbs, especially during fever. Symptoms seem to come and go.

Euphrasia. Bland nasal discharge, burning tears, grogginess, irritability, and sinus headache are what to observe; it's the opposite of Allium cepa (see above). This is an important remedy for hay fever. Open air relieves symptoms, though they turn worse as evening approaches.

Ferrum phosphoricum. Choose this remedy for the beginning of a fever or cold; the face can be pale or flushed. Also look for weakness and irritability. Lying down makes symptoms better, but they are worse at night.

Gelsemium. The four "Ds" describe this remedy—dull, droopy, drowsy, and dizzy. You don't feel like drinking anything, and your whole body feels stiff and maybe chilly. You want to hibernate in your bedroom and close the door on the world. Fright can bring your illness on or make it worse; lying down with your head propped feels good.

Graphites. This remedy works well for various skin conditions and constipation. Skin tends to be unhealthy-looking and can have a sticky ooze seeping from lesions. Those who fit this remedy startle easily, and often are fair-skinned and sometimes overweight.

Hamamelis virginica. This is homeopathic witch hazel and can also be used for varicose veins and hemorrhoids. This sign to note is a "bruised soreness of affected parts." Also, hemorrhoids tend to bleed profusely. Warmth makes these conditions feel worse.

Hepar sulphuris calcareum. This remedy works well for inflamed wounds that tend to form pus like abscesses. You might also find that you're very sensitive to pain and other annoyances, and feel chilly. Heat makes the sore feel better; touching it or covering the body makes it and you feel worse.

Ignatia. This is a classic remedy for grief. For those times when you're very sad, sigh a great deal, and can't stop crying, think of Ignatia. You feel like you have a lump in your throat; can also be used for hurt feelings after disappointment. Taking deep breaths eases your grief.

Ipecac. Ipecac syrup makes you vomit and is used in cases of poisoning. Homeopathic Ipecac works the opposite way and eases nausea and vomiting; bleeding may accompany this. Not surprisingly, irritability is part of this picture. You're not thirsty, though cold drinks may make you feel better. Vomiting makes you feel worse.

Kali bichromicum. Use this remedy for the later stages of a cold or for sinus infections where the mucus is thick and yellow-green, and there's pain under your eyes and around your nose. You can also use this for coughs associated with asthma and bronchitis that are hacking and rattle. Morning is worse, heat improves symptoms.

Kali muriaticum. This remedy is most suitable for chronic conditions of the middle ear. Often the glands around the ear are also swollen, and you might hear snapping noises. Eating fatty foods makes it worse.

Lachesis. This remedy—derived from the Bushmaster snake—has all the features associated with this animal: dislike of anything tight around the middle or neck (or a lump in the throat) and fear of snakes. Many of the symptoms are left-sided, or at the very least move from left to right. Bleeding disorders often fit this remedy, like nosebleeds and abnormal menstrual periods. Sleep or touch makes symptoms worse; expressing feelings makes things better.

Ledum. For puncture wounds, insect bites or stings, smashed digits, this is where you start. Also good for bruised sprains and sore feet. Cold makes the injuries feel better, and warmth and movement worse.

Lycopodium. Unlike Lachesis, this remedy's symptoms tend to be right-sided or move from right to left. You might find your sweet tooth is stronger than usual. People who fit this remedy often feel fearful inside, but hide it with bravado. Gas and bloating are predominant even after a small amount of food, including typical gaseous foods like cabbage and beans. You probably feel chilly though warmth makes you feel worse. You're better off with warm drinks, and in fact yearn for them.

Muriaticum acidum. This is a fine remedy for hemorrhoids that are swollen, itchy, dark blue, protruding and very sensitive; they're so sensitive, in fact, that even wiping yourself with toilet paper is agonizing. Women who get hemorrhoids during pregnancy are often helped by this remedy. One characteristic that separates Muriaticum from the others is that urination makes the itching and protrusion worse, and may even initiate involuntary stool evacuation. This remedy can also be used for conditions of the mouth like canker sores, ulcers on the tongue, and eczema on the back of the hands.

Natrum phosphoricum. In this book, I recommend Natrum phos for vaginal yeast that's characterized by a creamy or honey-colored, sour-smelling and sometimes watery discharge. This is a good remedy for yeast infections caused by antibiotic use. It can also be used for similar discharges from the eyes and mouth, greenish diarrhea, hives, and jaundice.

Nux vomica. This is the workaholic remedy. Your mind is obsessed with business, you're impatient and irritable, your muscles are tense, you have heartburn and constipation and insomnia. You're drawn to stimulants like coffee and tobacco as well as alcohol, and hot, fatty foods. Resting makes you feel better, and eating any of your desired foods makes you worse.

Petroleum. This is another good motion sickness remedy, but is distinguished by a drunk feeling that goes with it. Your stomach feels very empty, and is better when you eat. Also watch for very dry, cracking skin that bleeds because it's so chapped. Warm air makes both these situations better.

Phosphorus. A tendency to bleed bright red blood and bruise are featured here. This can mean nosebleeds, coughing up blood, or excessive periods. Cold drinks, especially pop or seltzer, go down easily. And you feel better with company. Spicy and warm foods make you worse.

Podophyllum. This is a fine diarrhea remedy, especially for the early morning explosive kind that comes with cramps and creates weakness. This diarrhea can stem from an intestinal infection like traveler's diarrhea, or overwork. Lying on your stomach feels good.

Pulsatilla. You feel like a little baby, happy one minute, crying the next. You want attention, but are indecisive. Any other symptoms you might have—infected eyes with yellow-green goop, cough, diarrhea, irregular periods—are also changeable. You crave creamy foods like ice cream, and are not thirsty. Being outside makes you feel better.

Rhus toxicodendron. Joints stiff after overexertion injuries like sprains, strains, and tendonitis, can be relieved with warmth and movement. You struggle to find a comfortable position. Warmth feels good; cold and wet feel bad.

Ruta graveolens or Ruta. This is another injury remedy. Here look for a bruised, sore, and achy feeling—especially of the ankles and wrists. Headaches caused by eye-strain can also be relieved with a dose of Ruta. An achy flu might be helped in cases where overdoing it makes you tired.

Sabadilla. This remedy targets the mucous membranes of the nose and eyes. Copious, watery nasal drainage, red runny eyes, itchiness inside the nose—somewhat like hay fever—are better outdoors in open air. Children's diarrhea with constant cutting pain can also be relieved with this remedy. Warm food and drinks make things better; cold makes them worse.

Sabina. This remedy offers help for a very specific type of trouble: paralytic pain in the small of the back. It feels worse with the smallest movement and heat, although cool fresh air brings some relief. Can also be applied to uterine problems (including hemorrhaging) and gout.

Sepia. This remedy is often used with women who are experiencing hormonal problems, though vaginal infections that discharge foul-smelling, white or yellow-green secretions are also indicated. Itching is also apparent. Irritability and crying can be present. Staying busy and exercising make symptoms better; skipping a meal makes them worse.

Silicea or Silica. Low stamina distinguishes this remedy, as well as infected lumps and bumps like boils, cysts, and abscesses. You can add swollen lymph glands to this list and conditions that go along with it like sore throats and ear infections. Constipation with "bashful" stools is also a part of this remedy. Warmth makes these conditions better.

Spongia. This is a good cough remedy, particularly for the dry, croupy, barking kind. Breathing can be difficult, and you might find yourself constantly clearing your throat. Hoarseness is also apparent. Warm drinks relieve these symptoms, while talking, singing, breathing (especially cold air) make them worse.

Sulphuricum acidum or Sulphur. When you have itchy, red, burning skin, turn to Sulphur. Burning, foul-smelling diarrhea and heartburn are also aided. Bathing and warmth make these symptoms worse; cool air makes them better.

Tabacum. If the smell of tobacco makes your travel sickness worse, think of Tabacum—homeopathic tobacco. This nausea is incessant, and moving makes you vomit. A terrible sinking feeling lies in the pit of your stomach, and your head aches horribly. Open your eyes, and the room (or car) spins. Fresh air makes you feel better.

Thuja occidentalis or Thuja. This is *the* wart remedy though it can be used for other bodily ailments, particularly of the skin and genitourinary system. Signs to look for when considering Thuja in vaginal yeast infections are a profuse, thick, white discharge (could be greenish too) and a very sensitive vagina. Symptoms increase at night while in bed and after drinking coffee or eating fatty foods.

Uranium nitricum. This unusual remedy is specific for both gastric and duodenal ulcers. Excessive thirst and a ravenous appetite set it apart from other ulcer remedies. Other distinguishing signs to take note of are nausea, vomiting, burning in the stomach, and a boring pain in a bloated abdomen.

Urtica urens. This is homeopathic stinging nettles (also called itch weed), so you should have no troubles remembering symptoms that match: stinging, itchy, painful, swollen sores. These can be skin rashes, bug bites, burns, herpes, hives, chicken pox, or others. Any cool application makes these symptoms worse.

Zincum metallicum or Zincum. Zincum is classic for depression that's not only mental but physical as well. Healing is slow; there might be anemia and profound fatigue. It also works well for large varicose veins of the legs that feel weak, tremble and twitch. You might find your soles are sensitive too. But most important, you're constantly moving your feet and legs. For women, menstruation makes it worse.

Appendix C

Resource List

There are many worthwhile books and magazines available on natural health. Below are a few to get you started. Also see Appendices A and B for herbal and homeopathic books to read. Some laboratories that specialize in tests that aid the natural health practitioner are listed below as well.

Books

Alternative Medicine: The Definitive Guide compiled by The Burton Goldberg Group, Future Medicine Publishing, 1993.

Total Wellness by Joseph Pizzorno, ND, Prima, 1996.

Dr. Wright's Guide to Healing with Nutrition by Jonathan Wright, MD, Keats, 1990.

Encyclopedia of Natural Medicine by Michael Murray, ND, and Joseph Pizzorno, ND, Prima, 1991.

Eat Right for Your Type by Peter D'Adamo, ND, G.P. Putnam's Sons, 1996.

Perfect Health by Deepak Chopra, MD, Harmony Books, 1991.

Encyclopedia of Nutritional Supplements by Michael T. Murray, ND, Prima, 1996.

Spontaneous Healing by Andrew Weil, MD, Alfred Knopf, 1995.

How to Eat Away Arthritis by Lauri M. Aesoph, ND, Prentice Hall, 1996.

Periodicals

Most of these magazines you'll find in your local bookstore, grocery store, or health food store. I've supplied addresses for ones you need to order.

Delicious!

Natural Health

Let's Live

Nutrition Insights

Vegetarian Times

Alive (Canada)

Humor and Health Letter
PO Box 16814
Jackson, MS 39236
(601) 957-0075

Bimonthly newsletter on the research and clinical use of humor.

Journal of Nursing Jocularity
PO Box 40416
Mesa, AZ 85274
(602) 835-6165

A quarterly journal about the funny side of nursing.

Laboratories

Great Smokies Diagnostic Laboratory
18A Regent Park Boulevard
Asheville, NC 28806
(800) 522-4762

Meridian Valley Clinical Laboratory
24030 132nd Avenue SE
Kent, WA 98042
(800) 234-6825

Appendix D

Natural Health Practitioners

While learning to care for your health is wonderful, there are times when you need the help of a skilled professional. Below I offer tips on how to assess natural health practitioners in your area; I also give you professional organizations that can refer you to trained natural health caregivers.

Twenty Questions to Ask Your Practitioner

1. Where were you trained?
2. Are you licensed to practice in this state (or province)? If your state doesn't license the practitioner you wish to see, ask if he or she is licensed in another state or, at the very least, is qualified to obtain a license in another state.
3. How long have you been in practice?
4. How many cases of my condition have you treated?
5. Do you practice full- or part-time? If part-time, how often?
6. Are you available 24 hours a day?
7. What kind of treatments do you use?
8. What do you do if your treatment doesn't work?
9. Do you perform physical exams?
10. Do you use laboratory tests? Which ones?
11. Do you believe in combining natural and conventional treatments? If so, how do you do this?

12. If I bring in new information, will you discuss it with me?

13. What do you do in case of emergencies?

14. Do you refer to other doctors or practitioners in the community?

15. Do you consult with other doctors in the community, or elsewhere?

16. Do you have privileges or a professional relationship with the local hospital?

17. Will you talk with my MD or family physician?

18. What do you charge?

19. Will my insurance cover your service, treatments and/or laboratory tests?

20. Do you carry malpractice insurance?

Professional Associations

Naturopathic Physicians

American Association of Naturopathic Physicians
601 Valley Street, Suite 105
Seattle, WA 98109
(206) 298-0125

Canadian Naturopathic Association
4174 Dundas Street, Suite 304
Etobicoke, Ontario
Canada M8X 1X3
(416) 233-1043

Holistic Doctors (MDs, osteopathic, naturopathic, chiropractic)

American Holistic Medical Association
4101 Lake Boone Trail, Suite 201
Raleigh, NC 27617
(919) 787-5181

Oriental Medical Doctors

American Association of Acupuncture and Oriental Medicine
433 Front Street
Capasauqua, PA 18032
(610) 433-2448

Herbalists

American Herbalists Guild
PO Box 746555
Arvada, CO 80006

Herb Research Foundation
1007 Pearl Street, Suite 200
Boulder, CO 80302
(303) 449-2265

Homeopaths

Homeopathic Academy of Naturopathic Physicians (HANP)
PO Box 69565
Portland, OR 97201
(503) 795-0579

International Foundation for Homeopathy (IFH)
PO Box 7
Edmonds, WA 98020
(206) 776-1499

National Center for Homeopathy
801 North Fairfax Street, Suite 306
Alexandria, VA 22314
(703) 548-7790

Humor Specialists

American Association of Therapeutic Humor
222 Meramec, Suite 303
St. Louis, MO 63105
(314) 863-6232

Appendix E

Feedback From Readers—Your Makeover Ideas!

A book like this develops with help from lots of people. If while completing *Your Natural Health Makeover*, you discovered some ideas, hints, or tricks of your own, let me know. I'd love to hear what worked for you, and with your permission, might include it in a future work.

Send *your* makeover ideas to:

Lauri M. Aesoph, ND
717 South Duluth Avenue
Sioux Falls, SD 57104

Or e-mail me at: aesoph@worldnet.att.net

For More Information

Lauri Aesoph, ND, delights in educating people about natural health care and responsible ways to begin incorporating these principles into their lives. She has also written *How to Eat Away Arthritis* (Prentice Hall, 1996), available in bookstores. If you're interested in reading more of her writings and what she does, look her up on the Internet (http://www.healthy.net/aesoph or http://www.naturopathic. org/nd.homepages/dr.aesoph).

If you'd like Dr. Aesoph to speak at your group meeting, association gathering, convention, or other get-together about *Your Natural Health Makeover* or related natural health topics, contact her at 605-339-3645 or write to her at 717 South Duluth Avenue, Sioux Falls, South Dakota 57104.

References

Part One

Chapter 1

1. Whelan J. Health care tradeoffs: comparing the Canadian single-payer and the American multipayer systems. Pacific Northwest Executive. October 1990:2.

2. US Dept of Health & Human Services (Public Health Service), *The Surgeon General's Report on Nutrition and Health*, 1988, Rocklin, CA: Prima Publishing.

3. Diamant M & B Diamant. Abuse and timing of use of antibiotics in acute otitis media. Archives of Otolaryngology 1974; 100: 226–232.

4. *Physician's Desk Reference 1996 (50th edition)*, Medical Economics Co., Montvale, NJ.

5. Caudell KA. Psychoneuroimmunology and innovative behavioral interventions in patients with leukemia. Oncology Nursing Forum 1996; 23(3):493–502.

6. Bryla CM. The relationship between stress and the development of breast cancer: a literature review. Oncology Nursing Forum 1996; 23(3):441–448.

7. Ginsburg IH. Psychological and psychophysiological aspects of psoriasis. Dermatologic Clinics 1995 Oct; 13(4):793–804.

8. Monteiro da Silva AM et al. Psychosocial factors in inflammatory periodontal diseases. A review. Journal of Clinical Periodontology 1995; 22:516–526.

9. Cohen S. Psychological stress and susceptibility to upper respiratory infections. American Journal of Respiratory & Critical Care Medicine 1995; 152:S53–S58.

10. Goddard NC. 'Spirituality as integrative energy': a philosophical analysis as requisite precursor to holistic nursing practice. Journal of Advanced Nursing 1995;22:808–815.

11. Miller MA. Culture, spirituality, and women's health. Journal of Obstetric, Gynecologic & Neonatal Nursing 1995; 24(3):257–263.

12. Turner JA et al. The importance of placebo effects in pain treatment and research. Journal of the American Medical Association. 1994; 271(20):1609–1614.

13. Rabinovitz M & DH Van Thiel. Hepatotoxicity of nonsteroidal anti-inflammatory drugs. The American Journal of Gastroenterology 1992; 87(12):1696–1704.

14. Graham NMH et al. Adverse effects of aspirin, acetaminophen, and ibuprofen on immune function, viral shedding, and clinical status in rhinovirus-infected volunteers. The Journal of Infectious Diseases 1990;162:1277–1282.

15. Trovato A et al. Drug-nutrient interactions. American Family Physician 1991; 44(5):1651–1658.

Chapter 3

1. Guyton AC. *Textbook of Medical Physiology* (6th ed). Philadelphia: WB Saunders, 1981.

2. Mozafar A. Enrichment of some B-vitamins in plants with application of organic fertilizers. Plant and Soil 1994;167: 305–311.

3. van de Laar MAFJ & JK van der Korst. Rheumatoid arthritis, food, and allergy. Seminars in Arthritis and Rheumatism 1991; 21(1): 12–23.

4. Egger J et al. Is migraine food allergy? The Lancet 1983, October 15: 865–869.

5. Burks AW et al. Atopic dermatitis: clinical relevance of food hypersensitivity reactions. The Journal of Pediatrics 1988; 113(3): 447–451.

6. Oehling A. Importance of food allergy in childhood asthma Allergol et Immonpathol. 1981; Supplementum IX:71–73.

7. Bogaards JJP et al. Consumption of Brussels sprouts results in elevated alpha-class glutathione S-transferase levels in human blood plasma. Carcinogenesis 1994;15(5): 1073–1075.

8. Kiso Y et al. Antihepatotoxic principles of Curcuma longa rhizomes. Planta Medica 1983;49:185–187.

9. Imai K & K Nakachi. Cross sectional study of effects of drinking green tea on cardiovascular and liver diseases.

10. Kirchchoff R et al. Increase in choleresis by means of artichoke extract. Phytomedicine 1994;1:107–115.

11. Hikino H et al. Antihepatotoxic actions of flavonolignans from Silybum marianum fruits. Planta Medica 1984; 50: 248–250.

12. Blanchet KD. Dandelion. Alternative & Complementary Therapies 1995 Jan/Feb: 115–117.

13. Kaptchuk T. *The Web that has no Weaver*. New York: Congdon & Weed, 1983, pp. 129–130.

14. Grady H. Immunomodulation through castor oil packs. The Journal of Naturopathic Medicine 1997; 7(10): 84–89.

Chapter 4

1. Thorburn AW et al. Slowly digested and absorbed carbohydrate in traditional bushfoods: a protective factor against diabetes? American Journal of Clinical Nutrition 1987; 45: 98–106.

2. Price WA. *Nutrition and Physical Degeneration* (50th anniversary edition). New Canaan: Keats Publishing, 1989.

3. Anon. Taco belles. Globe & Mail (Toronto). February 11, 1995, pg D8.

4. Block G. Dietary guidelines and the results of food consumption surveys. American Journal of Clinical Nutrition 1991; 53: 356S–357S.

5. Anon. Food timetables. Mother Earth News, Oct/Nov 1991; 128:26.

6. Greenberg ER et al. Mortality associated with low plasma concentration of beta carotene and the effect of oral supplementation. The Journal of the American Medical Association 1996; 275(9): 699–703.

7. Block G. Vitamin C and cancer prevention: the epidemiologic evidence. American Journal of Clinical Nutrition 1991; 53. 270S–282S.

8. Seddon JM et al. Dietary carotenoids, vitamins A, C, and E, and advanced age-related macular degeneration. Journal of the American Medical Association 1994; 272:1413–1420.

9. McNutt K. The individualized prescriptive foods era has dawned. Nutrition Today, May/June 1993: 43–47.

10. Johnston BT et al. Acid perception in gastro-oesophageal reflux disease is dependent on psychosocial factors. Scandinavian Journal of Gastroenterology 1995; 30(1): 1–5.

11. Herlofson BB & P Barkvoll. Oral mucosal desquamation of pre- and post-menopausal women. A comparison of response to sodium lauryl sulphate in toothpastes. Journal of Clinical Periodontology 1996; 23(6): 567–571.

Chapter 5

1. Covert C. New soft drinks surge into stores with a jolt. Star Tribune (Minneapolis), February 23, 1997: E1.

2. Robertson W et al. Prevalence of urinary stone disease in vegetarians. European Urology 1982; 8:334–339.

3. Avorn J et al. Reduction of bacteriuria and pyuria after ingestion of cranberry juice. Journal of the American Medical Association 1994; 271:751–754.

4. Ringsdorf WM et al. Sucrose, neutrophilic phagocytosis and resistance to disease. Dental Survey 1976; 52:46–48.

5. Sanchez A et al. Role of sugars in human neutrophilic phagocytosis. The American Journal of Clinical Nutrition 1973; 26:1180–1184.

6. Kilbourne JP. Cranberry juice in urinary tract infection. Journal of Naturopathic Medicine 1991; 2:45–47.

7. Ofek I et al. Anit-escherichia adhesion activity of cranberry and blueberry juices. New England Journal of Medicine 1991;324: 1599

8. Katzung BG. *Basic and Clinical Pharmacology (2nd edition).* Los Altos, CA: Lange Medical Publications, 1984, pg 180.

9. Adetumbi MA et al. *Allium sativum* (garlic)—a natural antibiotic. Medical Hypotheses 1983; 12:227–237.

10. Ghannoum MA. Studies on the anticandidal mode of action of *Allium sativum* (garlic). Journal of General Microbiology 1988;134: 2917–2924.

11. Davis LE et al. Antifungal activity on human cerebrospinal fluid and plasma after intravenous administration of *Allium sativum*. Antimicrobial Agents and Chemotherapy 1990; 34(4): 651–653.

12. Mirelman D et al. Inhibition of growth of *Entamoeba histolytica* by allicin, the active principal of garlic extract (*Allium sativum*). The Journal of Infectious Diseases 1987;156(1): 243–244 (Letter).

13. Tsai Y et al. Antiviral properties of garlic: in vitro effects on influenza B, herpes simplex and coxsackie viruses. Planta Medica 1985: 460–461.

14. Pantoja CV et al. Diuretic, natriuretic and hypotensive effects produced by *Allium sativum* (garlic) in anaesthetized dogs. Journal of Ethnopharmacology 1991; 31: 325–331.

15. Brenner BM (ed). *Brenner & Rector's: The Kidney* (5th ed), Volume II. Philadelphia: WB Saunders Co, 1996.

16. Scott R et al. The importance of cadmium as a factor in calcified upper urinary tract stone disease—a prospective 7-year study. British Journal of Urology 1982; 54: 584–589.

17. Rose G. The influence of calcium content of water, intake of vegetables and fruit and of other food factors upon the incidence of renal calculi. Urological Research 1975; 3: 61–66.

18. Shaw P et al. Idiopathic hypercalciuria: its control with unprocessed bran. British Journal of Urology 1980; 52:426–429.

19. Griffith H et al. A control study of dietary factors in renal stone formation. British Journal of Urology 1981; 53: 416–420.

20. Thom J et al. The influence of refined carbohydrate on urinary calcium excretion. British Journal of Urology 1978; 50: 459–464.

21. Lemann J et al. Possible role of carbohydrate-induced hypercalciuria in calcium oxalate kidney-stone formation. New England Journal of Medicine 1969; 280: 232–237.

22. Zechner O et al. Nutritional risk factors in urinary stone disease. Journal of Urology 1981; 125: 51–55.

23. Harvey JA et al. Calcium citrate: reduced propensity for the crystallization of calcium oxalatein urine resulting from induced hypercalciuria of calcium supplementation. Journal of Clinical Endocrinology and Metabolism 1985; 61(6): 1223.

24. Harvey JA et al. Dose dependency of calcium absorption: a comparison of calcium carbonate and calcium citrate. Journal of Bone and Mineral Research 1988; 3(3): 253.

25. Curhan GC et al. Comparison of dietary calcium with supplemental calcium and other nutrients as factors affecting the risk for kidney stones in women. Annals of Internal Medicine 1997; 126(7): 497–505. ("calcium"-abstract)

Chapter 6

1. Ringsdorf WM et al. Sucrose, neutrophilic phagocytosis and resistance to disease. Dental Survey 1976; 52: 46–48.

2. Covert C. New soft drinks surge into stores with a jolt. Star Tribune (Minneapolis), February 23, 1997:E1.

3. Sanchez A et al. Role of sugars in human neutrophilic phagocytosis. The American Journal of Clinical Nutrition 1973; 26: 1180–1184.

4. Dale DC & DD Federman (eds). *Scientific American Medicine*. NYC: Scientific American, Inc, 1978–1997; Chapter XXIV, "Pathophysiology of Fever and Fever of Undetermined Origin."

5. Horowith BJ et al. Sugar chromatography studies in recurrent candida vulvovaginitis. The Journal of Reproductive Medicine 1984; 29:441–443.

6. Lefkowith JB. Do dietary fatty acids affect the interactions among macrophages, endothelial lesions, and thrombosis? American Journal of Clinical Nutrition 1992; 56: 808S.

7. Nirgiotis JG et al. Low-fat, high-carbohydrate diets improve wound healing and increase protein levels in surgically stressed rats. Journal of Pediatric Surgery 1991; 26(8): 925–29.

8. Pollmacher T et al. Influence of host defense activation on sleep in humans. Advances in Neuroimmunology 1995; 5(2):155–169.

9. Moldofsky H. Central nervous system and peripheral immune functions and the sleep-wake system. Journal of Psychiatry & Neuroscience. 1994; 19(5): 368–374.

10. Chandra RK. Effect of vitamin and trace-element supplementation on immune responses and infection in elderly subjects. Lancet 1992; 340: 1124–1127.

11. Prinz W et al. The effect of ascorbic acid supplementation on some parameters of the human immunological defence system. International Journal of Vitamin and Nutritional Research 1977; 47: 248–257.

12. Semba RD et al. Abnormal T-cell subset proportions in vitamin-A-deficient children. The Lancet 1993; 341: 5–8.

13. Beisel WR et al. Single-nutrient effects on immunologic functions. Journal of the American Medical Association 1981; 245(1): 53–58.

14. Lakshman K et al. Monitoring nutritional status in the critically ill adult. Journal of Clinical Monit 1986; 2(2): 114–120.

15. Caudell KA. Psychoneuroimmunology and innovative behavioral interventions in patients with leukemia. Oncology Nursing Forum 1996; 23(3): 493–502.

16. Cohen S. Psychological stress and susceptibility to upper respiratory infections. American Journal of Respiratory Critical Care Medicine 1995;152: 553–558.

17. Monteiro da Silva AM et al. Psychological factors in inflammatory periodontal diseases. Journal of Clinical Periodontology 1995; 22: 516–526.

18. Ginsburg IH. Psychological and psychophysiological aspects of psoriasis. Dermatologic Clinics 1995;13(4): 793–804.

19. Kiecolt-Glaser JK et al. Slowing of wound healing by psychological stress. Lancet 1995; 346:1194–1196.

20. Cohen S et al. Psychological stress and susceptibility to the common cold. The New England Journal of Medicine 1991; 325:606–612.

21. Anon. State-specific estimates of smoking-attributable mortality and years of potential life lost-United States, 1985. Journal of the American Medical Association 1989; 261(1): 23–25.

22. Anon. Smoking and immunity. The Lancet 1990; 335: 1561–1563.

23. Lowinson JH et al (eds). *Substance Abuse, A Comprehensive Textbook (2nd ed)*. Baltimore: Williams & Wilkins, 1992.

24. Piyathilake CJ et al. Local and systemic effects of cigarette smoking on folate and vitamin B-12. American Journal of Clinical Nutrition 1994; 60: 559–566.

25. American Thoracic Society, Medical Section of American Lung Assoc. Cigarette smoking and health. American Review of Respiratory Disease 1985; 132(5): 1133–1136.

26. American Thoracic Society, Medical Section of American Lung Assoc. Health effects of smoking on children. American Review of Respiratory Disease 1985; 132(5): 1137–1138.

27. Dunnet B. Drugs that suppress immunity. American Health; Nov 1986: 43.

28. Bayer BM et al. Acute infusions of cocaine result in time-and-dose-dependent effects on lymphocyte responses and corticosterone secretion in rats. Immunopharmacology 1995; 29(1): 19–28.

29. Kreek MJ et al. Drugs of abuse and immunosuppression. NIDA Research Monograph 1994;140: 89–93.

30. Mohs ME et al. Nutritional effects of marijuana, heroin, cocaine, and nicotine. Journal of the American Dietetic Association 1990; 90: 1261–1267.

31. Brayton RG et al. Effect of alcohol and various diseases on leukocyte mobilization, phagocytosis and intracellular bacterial killing. The New England Journal of Medicine 1970; 282(3): 123–128.

32. Graham NMH et al. Adverse effects of aspirin, acetaminophen, and ibuprofen on immune function, viral shedding, and clinical status in rhinovirus-infected volunteers. Journal of Infectious Disease 1990;162:1277–1282.

33. Fujii T et al. Inhibitory effect of erythromycin on interleukin 8 production by 1 alpha, 25-dihydroxyvitamin D3-stimulated THP-1 cells. Antimicrobial Agents & Chemotherapy 1996;40(6): 1548–1551.

34. Rosaschino F et al. Evaluation of the immune status of children never treated with chemoantibiotics (children 3 to 6 years old). Minerva Pediatrica 1994; 46(11): 481–500.

35. Vojdani A et al. Immune alterations associated with exposure to toxic chemicals. Toxicology and Industrial Health 1992; 8(5): 239–254.

36. Miyakoshi H, Aoki T. Acting mechanisms of lentinan in humans—I. Augmentation of DNA synthesis and immunoglobulin production of peripheral mononuclear cells. International Journal of Immunopharmacology 1984; 6(4): 365–371.

37. Srivastava KC, T Mustafa. Ginger (*Zingiber officinale*) in rheumatism and musculoskeletal disorders. Medical Hypotheses 1992; 39: 342–348.

38. Jeevan A, Kripke ML. Ozone depletion and the immune system. The Lancet 1993; 342:1159–1160.

Chapter 7

1. Associated Press. Fatty diet hurts ability to deal with stress. Argus Leader, October 31, 1992, pg 3a.

2. Bolton S et al. A pilot study of some physiological and psychological effects of caffeine. The Journal of Orthomolecular Psychiatry;13(1): 34–41.

3. Brown DJ. *Herbal Prescriptions for Better Health*. Rocklin: Prima Publishing, 1996

4. Cousins N. *Anatomy of an Illness*. New York: Bantam Books, 1979.

5. Wooten P. Humor: an antidote for stress. http://www.mother.com/JestHome/anti-stress.html.

6. Berk L. Neuroendocrine and stress hormone changes during mirthful laughter. American Journal of Medical Sciences. 1989; 298: 390–396.

7. Berk L. Eustress of mirthful laughter modifies natural killer cell activity. Clinical Research 1989; 37(115).

Chapter 8

1. Komatsu A & I Sakurai. A study of the development of atherosclerosis in childhood and young adults: risk factors and the prevention of progression in Japan and the USA. The Pathobiological Determinants of Atherosclerosis in Youth (PDAY) Research Group. Pathology International 1996; 46(8): 541–547.

2. Kottke BA et al. Apolipoproteins and coronary artery disease. Mayo Clinic Proceedings 1986; 61.

3. Blieden LC et al. Non-traditional risk factors for atherosclerosis in high risk children. Israel Journal of Medical Sciences 1996; 32(12): 1255–61.

4. Ornish D et al. Can lifestyle changes reverse coronary heart disease? The Lancet 1990; 336:129–133.

5. Sacks FM & WW Willett. More on chewing the fat. The good fat and the good cholesterol. The New England Journal of Medicine 1991; 325(24):1740–1742.

6. Steinberg D. et al. Lipoproteins and atherogenesis. Journal of the American Medical Association 1990; 264:3047–3052.

7. Lichenstein AH. Trans fatty acids and hydrogenated fat—what do we know? Nutrition Today 1995; 30(3):102–107.

8. Blair SN et al. Physical fitness and all-cause mortality. Journal of the American Medical Association 1989; 262(17): 2395–2401.

9. Davidson MH et al. The hypocholesterolemic effects of beta-glucan in oatmeal and oat bran. Journal of the American Medical Association 1991; 265(14):1833–1839.

10. Glore SR et al. Soluble fiber and serum lipids: a literature review. Journal of the American Dietetic Association 1994; 94(4):425–436.

11. Hertog MGL et al. Dietary antioxidant flavonoids and risk of coronary heart disease: the Zutphen Elderly Study. The Lancet 1993; 342:1007–1011.

12. Riemersma RA et al. Risk of angina pectoris and plasma concentrations of vitamins A, C, and E and carotene. The Lancet 1991; 337(8732):1–5.

13. Manson JE et al. A prospective study of vitamin C and incidence of coronary heart disease in women. Circulation 1992; 85: 865.

14. Whang R et al. Refractory potassium repletion: a consequence of magnesium deficiency. Archives of Internal Medicine 1992;152:40–45.

15. Woods KL et al. Intravenous magnesium sulphate in suspected acute myocardial infarction: results of the second Leicester Intravenous Magnesium Intervention Trial (LIMIT-2). The Lancet 1992; 339:1553–1558.

16. Clarke R et al. Hyperhomocysteinemia: an independent risk factor for vascular disease. The New England Journal of Medicine 1991; 324(17):1149–1155.

17. Ferrannini E et al. Insulin resistance in essential hypertension. The New England Journal of Medicine 1987; 317:350–357.

18. Hodges RE & T Rebello. Carbohydrates and blood pressure. Annals of Internal Medicine 1983; 98(part 2):838–841.

19. Hall JH et al. Long-term survival in coenzyme Q10 treated congestive heart failure patients. Circulation 1990; 82(4), supplement III: 675.

20. Ernst E et al. Garlic and blood lipids. British Medical Journal 1985; 291:139.

21. Gujral S et al. Effects of ginger (*Zingebar officinale roscoe*) oleoresin on serum and hepatic cholesterol levels in cholesterol fed rats. Nutrition Reports International 1978;17: 183–189.

22. Wang J-P et al. Antiplatelet effect of capsaicin. Thrombosis Research 1984;36:497–507.

23. Shoji N et al. Cardiotonic principles of ginger (Zingiber officinale roscoe). Journal of Pharm Science 1982;10:1174–75.

24. Kiuchi F et al. Inhibitors of prostaglandin biosynthesis from ginger. Chem Pharm Bull 1982; 30: 754–757.

25. Srivastava K. Effects of aqueous extracts of onion, garlic and ginger on the platelet aggregation and metabolism of arachidonic acid in the blood vascular system: In vitro study. Prost Leukotri Med 1984;13: 227–35.

26. Wahlqvist M. Fish intake and arterial wall characteristics in healthy people and diabetic patients. The Lancet 1989; 944: 946.

27. Sharp DS & NL Benowitz. Pharmacoepidemiology of the effect of caffeine on blood pressure. Clinical Pharmacol Ther 1990;47:57–60.

28. Urgert R et al. Effects of cafestol and kahweol from coffee grounds on serum lipids and serum liver enzymes in humans. American Journal of Clinical Nutrition 1995; 61:144–145.

29. Imai K, Nakachi K. Cross sectional study of effects of drinking green tea on cardiovascular and liver diseases. British Medical Journal 1995; 310: 693–96

30. Facchini FS et al. Insulin resistance and cigarette smoking. The Lancet 1992;339:1128–1130.

31. Zhu B & WW Parmley. Hemodynamic and vascular effects of active and passive smoking. American Heart Journal 1995;130:1270–1275.

32. Timmreck TC & JF Randolph. Smoking cessation: clinical steps to improve compliance. Geriatrics 1993; 48(4): 63–70.

33. Rimm EB et al. Prospective study of alcohol consumption and risk of coronary disease in men. The Lancet 1991; 338: 464–468.

34. Regan TJ. Alcohol and the cardiovascular system. Journal of the American Medical Association 1990; 264(3): 377–381.

35. Longnecker MP et al. A meta-analysis of alcohol consumption in relation to risk of breast cancer. Journal of the American Medical Association 1988; 260(5): 652–656.

36. Yeung AC et al. The effect of atherosclerosis on the vasomotor response of coronary arteries to mental stress. The New England Journal of Medicine 1991; 325: 1551–1556.

37. Anon. Essence of stress. The Lancet 1994; 344:1713–1714.

38. Raymond C. Distrust, rage may be "toxic core" that puts "Type A" person at risk. Journal of the American Medical Association 1989; 261(6): 813.

39. Chopra D. Longevity Magazine 1989.

Chapter 10

1. Anon. Chronobiology and chronotherapy in medicine. Disease-a-Month 1995;16(8):506–575.

2. Tjoa WS et al. Circannual rhythm in human sperm count revealed by serially independent sampling. Fertility and Sterility 1982; 38:454–459.

3. Lieber CS. The metabolism of alcohol. Scientific American 1976, March: 25–33.

4. Gavaler JS et al. Alcohol and estrogen levels in postmenopausal women: the spectrum of effect. Alcoholism: Clinical and Experimental Research 1993;17(4): 786–790.

5. Dawood MY, JL McGuire, LM Demers (ed). *Premenstrual Syndrome & Dysmenorrhea*. Baltimore-Munich: Urban & Schwarzenberg, 1985.

6. Feldman HA et al. Impotence and its medical and psychosocial correlates: results of the Massachusetts Male Aging Study 1994;151: 54–61.

7. Nielsen FH et al. Effect of dietary boron on mineral, estrogen, and testosterone metabolism in postmenopausal women. Federation of American Societies for Experimental Biology 1987;1:394–397.

8. Snively WD, RL Westerman. Minnesota Medicine, June 1965.

9. Gonzalez-Reimers E et al. Relative and combined effects of ethanol and protein deficiency on gonadal function and histology. Alcohol 1994;11(5):355–360.

10. Porikos KP, TB Van Itallie. Diet-induced changes in serum transaminase and triglyceride levels in healthy adult men. Role of sucrose and excess calories. American Journal of Medicine 1983; 75: 624.

11. Shils ME, VR Young. *Modern Nutrition in Health and Disease (7th ed)*. Philadelphia: Lea & Febiger, 1988.

12. Nielsen FH. Nutritional requirements for boron, silicon, vanadium, nickel, and arsenic: current knowledge and speculation. Federation of American Societies for Experimental Biology 1991;5:2661–2667.

13. Takihara H et al. Zinc sulfate therapy for infertile male with or without varicocelectomy. Urology 1987; 29(6): 638–641.

14. Dincer SL et al. Thalassemia, zinc deficiency, and sexual dysfunction in women. Hospital Practice 1992; 27(4A): 35.

15. Morales A et al. Oral and topical treatment of erectile dysfunction. Urologic Clinics of North America 1995; 22(4): 879–886.

Chapter 11

1. Wisneski LA. Clinical management of postmenopausal osteoporosis. Southern Medical Journal 1992; 85: 832–39.

2. Nelson ME et al. A 1-y walking program and increased dietary calcium in postmenopausal women: effects on bone. American Journal of Clinical Nutrition 1991; 53: 1304–1311.

3. Ott SM. Bone density in adolescents. New England Journal of Medicine 1991; 325: 1646–1647.

4. Licata AA. Therapies for symptomatic primary osteoporosis. Geriatrics 1991; 46: 62–67.

5. Slemenda CW et al. Long-term bone loss in men: effects of genetic and environmental factors. Annals of Internal Medicine 1992; 117: 286–291.

6. Hernandez-Avila M et al. Caffeine, moderate alcohol intake, and risk of fractures of the hip and forearm in middle-aged women. American Journal of Clinical Nutrition 1991;54:157–163.

7. Mickelsen O & AG Marsh. Calcium requirement and diet. Nutrition Today, Jan/Feb 1989:28–32.

8. Eaton SB et al. *The Paleolithic Prescription*. New York: Harper & Row, Publishers, 1988.

9. Johnson K & EW Kligman. Preventive nutrition: disease-specific dietary interventions for older adults. Geriatrics 1992;47: 39–40, 45–49.

10. Werbach MR. *Nutritional Influences on Illness*. Tarzana: Third Line Press, 1988.

11. Andon MB et al. Spinal bone density and calcium intake in healthy postmenopausal women. American Journal of Clinical Nutrition 1991;54: 927–929.

12. Stevenson JC et al. Dietary intake of calcium and postmenopausal bone loss. British Medical Journal 1988; 297:15–17.

13. Iseri LT & JH French. Magnesium: nature's physiologic calcium blocker. American Heart Journal 1984;108: 188–193.

14. Medalle R et al. Vitamin D resistance in magnesium deficiency. American Journal of Clinical Nutrition 1976; 29: 854–858.

15. Nielsen FH et al. Effect of dietary boron on mineral, estrogen, and testosterone metabolism in postmenopausal women. Federation of American Societies for Experimental Biology 1987;1:394–397.

16. Raloff J. Reasons for boning up on manganese. Science News 1986; 130: 199.

17. Gaby AR & JV Wright. Nutrients and bone health. Published by: Wright/Gaby Nutrition Institute (1988): PO Box 21535, Baltimore, MD 21208.

18. McCaslin FE Jr & JM Janes. The effect of strontium lactate in the treatment of osteoporosis. Proceedings of Staff Meetings Mayo Clinic 1959; 34: 329–334.

19. Nielsen FH. Nutritional requirements for boron, silicon, vanadium, nickel, and arsenic: current knowledge and speculation. FASEB 1991; 5: 2661–2667.

20. Fehily AM et al. Factors affecting bone density in young adults. American Journal of Clinical Nutrition 1992; 56: 570–586.

21. Hart JP et al. Circulating vitamin K1 levels in fracture neck of femur. The Lancet 1984; II: 283.

22. Turnlund JR et al. Vitamin B6 depletion followed by repletion with animal or plant source diets and calcium and magnesium metabolism in young women. American Journal of Clinical Nutrition 1992; 56.

23. Thom J et al. The influence of refined carbohydrate on urinary calcium excretion. British Journal of Urology 1978; 50: 459–464.

24. Lemann J et al. Possible role of carbohydrate-induced hypercalciuria in calcium oxalate kidney-stone formation. New England Journal of Medicine 1969; 280: 232–237.

25. Mazess RB & HS Barden. Bone density in premenopausal women: effects of age, dietary intake, physical activity, smoking and birth-control pills. American Journal of Clinical Nutrition 1991; 53: 132–142.

26. Rao C et al. Influence of bioflavonoids on the metabolism and crosslinking of collagen. Italian Journal of Biochemistry 1981; 30: 259–270.

27. Sutton PRN. Acute dental caries, mental stress, immunity and the active passage of ions through the teeth. Medical Hypotheses 1990; 31:17.

28. Herlofson BB & P Barkvoll. Oral mucosal desquamation caused by two toothpaste detergents in an experimental model. European Journal of Oral Sciences 1996; 104(1): 21–26.

29. Skaare A et al. The effect of toothpaste containing triclosan on oral mucosal desquamation. A model study. Journal of Clinical Periodontology 1996; 23(12):1100–1103.

30. Herlofson BB et al. Increased human gingival blood flow induced by sodium lauryl sulphate. Journal of Clinical Periodontology 1996; 23(11):1004–1007.

31. Herlofson BB & P Barkvoll. Oral mucosal desquamation of pre- and postmenopausal women. A comparison of response to sodium lauryl sulphate in toothpastes. Journal of Clinical Periodontology 1996; 23(6): 567–571.

32. Addy M et al. Dentine hypersensitivity—effects of some proprietary mouthwashes on the dentine smear layer: a SEM study. Journal of Dentistry 1991;19(3):148–152.

33. Subcommittee on Risk Management of the Committee to Coordinate Environmental Health and Related Programs. *Dental Amalgam: A scientific review and recommended public health service strategy for research, education and regulation.* January 1993. Department of Health and Human Services. Public Health Service.

34. Nylander M et al. Mercury concentrations in the human brain and kidneys in relation to exposure from dental amalgam fillings. Swedish Dental Journal 1987;11:179–187.

35. Bland JS. Can mercury in dental fillings make you sick? Delicious! April 1995: 64.

36. Siblerud RL. The relationship between mercury from dental amalgam and mental health. American Journal of Psychotherapy 1989;XLIII(4):575–587.

37. Newman NM & RSM Ling. Acetabular bone destruction related to non-steroidal anti-inflammatory drugs. The Lancet 1985; July 6: 11–14.

38. Hudson TS. Osteoporosis: an overview for clinical practice. Journal of Naturopathic Medicine 1997; 7(1): 27–33.

Chapter 12

1. Sindrup JH et al. Nocturnal temperature and subcutaneous blood flow in humans. Clinical Physiology 1995; 15(6): 611–622.

2. Marshall LA. How pure is your water? Delicious! April 1995, pg 38.

3. Krause MV & LK Mahan. *Food, Nutrition, and Diet Therapy (7th ed)*. Philadelphia: WB Saunders Co, 1984.

4. Trevithick JR et al. Topical tocopherol acetate reduces post UVB, sunburn associated erythema, edema, and skin sensitivity in mice. Archives of Biochemistry and Biophysiology 1992; 296: 575–582.

5. Garland CF et al. Could sunscreens increase melanoma risk? American Journal of Public Health 1992; 82(4): 614–615.

6. Roan S. Worship your skin. Argus Leader, July 30, 1996.

7. Perasalo J. Traditional use of the sauna for hygiene and health in Finland. Annals of Clinical Research 1988; 20: 220–223.

Chapter 13

1. Age-related Macular Degeneration Study Group. Multicenter ophthalmic and nutritional age-related macular degeneration study—part 1: design, subjects and procedures. Journal of the American Optometric Association 1996; 67(1): 12–29.

2. Christen WG et al. A prospective study of cigarette smoking and risk of age-related macular degeneration in men. Journal of the American Medical Association 1996; 276(14): 1147–1151.

3. Schectman G et al. The influence of smoking on vitamin C status in adults. American Journal of Public Health 1989; 79(2):158–162.

4. Klein R, BEK Klein. Smoke gets in your eyes too (editorial). Journal of the American Medical Association 1996; 276(14): 1178–1179.

5. Hankinson SE et al. Nutrient intake and cataract extraction in women: a prospective study. British Medical Journal 1992; 305: 335–339.

6. Ritter LL et al. Alcohol use and lens opacities in the Beaver Dam Eye Study. Archives of Ophthalmology 1993;111:113–117.

7. Forman MR et al. Effect of alcohol consumption on plasma carotenoid concentrations in premenopausal women: a controlled dietary study. American Journal of Clinical Nutrition 1995; 62:131–135.

8. Munoz B et al. Alcohol use and risk of posterior subcapsular opacities. Archives of Ophthalmology 1993; 111:110–112.

9. Seddon JM et al. Dietary carotenoids, vitamins A, C, and E, and advanced age-related macular degeneration. Journal of the American Medical Association 1994; 272:1413–1420.

10. Murray M. *The Healing Power of Herbs*. Rocklin, CA: Prima Publishing, 1995.

11. Shils ME, VR Young. *Modern Nutrition in Health and Disease (7th ed)*. Philadelphia: Lea & Febiger, 1988.

12. Berson EL et al. A randomized trial of vitamin A and vitamin E supplementation for retinitis pigmentosa. Archives of Ophthalmology 1993;111:761–772.

13. Fishbein S & S Goodstein. The pressure lowering effect of ascorbic acid. Annals of Ophthalmology 1972;4:487–491.

14. Anon. Vitamin C may enhance healing of caustic corneal burns. Journal of the American Medical Association 1980; 243(7): 623.

15. Newsome DA et al. Oral zinc in macular degeneration. Archives of Ophthalmology 1988;106:192–198.

16. Swanson A, A Truesdale. Elemental analysis in normal and cataractous human lens tissue. Biochem. Biophys. Res. Comm 1971; 45:1, 488–496.

17. Albert DM, FA Jakobiec. *Principles and Practice of Ophthalmology (vol 1)*. Philadelphia: WB Saunders, 1994.

18. The Revolutionary Health Committee of Hunan Province. *A Barefoot Doctor's Manual* (revised and enlarged edition), Seattle: Madrona Publishers, 1977.

Chapter 14

1. Anderson GH. Diet, neurotransmitter and brain function. British Medical Bulletin 1981; 37(1): 95–100.

2. DeLong GR. Effects of nutrition on brain development in humans. American Journal of Clinical Nutrition Supplement 1993; 57: 286S–290S.

3. Benton D & JP Buts. Vitamin/mineral supplementation and intelligence. The Lancet 1990; 335:1158–1160.

4. LaRue A et al. Nutritional status and cognitive functioning in a normally aging sample: a 6-y reassessment. American Journal of Clinical Nutrition 1997; 65: 20–29.

5. Pizzorno J. *Total Wellness*. Rocklin, CA: Prima Publishing, 1996.

6. Guyton AC. *Textbook of Medical Physiology* (6th ed). Philadelphia: WB Saunders, 1981.

Part Two

1. Psychiatry Research, 1992; 43: 253–62.

2. Das SK et al. Deglycyrrhizinated liquorice in apthous ulcers. Journal of the Association of Physicians of India (JAPI) 1989; 37: 647.

3. Jacobs J et al. Treatment of acute childhood diarrhea with homeopathic medicine: a randomized clinical trial in Nicaragua. Pediatrics 1994; 93(5): 719–725.

4. Diamant M, B Diamant. Abuse and timing of use of antibiotics in acute otitis media. Archives of Otolaryngology 1974;100: 226–232.

5. Dale DC & DD Federman (eds). *Scientific American Medicine*. NYC: Scientific American, Inc, 1978–1997; Chapter XXIV, "Pathophysiology of Fever and Fever of Undetermined Origin."

6. Ball GV & LB Sorensen. Pathogenesis of hyperuricemia in saturnine gout. New England Journal of Medicine 1969; 280: 1199–1202.

7. Stein HB. Ascorbic acid-induced uricosuria: a consequence of megavitamin therapy. Annals of Internal Medicine 1976; 84: 385–388.

8. Gershon SL & IH Fox. Pharmacological effects of nicotinic acid on human purine metabolism. Journal of Laboratory and Clinical Medicine 1974; 84: 179–186.

9. Grant ECG. Food allergies and migraine. The Lancet 1979, May 5: 966–969.

10. Egg J et al. Is migraine food allergy? A double-blind controlled trial of oligoantigenic diet treatment. The Lancet, 1983, October 15: 865–869.

11. Mauskop A. Intravenous magnesium sulfate relieves migraine attacks in patients with low serum ionized magnesium levels: A pilot study. Clinical Science 1995; 89: 633–636.

12. Scattner P & D Randerson. Tiger Balm as a treatment of tension headache: A clinical trial in general practice. Australian Family Physician 1996; 25:216–222.

13. Kraft JR. Detection of diabetes mellitus in situ (occult diabetes). Laboratory Medicine 1975; 6(2):10.

14. Macintosh A. Dysglycemia: a misunderstood functional illness. Journal of Naturopathic Medicine 1997; 7(1): 78–83.

15. Ferrannini E et al. Insulin resistance in essential hypertension. New England Journal of Medicine 1987; 317: 350.

16. Facchini FS et al. Insulin resistance and cigarette smoking. The Lancet 1992; 339: 1128–1130.

17. Eby GA et al. Reduction in duration of common colds by zinc gluconate lozenges in a double-blind study. Antimicrobial Agents and Chemotherapy 1984; 25(1): 20–24.

18. Anon. Bugged by an ulcer? You could have a bug. Discover 1987 (May); pg 10.

Index